Lau v. Nichols and Chinese American Language Rights

BILINGUAL EDUCATION & BILINGUALISM

Series Editors: **Nancy H. Hornberger** *(University of Pennsylvania, USA)* and **Wayne E. Wright** *(Purdue University, USA)*

Bilingual Education and Bilingualism is an international, multidisciplinary series publishing research on the philosophy, politics, policy, provision and practice of language planning, Indigenous and minority language education, multilingualism, multiculturalism, biliteracy, bilingualism and bilingual education. The series aims to mirror current debates and discussions. New proposals for single-authored, multiple-authored, or edited books in the series are warmly welcomed, in any of the following categories or others authors may propose: overview or introductory texts; course readers or general reference texts; focus books on particular multilingual education program types; school-based case studies; national case studies; collected cases with a clear programmatic or conceptual theme; and professional education manuals.

All books in this series are externally peer-reviewed.

Full details of all the books in this series and of all our other publications can be found on http://www.multilingual-matters.com, or by writing to Multilingual Matters, St Nicholas House, 31–34 High Street, Bristol, BS1 2AW, UK.

Front cover image description

During the 1971–1972 school year, Miss Lucinda Lee taught in the Cantonese-bilingual pilot program at Commodore Stockton Elementary School (now Gordon J. Lau Elementary), the largest school in San Francisco's Chinatown. Her classroom, 10M was located in the basement. Lucinda's students came from across the city due to mandatory busing orders for racial integration (Johnson v. SFUSD, 1971). The school once homogeneously Chinese and Cantonese speaking would change dramatically with students coming from Noe Valley, the Mission, and Hunter's Point, representing students from different linguistic and racial identities. Drawing strongly from her training in early childhood and project based learning, alongside the bicultural emphasis of the burgeoning bilingual program, she took her students across the greater Bay Area to explore parks, the planetarium, and the aquarium. Locally, she took children across the street to area restaurants and markets where they would eat Chinese foods distinctive of the season, discussing the historical context of the cuisine with the children. During that school year, children identified a field trip of 'impression' and were assigned a part of the Commodore Stockton wall that encased their concrete playground. The Chinese children, many of whom had not traversed beyond the community of Chinatown drew pictures of Fairyland, the aquarium, and the planetarium. Students outside of Chinatown painted images of their buses that brought them to Chinatown and the community of Chinatown that was unfamiliar to them. The mural is now painted over, but prior to its cover up, Linda Chu, a student in Lucinda's classroom in the 1971–1972 school year had a boyfriend who was an excellent listener and photographer. Hearing Linda's stories about her days at Commodore Stockton, her then boyfriend, William Tsui took pictures of the spaces she traversed as a young child and assembled it into a photo album for her. Later, they would marry. Thank you William for preserving this distinct period in time which captures the intersectional exploration of racial and linguistic integration.

BILINGUAL EDUCATION & BILINGUALISM: 145

Lau v. Nichols and Chinese American Language Rights

The Sunrise and Sunset of Bilingual Education

Trish Morita-Mullaney

MULTILINGUAL MATTERS
Bristol • Jackson

DOI https://doi.org/10.21832/MORITA7069
Library of Congress Cataloging in Publication Data
A catalog record for this book is available from the Library of Congress.
Names: Morita-Mullaney, Trish, author.
Title: *Lau v. Nichols* and Chinese American Language Rights: The Sunrise and Sunset of Bilingual Education/Trish Morita-Mullaney.
Other titles: *Lau vs. Nichols* and Chinese American Language Rights
Description: Jackson: Multilingual Matters, 2024. | Series: Bilingual Education & Bilingualism: 145 | Includes bibliographical references and index. | Summary: "This book employs a narrative portraiture approach to recenter the stories of those involved in the *Lau v. Nichols* court case. It brings Chinese and Chinese American voices to the forefront, filling a significant gap in narration, representation and retrospective research"— Provided by publisher.
Identifiers: LCCN 2024006304 (print) | LCCN 2024006305 (ebook) | ISBN 9781800417052 (paperback) | ISBN 9781800417069 (hardback) | ISBN 9781800417076 (pdf) | ISBN 9781800417083 (epub)
Subjects: LCSH: Education, Bilingual—Law and legislation—United States. | Language policy—United States. | Lau, Kinney Kinmon—Trials, litigation, etc. | San Francisco (Calif.). Board of Education—Trials, litigation, etc.
Classification: LCC KF228.L278 M67 2024 (print) | LCC KF228.L278 (ebook) | DDC 344.73/079—dc23/eng/20240222
LC record available at https://lccn.loc.gov/2024006304
LC ebook record available at https://lccn.loc.gov/2024006305

British Library Cataloguing in Publication Data
A catalogue entry for this book is available from the British Library.

ISBN-13: 978-1-80041-706-9 (hbk)
ISBN-13: 978-1-80041-705-2 (pbk)

Multilingual Matters
UK: St Nicholas House, 31–34 High Street, Bristol, BS1 2AW, UK.
USA: Ingram, Jackson, TN, USA.

Website: https://www.multilingual-matters.com
X: Multi_Ling_Mat
Facebook: https://www.facebook.com/multilingualmatters
Blog: https://www.channelviewpublications.wordpress.com

Copyright © 2024 Trish Morita-Mullaney.

All rights reserved. No part of this work may be reproduced in any form or by any means without permission in writing from the publisher.

The policy of Multilingual Matters/Channel View Publications is to use papers that are natural, renewable and recyclable products, made from wood grown in sustainable forests. In the manufacturing process of our books, and to further support our policy, preference is given to printers that have FSC and PEFC Chain of Custody certification. The FSC and/or PEFC logos will appear on those books where full certification has been granted to the printer concerned.

Typeset by Techset Composition India(P) Ltd, Bangalore and Chennai, India.

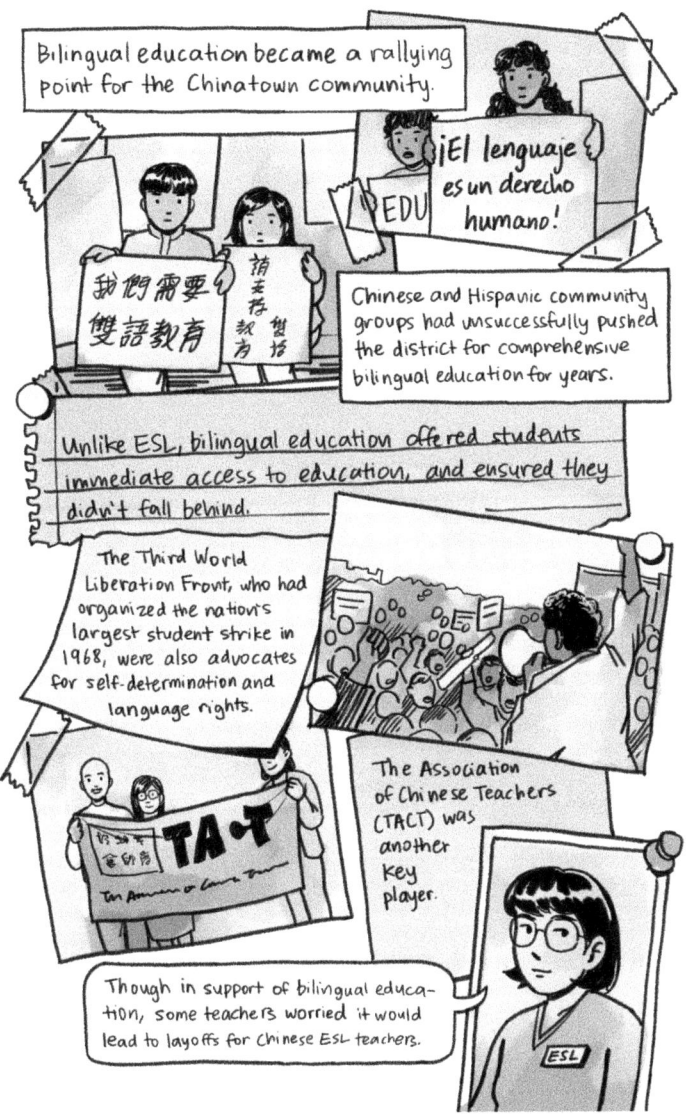

Chinese for Affirmative Action, 826 Valencia & San Francisco Unified Schools (2024) *Language is a Superpower: A Zine* (J. Jiang, Illus.). Chinese for Affirmative Action.

Contents

Acknowledgements	ix
Foreword	xv
Betina Hsieh	
Introduction	xxi

Section 1 Before Lau: The Sunrises

1. Before Lau: Chinese Exclusion — 3
   Mamie Tape as Excluded
2. Before Lau, there was Mrs Lau — 12
   Lucinda Wong Lee Katz, Kinney Kinmon Lau's Teacher
3. Before Lau, There Was School Desegregation and Bilingual Education — 22
   Lucinda Lee, Commodore Stockton Chinese Bilingual Teacher and Her Students
4. Before Lau: Personalized Curriculum Writers, not Publishers — 37
   Gordon Lew, the Chinese Curriculum Writer
5. Before Lau, Chinese Educators Were Assigned Outside of Chinatown — 45
   Victor Low, the Bilingual Educator and Administrator
6. Before Lau, Collective Advocacy Had Many Tentacles — 56
   The Association for Chinese Teachers (TACT)
7. Before Lau, Community Agencies at the Core — 66
   Ling-Chi Wang and the Chinese for Affirmative Action (CAA)
8. Before Lau, a 'Reggie' Found a Way — 76
   Edward Steinman, J.D., the Lau Lawyer
9. Before Lau, An Idealistic Lawyer and Public Servant is Appointed to the School Board — 90
   Alan Nichols, J.D., School Board President
10. Before Lau, There Was School Desegregation and Mandatory Busing — 99
    Enter the Freedom Schools of Chinatown

Section 2 After Lau: The Sunrising Quickly

11 After Lau: Remedies and More Remedies 111
The Lau Consent Decrees

12 After Lau: California's Proposition 227 and
English for the Children 125
Federal Decrees Combat State Language Policy

13 A Third World Rights Federation Activist in the Midst 132
Laureen Chew, EdD

14 Remedies and Remediation in Higher Education 142
Interpreting Language Rights at the University

Section 3 Beyond Lau: The Sun Setting

15 Post Lau: The Association of Chinese Teachers 153
TACT Advances its Advocacy in Bicultural Identity

16 Post Lau: The Chinese Principals 165
Interpreting and Implementing Lau

17 The Modified Lau Consent Decree to the Sunset 178

18 Sunset and Beyond: Language as Problem, Right,
Resource or Choice? 186

19 Sunsetting and Choice: Co-Articulating Language Rights,
Affirmative Action and Voting Rights 193

References 198

Index 210

Acknowledgements

In the Spring of 2013, I was a graduate student attending the American Educational Research Association's annual conference in San Francisco, California – city of my birth. I attended a Sunday morning presidential panel entitled, 'The State of Language Minority Education 40 Years After *Lau v. Nichols*'. Mary Carol Combs of the University of Arizona chaired the session and Patricia Gándara of the University of California of Los Angeles, Edward Steinman of Santa Clara University and Ling-Chi Wang of the University of California at Berkeley served as panelists. The panel resonated with me for two central reasons. First, Dr Ling-Chi Wang, a Chinese American activist, scholar and original recruiter for plaintiffs in the Lau case was not listed in the AERA program. I wondered if the absence of his name was an oversight, or if he was a later addition? After all, we were in San Francisco, the birthplace of Lau and Ling-Chi was central to framing linguistic rights for the Chinese and Chinese American community in his then role as director and co-founder of the Chinese for Affirmative Action. Whether blatant or an oversight, the omission was reminiscent of the historic erasure of Asian voices, one that I was experiencing in my current job as a bilingual district administrator as an Asian woman seeking to carve out language rights for our small Asian community. My contributions were often dismissed and the absence of my name on invitations was often described as an oversight. Secondly, Edward Steinman, the lead lawyer who collaborated with Ling-Chi to recruit the plaintiffs stated on the panel, 'Lau should have been Lopez versus Nichols' due to the higher proportion of Latine families within the San Francisco Unified Schools. Ed received much pressure and criticism from Latine groups, as they had a political force that was local and strong. Yet Ed argued that the proportional harm to Chinese youth was much higher and the likelihood of them having no language support or services was much higher. Ed stood his ground alongside of the Chinese community of Chinatown, despite the immense political pressure. The combination of resistance and advocacy of Ling-Chi and Ed drew me inward, examining why the voices of Asian and Asian Americans were absent or less represented in the collective and historical narrative of bilingual education. I thank them for building this flame of inquiry.

After I graduated, I got busy with my new role as an Assistant Professor but continued to remember and heed Ling-Chi's and Ed's comments about resisting erasure and pushing for the recentering of Chinese and Chinese American families. In the summer of 2019, I contacted Ed by phone and asked if he would be willing to meet with me about his 'Lopez versus Nichols' statement as I was in the Bay Area visiting family. He agreed and in July 2019, he came to my Dad's house in a red convertible with his two golden retrievers in tow. Scout, then just a puppy came inside, and we sat at my dad's dining room table talking about Lau with Scout at our feet. Ed is a lawyer, so his comments were specific to codes and constructs, a discourse that was unfamiliar and daunting. But, as he began talking about the different players in the case, my ears began to perk as he humanized how the law was embodied by the Chinese American Lau architects. From there, the snowball grew as he shared that Alan Nichols, the defendant, lived up the street from my Dad, and Lucinda Lee Katz, Kinney Lau's first teacher was in the city and of course, Ling-Chi Wang was too. As I talked in person or by phone with them prior to the COVID-19 pandemic, the landscape of Chinatown and language rights before, during and after Lau came to the fore. I acknowledge Ling-Chi Wang, Edward Steinman, Alan Nichols and Lucinda Lee Katz as being first to introduce me to architecture of language policy and planning for bilingual education from the ground up in Chinatown: The birthplace of Lau.

The Association of Chinese Teachers or TACT, a Chinese American teacher group founded in 1969 was central in providing primary documents, identifying participants, and helping me interpret the larger context of San Francisco at the time. Darlene Lim, bilingual teacher, principal and Enrollment Center Director provided the original newsletters, filmstrips, documents shared with the school board, and their greater political advocacy throughout the state of California. Laureen Chew, Pat Chew, Irene Dea Collier, Sophie Lee, John Lum, Lonnie Chin, Helen Lew and Victor Low helped make sense of the piles of documents, interpreting the story and bringing light to their identities as teachers and leaders advocating for Cantonese-Chinese language rights and Chinese representation in textbooks and lessons. Their current president, Cynthia Cen was instrumental in bringing current and historic TACT members to collectively review the TACT chapters to ensure that their history of advocacy and resistance represented their distinct multivocality of the present and past.

The Chinese for Affirmative Action was instrumental in illuminating the historic and present context of Chinatown and how the fight for language rights is nested within a larger social struggle for housing, healthcare, employment and voting rights. I thank the historic director, Henry Der for his insight and threading together important events and Ling-Chi Wang for situating its origins. I am grateful to the current educational leadership of Sally Chen and Alice Cheng who engaged with the greater SFUSD community-around language rights, conducting workshops with families about what it means to be multilingual 50 years after Lau. Sally and Alice are the modern day and future architects of language policy and planning.

The San Francisco Unified Schools were supportive in locating the Lau consent decree reports filed from 1976 to 2019. I am especially grateful to Christina Wong, a district and community leader who contextualized the long history of bilingual education and how it has transformed to its present naming convention of the Multilingual Pathways Department. Victor Tam, formerly of the Fred and Anita Lee Newcomer Center provided deep context on the present implementation of Lau and introduced me to key players throughout the city. Additional educators throughout SFUSD (represented as a collective) detailed how parent choice and the elimination of race as a factor in school assignment and the rapid language shift from Cantonese to English creates a complexity for language provisions.

The libraries of the greater Bay Area were staffed with wonderful people who had deep context of the Asian American community in San Francisco. Librarian Tami Suzuki of the San Francisco Public Library History Center on the sixth floor hosted carts of archives and ensured I had ready access to scanning and other supporting resources within the library. Her connection to the greater SFUSD as a long-term resident of the city guided me in understanding how teachers across the city interpret and embody bilingual education. Sine Hwang Jenson, librarian at the Ethnic Studies Library at UC Berkeley dug through dusty boxes to find the original *East West* news weeklies and other media materials including *Bean Sprouts* and filmstrips originally developed by the Association of Chinese Teachers. The National Archives at San Francisco or NARA assisted in finding all primary legal documents from the Lau case, including primary testimony from the plaintiffs in Lau. Special thanks to Charles Miller for managing my multiple requests and those that would change in flight.

Harry Chuck of the Cameron House, a social agency for Chinatown youth described how Chinatown was transforming in the late 1960s and the war on poverty brought needed resources to the community. He described the generational divides between immigrant parents and their US born children and how he worked with various Lau educators to mitigate the tensions. His seminal documentary work with his son, Josh Chuck, called *Chinatown Rising* illuminated a rich history that set the larger stage for Chinese language rights. David Lei, regarded as a walking history of Chinatown, and worked at the YMCA, detailed the challenges of first and second generation Chinese gangs and how this was polarized by lack of employment and poor educational provisions in the lead up to Lau. David was instrumental in pointing me to places to find archives and facilitated communications with the Chinese Six Companies. He and a team of volunteer archivists regularly comb the area libraries and community centers to ensure ready access for researchers studying the history of the Chinese.

Dr Lily Wong-Fillmore, emeritus professor at UC Berkeley introduced me to pivotal moments in Chinatown's history including the formation of the Freedom Schools and introduction to local Chinese activists in the city. At UC Berkeley, I also worked with Kenny Pui Gin Li, an undergraduate from Hong Kong who meticulously translated primary documents from *East West*, nesting them within a larger social context of San Francisco, given his interests in Asian American studies. At Purdue, Bryan Zhibo Li, recommended by Dr Haiyan Li continued the translation of *East West* after Kinney graduated from UC Berkeley. Zhibo was inspired by the rich history of Guangzhou, China where he is from, and appreciated the affirmation of the historical sojourn of the Chinese to the US. Pui and Zhibo's attention to detail captured nuances that allowed the narratives of the Chinese to be represented more fully. Other academic mentors include Drs Beth Berghoff and Annela Teemant that told me to embrace narrative fully and from there, the ideas would emerge. Thanks for building this early notion of trusting when confused.

Multilingual Matters has been such a supportive publisher, ushering through items in a timely manner and making the process transparent and actionable at all stages of the project. Thanks to Rosie for taking the proposal and advertising the book on the road at conference venues and introducing me to the Multilingual Matters family who have helped me at different stages: Elinor, Sarah, Flo and Praveena – I thank you. Another special thanks to the editors of the Bilingual Education and Bilingualism series: Drs Nancy Hornberger and Wayne Wright. My questions were always answered, and encouragement came just when I needed it.

My Purdue family, including colleagues and students were ardent cheerleaders, always asking about the project and listening to the stories of the Lau architects. To my colleagues: Wayne Wright, Virak Chan, Jennifer Renn, Ofelia Castro Schepers, Brenda Sarmiento and Anne Garcia. To the students in the ELL/bilingual program at Purdue (both current and past), I thank you for sharing your language identities with me and how it is uniquely shaping your current and future work. Special thanks to Drs Haiyan Li and David Song for providing important interpretation advice in Mandarin and Cantonese.

The fierce Asian American feminist icons, Drs Diep Nguyen, Christine Leider and Shengxiao Sole Yu pointed me to the deepest parts of my soul and identity, helping me understand the nuance in the narratives of the Lau story. I thank them for their laughter, support and insight as they continue to transform Asian women across the country in their professional pursuits.

To my Lawrence Township family of Indianapolis where I spent much of my career as a language educator, where my children attended; thank you for your unapologetic advocacy and fierce resistance to the policies that usurp the rights and needs of multilingual students. Thank you for always speaking out and up and continuing the legacy of Lau in your daily work. I thank my life-long friends and the mothers of bilingual education: Julie Majercak, Erika Tran, Michelle Greene and Cammie Moody for reminding me of where we started.

This work would not have been possible without the support of my wonderful family. My life-long partner, Jeffrey Mullaney wove out my doubt, asked questions and assured me that the finish line was near. To my children, Sachiko and Micah, heritage learners of Japanese, often reminded me that language reclamation is beautifully possible and to keep writing about language. My daughter, Sachiko Rose provided constant encouragement, and my son, Micah Thomas found picture archives and photoshopped them for the book. My siblings, Pam, Laura and Marc offered fresh perspectives when my ideas felt muddled. My niece, Audrey Yeun created the icons used in the book to help you as a reader. Thank you for your creativity and voice. Lastly, my Dad, Dr Eugene Takashi Morita shared his stories of language shift and loss from his childhood to the present and how such should not be repeated. When I finished the book, my Dad said, 'I'm just delighted, Trish' and cracked a smile. Thank you Dad for your inspiration, and your affirmation of identity work – always done with delight.

Foreword

Growing up, I remember my Taiwanese immigrant mother telling me that her American graduate school professors counseled her to speak only in English and raise her future children to speak 'perfectly accent-free' English, if she wanted to give them (us) better chances of having successful futures. She was told by her professors (much like Laureen Chew and Lucinda Lee were told on the Washington Irving Elementary playground) that speaking Chinese (herself, and to us, her children) would hinder development of English language skills. My mom did speak English to me, and outside of my home I was constantly immersed in English growing up in a predominantly white suburb of Los Angeles. However, at home, Mandarin and Taiwanese Hokkien flowed freely among the adults (until my maternal grandmother passed away when I was 7) leading to my dismay when my mother indicated, as she was registering me for kindergarten, that everyone spoke English at home and that I only spoke English. At the time, Mandarin, Hokkien, and gesturing were the only ways that I could functionally communicate with my grandmother who helped raise me. My mother later told me that when she had enrolled my brother in school, honestly stating that the adults in the house spoke Chinese, he had been taken out of his honors English class to be tested for English proficiency (as was required by the state). She didn't want me to suffer the same fate. My mother wanted me to learn Mandarin, even asking my estranged father to send basal reader textbooks with Zhuyin phonetic guides from Taiwan when I was in upper elementary school, but she prioritized my success in English as my chance at an easier life than she had with her ever-present access. However, by the time the textbooks arrived from my father, I had so internalized that speaking Chinese would make me stand out as different from my (white) classmates, who seemed so self-assured and popular, that I rejected her attempts to teach me and resisted any suggestion of attending a Chinese heritage language school on the weekends. Given that we were a 30-minute drive from the nearest heritage language school and that my single mother was not the biggest fan of freeway driving, she let it go, and my early childhood Mandarin proficiency all but disappeared after my grandmother passed away.

    My mother herself passed away when I was in high school. With her passing, I lost the remaining positive associations I had with being

Taiwanese American. My limited knowledge of Taiwanese culture, Taiwanese Hokkien and Mandarin made me feel like I was 'incomplete', missing a part of myself that I had long rejected. Well-intentioned, but painful questions about where I was really from and compliments about how good my English was, reminded me that even though I spoke 'perfect, accent-free' (American) English, it did not afford me complete access to the dominant culture promised to my mother by her professors. I did go on to be successful, perhaps ironically, as an English Language Arts teacher and later a literacy teacher educator. Yet today, when I look at photographs my mother took of her years in Taiwan and early years in the United States and I see her handwriting in Chinese, I acutely feel the loss of a bicultural and biliterate identity based in my heritage culture.

I first learned about the *Lau v. Nichols* case when I was in graduate school studying English education in the San Francisco Bay Area. At the time, having never thought of myself as an 'English Language Learner', I thought it was interesting and important that such a significant Civil Rights Act was linked to a local Chinese American family, and that content and language support, including supplemental language instruction as student rights were relatively recent concepts. I appreciated the need to learn scaffolding strategies to support non-English dominant multilingual learners that I would teach, from newcomers in early English Language Development courses to 'long term English Learner' students in grade level English courses. Since I taught in majority immigrant communities, these supports for English acquisition were helpful teaching tools. I was grateful to the families involved in the Lau case for advocating that 'language minority' students (as they were sometimes labeled by the state during the time I was learning to teach) have access to the curriculum. I thought that this access was always conceptualized through English Language Development (or English as a Second Language) courses and strategies to scaffold (English) language acquisition, promoting conceptual understanding alongside the development of comprehension and communication skills in English.

I embraced language scaffolds as a student teacher in a high school newcomer setting and later as a middle school teacher to support multilingual learners in my English Language Arts classes. As a teacher educator, in my preservice teacher education courses, I turned the tables on English-dominant teacher candidates, often teaching an entire lesson on language scaffolding strategies in academic French. Many teacher candidates, who were not multilingual and sometimes came into the class completely unfamiliar with how to support English Learners, reacted with various levels of discomfort and coping strategies, from immediate disengagement, to attempts to use verbal scaffolds and their existing language systems to make meaning, to relying on strategies like gestures, objects and translation apps. This lesson often had a powerful impact on teacher candidates, multilingual and monolingual. Monolingual English speakers noted that being placed in an experience where they were taught credential program content (i.e. content at a post-baccalaureate level) in a language they had an emergent (at best) understanding of, even for 20-30 minutes, gave them a deep appreciation for the effort of non-English dominant emergent multilingual students who are trying to learn grade level content in English for eight or more hours a day. Multilingual teacher candidates often recounted painful stories of language loss, a continued sense of inadequacy in relation to their academic English, or identified with strategies that could be used to support language development.

I knew personally that language was important to identity. I knew professionally that language was essential to understanding content. Still, I was missing a crucial connection. I did not fully appreciate the power of bilingual/ bicultural education to bridge and affirm cultural, linguistic, literate, and social understandings (even as the parent of children who have deeply benefited from bilingual/bicultural education programs), nor did I fully understand the political and social dynamics related to language equity as a Civil Right and bilingual/bicultural education programs. Intellectually all the pieces were there, but the connection that was missing was a connection to my heart, a connection that comes from seeing oneself in another's story.

Before reading *Lau v. Nichols and Chinese American Language Rights*, I recognized *Lau v. Nichols* as a critically important Supreme Court case that moved public school policy towards providing more equitable opportunities for non-English dominant families and students. For me, Lau was about access to English, the language of power, not about a fight for access to content through language, and as a significant opening for identity affirming and bridge-building bilingual/bicultural education. I did not know the stories behind the case nor the intent of the original consent decree. I did not know about the context of *Lau* within larger place-based and historically situated movements, in SFUSD, in the state and across the nation, movements which spanned decades. Knowing these stories and this context matters, just as my own stories, experiences and contexts matter equally as much as the policy that has shaped the opportunities available to me.

By centering the interwoven stories of key figures related to the *Lau v. Nichols* case through her use of narrative policy portraiture, Dr Morita-Mullaney humanizes and contextualizes language education policy in San Francisco Unified School District (SFUSD) and beyond, through the people who played critical roles in its realization, actualization and implementation. *Lau v. Nichols* as a decision established a critical legal precedent that would influence SFUSD language policy for multilingual students directly for 45 years (as well as language policy nationally for multilingual learners in important ways to this day). Yet, the story of *Lau* is compelling beyond these policy implications when one is able to see the way *Lau*'s implementation and implications are situated within and adjacent to larger social movements, including immigrant rights, Civil Rights (including racial and linguistic segregation), and school choice. Discriminatory education policy precursors towards Asian Americans in San Francisco predate the *Lau* decision by nearly 100 years and the debate over implementation of *Lau*'s remedies have continued, even five years since the sunset of its mandatory consent decrees. The narratives found within this book, and the choices, policies, documents and lives they are tied to, amplify not only the significance of the *Lau* case, but also its power to connect with larger audiences of parents, educators and teacher educators concerned with equitable educational opportunities, bilingual/bicultural education, curriculum development, bilingual teacher support, and with language policy implementation, interpretation and legacies.

Prior to the *Lau* decision, Dr Morita-Mullaney highlights the stories of students and teachers who were part of the emergent bilingual/bicultural Cantonese pilot program, done in conjunction with mandated integration through busing. As a parent of children who have been in dual language immersion programs, I was fascinated by the stories of bicultural exchange from former students (both Cantonese dominant and English dominant) which can be rare, particularly in 'status' (e.g. Mandarin) Chinese dual language immersion programs today. English dominant students who were bussed into the community spent time exploring a neighborhood that was only a few miles from them but was culturally a new world for them. Cantonese-dominant students from the Chinatown community got to visit places in the Bay Area outside of their community which previously felt exclusive to them. Both groups of children learned about one another, and the community's cultural assets as well as the larger Bay Area's cultural offerings were affirmed alongside one another. The connection between this early bilingual program to which Kinney Kinmon Lau did not have access, and his own education, through his first-grade teacher, Mrs Lucinda Lee Katz was fascinating. If the pilot program had started sooner, and Kinney had access to learn content through Cantonese, one wonders how the story may have shifted, and if another plaintiff would have emerged.

After the *Lau* decision, SFUSD's reports tell one part of the story about Cantonese bilingual/bicultural education's (BBE) existence and its evolution, but also reveal gaps in access to these programs, particularly for emergent bilingual Cantonese-dominant speakers, many of whom received no language support while a large number of their English-dominant peers were bussed into their neighborhood schools (under the protection of school staff) to participate in Cantonese BBE. While who benefits and who has access to BBE remains a theme throughout the book, another important take away from this period is the resilience of those who made Cantonese BBE possible. Dr Morita-Mullaney's interviewees share stories of navigating multiple barriers to make bilingual/bicultural classrooms a reality. From designing specialized curricula for the program when none was available to recruiting and retaining bilingual teachers (including building a language certification program at SF State), we see the impact policy has on people and the resources implementation demands. As a teacher educator who thinks deeply about both curricular design and the recruitment and retention of teachers, these chapters were so important in emphasizing the importance of local, contextualized knowledge (speaking back to one-size-fits-all boxed curricula which so often leave many students on the margins) and the challenge of equitably preparing and supporting teachers, particularly teachers from linguistically diverse immigrant communities.

Given that *Lau* focuses on the Cantonese speaking community in San Francisco, a traditional language majority community in SF Chinatown, but a minoritized/non-dominant Chinese language community (i.e. among Chinese speakers, for whom Mandarin is the status or dominant language), the book raises issues of ethno-linguistic power dynamics prevalent across many language communities, but often obscured or unknown by those that are not part of such communities. The overlap of the Lau Consent Degrees with racial integration initiatives in SFUSD, from busing to the SFUSD Diversity Index, also show somewhat parallel shifts from court-enforced equity-grounded initiatives based on Civil Rights principles to school choice initiatives which report racial (and linguistic) diversity but do little to affect racial (and linguistic) segregation, equitable access to educational resources, or to challenge existing dominant power structures. Within these paradigms, readers see how bilingual education (through dual language immersion programs) has become, in many cases, an 'additive advantage' that allows certain children to have more 'marketable' language skills, a far departure from its origins as a Civil Right initiative that allows linguistically marginalized children to have culturally affirming education that supports their access to appropriate curriculum.

Reading about this evolution of BBE brings me back to the heart and the stories of mothers. It makes me wonder what Mrs Lau would have said about the 'boutiquing' and gentrification of BBE and whether current forms of dual immersion actually fulfill her intention that her son have access to the curriculum through his primary language. I wonder how many children like Kinney still face exclusion 'by lottery' or have access only to limited support as they learn in their local schools. I also think about my mother, how her perspectives about her professors' advice to her about only speaking English may have shifted (or not) given my own professional trajectory, and what she would have thought about my commitment to raising multilingual children. Her words that one day I would regret not learning Mandarin from her echo often in my mind. Finally, I think about my own mothering and the choices I've made and had the privilege to make in terms of bilingual/bicultural education for my own children, one of whom learned Mandarin in dual language immersion programs and weekend heritage schools for nine years, and the other who is learning Korean (not one of her heritage languages) in a dual language program in our neighborhood school. I think about what it means to try to reclaim my own (significantly if not fully) severed language and cultural connection to my Taiwanese American identity through my multiracial children embracing the fullness of their cultural and linguistic identities. I think about 'choices' that I can and cannot make based on my socioeconomic status and access my children have (and have had) to (quality) bilingual/bicultural education programs. I also consider my lingering sense of imposter syndrome, having not had access to culturally and linguistically affirming (or public school-sponsored) BBE as a child. I wonder how my own development might have been different if I had not struggled so much to embrace my own cultural and linguistic identity and had external spaces that fully acknowledged who I am. I wonder how my perspectives of my professional identity and what was possible for me as an educator might have been impacted by having an Asian American teacher in my K-12 public schooling.

It is the reflection, connection and wonderings that this book prompts that make it so special. What is perhaps most striking about *Lau v. Nichols and Chinese American Language Rights* is its reminder that behind every policy, there are people, and that policies, like people, continue to evolve within social contexts that reflect both continuity and change. The power of this text is in the power of visibility as a way to continue moving towards linguistic justice. It is in the power of telling stories that touch our shared humanity. It is in the liminality of what is between the lines of policy documents and implementation reports and in the possibility of a future that can be more, based on a past that cannot be erased. These stories are much needed in this moment, reminding us that the language struggles of marginalized communities are Asian American struggles just as they are shared struggles with other immigrant communities, that Civil Rights is an Asian American issue just as they are issues for other marginalized groups, that solidarity and working through cross-racial tensions are critical parts of Asian American histories just as they must be for Asian American futures.

May this book help us move forward together, honoring and affirming our shared humanity, in all of its cultural and linguistic richness and diversity.

Betina Hsieh
Boeing Professor of Teacher Education
University of Washington (Seattle), USA

Introduction

Linking Asian American Studies and Language Policy

Asian American Studies

During World War II, my father, Eugene Takashi Morita, a US-born Japanese American was incarcerated in Tule Lake, California and Amache, Colorado prison camps as a young child with his four siblings, mother, and father, all of whom were US citizens or legal residents. After the bombing of Pearl Harbor, Hawaii by the Japanese of Japan on December 8, 1941, my dad, and his family were regarded as a suspect class and potential conspirators of Japan along with another 120,000 Japanese and Japanese Americans. President Franklin Roosevelt quickly created the War Relocation Authority following the bombing and administered Executive Order 9066 on February 21, 1942, requiring that anyone of Japanese descent, regardless of citizenship status, was to be detained in internment camps under authority of the Secretary of War. Dad, his parents and four siblings lived in a barrack with a pot-bellied stove, and ate their meals in a communal cafeteria and attended school during the day. The focus of school was on all subjects, but also had a heavy emphasis on Americanization and loyalty, a consistent reinforcement of the power of English and the evacuation of anything Japanese. With armed guards living among them and guarding them by tower, the message was not lost about what they needed to release: Japanese. Rapid language shift ensued: My dad and most of his siblings have limited to no proficiency in Japanese. My dad and his extended family often said 仕方がない or shikata ga nai: 'It must be done, it can't be helped' to endure events of hardship, even those that were perniciously executed by normalizing the deletion of Japanese language use and 'reeducating' them on what was regarded as American ideals. This construct of endurance in large part describes why my father, a second-generation Japanese American, Nisei and his father, an Issei, a Japanese immigrant, and a legal resident largely did not speak of their incarceration. I would learn of his imprisonment after reading books by Yoshiko Uchida when I was in elementary school (Uchida, 1971). Growing up with my father, the construction of shikata ga nai was used as a method to get through challenging times, and to endure. I also recognize how such a construction was subverted and successfully arbitrated the agenda of those with power, in his case, the US government during his incarceration or what dad calls 'camp'.

In Chinese, there is a similar construct called mou de gan or 冇得拣. Mou de gan articulates that persecution was real and for that reason, many Chinese in Southern China had to leave their hometowns. Importantly, the construct details that once a particular threshold is reached, then mou de gan should be invoked, but also has allowances for endurance and resistance in the interim. Mou de gan can also mean that there is no solution and thus, resignation becomes necessary: there is no possible way. Thus, mou de gan or 冇得拣 like shikata ga nai can be a way of testing the waters of when thresholds of resistance are met or when tinkering can take place. More directly, shikata ga nai or mou de gan or 冇得拣[1] depending on social location and power relations, can be a racial project of assimilation and subjugation.

Racial plotting and continuums

Within the racially diverse US landscape, the racial continuum of Black to White positions AAPIs in the perpetual in-between space. Thus, Asian and Asian Americans may experience a racial homelessness where they are not Black, and not White (Alcoff, 2003; Morita-Mullaney, 2014b; Perea, 1997). Asians, Latinos and First Nations people have also described the in-betweeners as perpetual foreigners, as they are ascribed as non-English speaking immigrants or migrants, regardless of language proficiency or generational status (Leonardo, 2002).

The positioning of the Chinese community for whom this book is centered as in-betweeners constitutes a relative comparison across groups of color. The Chinese stand in relationship to the racial ordering instead being fixed between Black and White bookends. Claire Jean Kim (1999, 2000, 2018, 2023) has critiqued and historicized Omi and Winant's (1986) racial hierarchy recognizing that the subjectivities of different groups of color is dependent on context and social relations. AAPIs are ascribed in relationship to the White/Black binary constructed along two axis points as superior or inferior and another axis being ostracized or valorized. For example, Asians may be valorized as cooperative or preferred immigrants (Hsu, 2015; Morita-Mullaney, 2019; Wu, 2013) and thus are positioned in relative adjacency to Whites, reaching toward superior and marking them as a racial bourgeoise (Matsuda, 1996). In contrast, the Chinese experienced a different positioning in the 1880s, ascribed as disease-ridden Mongolians and thereby, segregated from White schools or denied enrollment altogether. The enterprise of situating Asians along this continuum of cooperative to barbaric, unassimilable Mongolians is a placement that is reliant on the social conditions that benefit the aims of Whiteness.

The construction of Asian superiority, meriting White adjacency is also a narrative that can be constructed as anti-Black (Kim, 2023). If Asians have materially and discursively met the conditions of Whiteness, they are constructed as a more willing and able student in comparison to Blacks (Morita-Mullaney, 2019). With such constructions, Asians can be used as pawns to mediate conflicts between Whites and Blacks, a frequent occurrence within integrated schools as Asians are positioned as neutral interlocutors (Morita-Mullaney & Nguyen, 2023). Yet this positioning is always laden with the politics of instrumental versus genuine inclusion. During the mandatory racial desegregation of San Francisco schools, mainly focused on correcting de jure policies of school segregation of Blacks, Chinese and Latino groups also adopted discursive frames that unsettled racial desegregation as solely a Black–White project (Quinn, 2020).

Language policy

The focus of the Lau case was on *positive liberty:* furnishing an accessible education inside the classroom that newcomer Chinese students could understand. Positive liberty is a construct that posits freedom to or freedom toward a given experience (Berlin, 1958; Thompson, 2013). This was the foundational premise on which Lau laid, but it stood in tension with the Johnson v. SFUSD (1971) and SFNAACP v. SFUSD (1978), which contextualized Lau's passage; cases based on racial integration in schooling. Johnson v. SFUSD (1971) dictated mandatory busing to meet racially integrative aims in the schools, and its construct was founded on *negative liberty*. Negative liberty suggests freedom from, or more specifically, freedom from being harmed by an unequal education. These two monikers of equity serve to differentiate how language rights were arbitrated across lines of integration, access and opportunity.

Narrative Policy Portraiture

My early memories of history lessons in school were the discrete memorization of dates and events with a nod to the characters who were wearing old clothes, donning a constricting uniform and bearing arms on some battlefield. Most of them were White faces and did not look like me. Usually during that time, I would daydream about a book I would rather read or when the bell would ring for recess. This exercise of social imagination during history time persisted into my college years until I took the course, Portraits of America, taught by History Professor, Dr Jim Hunt. For my four-week intensive January term, we read a portrait each week and were invited into the historical narratives of one person. Instead of copious lists of dates and events with exhaustive historical depictions, I came to know four characters well as they were foregrounded in the story. Thereafter, the dates and the events were cast in relationship to the person I had come to know more deeply and then the history came into view. Dr Jim Hunt showed me that history can be humanizing. By drawing me into a relationship with these central characters, my future approach to understanding the past was transformed and any historical resource I would seek out would be narratively expressed either in print or speech.

My father was also instrumental in the formation of the methodology I employ in the book. As a photographer, my father taught me the importance of foregrounding in storytelling, a technique he often uses when he is taking pictures. A photograph using foregrounding places the subjects closest to the camera, where their faces, stances and movements are in sharp focus and the first to grab your attention. Yet, the background contextualizes and humanizes them in a time and place. Metaphorically, I consider the background to be the nauseating locations and dates I had to memorize in school, which meant nothing without the foregrounding. When narrated in first-person, the background, dates and events became accessible, integrated and real; I had a richer and contextualized portrait.

When I learned about narrative portraiture and photographic foregrounding, I was drawn to this as a methodology for engaging with participants. At first, I did comb through primary legal documents on *Lau v. Nichols* and became overwhelmed by the legal discourse of amicus briefs and daunting codes that seemed to have no pattern. I then set such approaches aside and began to speak with the characters of *Lau v. Nichols*. I originally identified five different sets of people to talk to, including lawyers, administrators, teachers, activists and students who lived or worked in Chinatown. The group was quite small and manageable. But as I met each person, they were invariably connected to a larger network, and the list of people grew. This elegant web of narratives then led me back to the primary documents. Then, the dates and events brought the characters into the foreground in the landscape of their past. I thus coin this methodology, *narrative policy portraiture* as it draws from first-person interviews in conjunction with reviews of varied primary documents with participants. On occasion you will see the braiding of my family's language history as it facilitated a deeper shared analysis of our family's language rights.

Narrative policy portraiture is well suited for a study of this scale and depth as it recenters the participants within the retrospective social context and captures 'nuances that are often overlooked' (Rodríguez-Dorans & Jacobs, 2020: 613). Importantly, this narrative portraiture is focused primarily on Chinese and Chinese Americans as they were the original plaintiffs in *Lau v. Nichols* (1974) and were the unlikely ones. Much pressure came from Mexican American Legal Defense and Education Fund (MALDEF) and League of United Latin American Citizens (LULAC), Hispanic legal advocates who claimed it was more politically savvy to have Hispanics lead as plaintiffs given the sizeable representation within the San Francisco Schools and throughout the US. Yet, as you will learn, the legal aid lawyer, Edward Steinman had other ideas about the Chinese community and language education.

Following the Trail

The linguistic landscape of Chinatown, San Francisco sets the stage for this inquiry, beginning in 1882. Chinatown was home to speakers of Cantonese, coming from six different districts in southern China; the Canton region. Cantonese has nine different tones whereas Mandarin Chinese has seven. To speak Cantonese is to use a different tonal repertoire. Functionally however, reading and writing are relatively the same with some variations.

This book is organized by time periods beginning with *Chinese Exclusion* from 1882–1965 to set the historic landscape for policy agents we will meet. *Teaching as activism* covers the period of 1968–1974 in the lead up to the *Lau v. Nichols* case with mandatory busing and the Civil Rights movement at its peak. The years 1974–1985 cover the implementation of *Lau and its remedies*. The section called *Remedial remedies* covers 1986–2018, documenting the lead up to the passage of California's Proposition 227, diminishing bilingual education provisions. The last section called *Choosing equity* captures a small window of time between 2019–2024 and the state of Cantonese-Chinese bilingual education today. The arc of the Lau case from before, during and after, demonstrates the rise or the *sunrising* of bilingual education and how over time, it began to

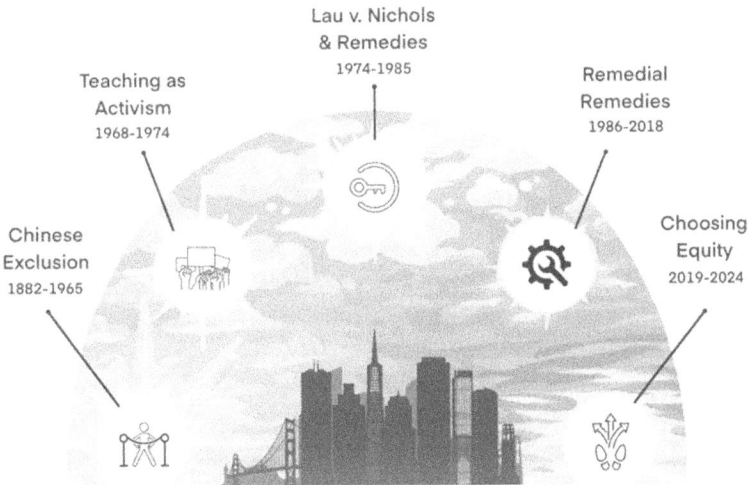

Figure 0.1 History of Chinese Language Rights in San Francisco (Illustrated by Audrey Yeun, 2023)

sunset, moving towards more English-medium models of instruction (Figure 0.1).

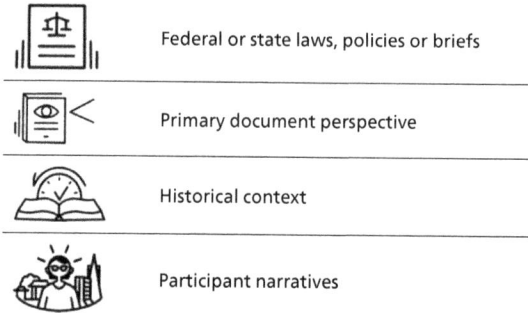

Table 0.1 Roadmap for narrative policy portraiture (Illustrated by Audrey Yeun, 2023)

Federal or state laws, policies or briefs

Primary document perspective

Historical context

Participant narratives

Icons are furnished to navigate the text. As I toggle between talking with participants and then referencing policy documents or contextualizing the history, the icons will assist in making the mental transitions. This strategy is consistent with the approach of *narrative policy portraiture,* so the threads are braided together into a coherent narrative (Table 0.1). Welcome to the *sunrise and sunset* of the language rights of the Cantonese Chinese of San Francisco, California.

Note

(1) 没有办法 (méiyǒu bànfǎ) is the Mandarin interpretation of the Cantonese 冇得拣 (mou de gan).

Section 1
Before Lau: The Sunrises

1 Before Lau: Chinese Exclusion
Mamie Tape as Excluded

Chinese and Chinese Americans were the first to advocate for school integration and their right to a free and public education, 70 years preceding the *Brown v. Board of Education* (1954, 1955) case that would racially integrate schools across the US. Such a story begins in the mid-1800s, in the Western Addition of San Francisco where the Tape family lived, a two-mile walk or carriage ride to the Chinese Quarter. The Chinese, Christian family would set the early precedent for equality in education, grooming the stage for the US Supreme Court case of *Lau v. Nichols* of 1974.

The number of Chinese and Chinese Americans in the US in 1880s was proportionally small, but this differed in California, a main port of entry for the Chinese due to history of the Gold Rush and the needed labor to build the transcontinental railroad that spanned from Northern California's Sacramento to the Midwest, connecting the eastern railways with the west. The density of Chinese in San Francisco proper was the highest in the US and many lived in what was then called the Chinese Quarter or what we reference today as Chinatown.

Consisting of just four city blocks in the 1880s, the population of the Chinese Quarter was 22,000. The majority were men directly due to the historic importation of male labor to build the railroads and the Page Act (1875), which restricted specific Chinese laborers and women from entry, as their professions were regarded as immoral. This law was an effort to restrict Chinese immigration, virtually controlling the birth rate of future generations of Chinese. An all-male workforce met the labor demands of the city. This import of labor preceded the Chinese Exclusion Act of 1882 that barred virtually all immigration to the US, further restricting the birth rate as intermarriage across races was illegal and also regarded as aberrant and non-Christian.

Jeu Dip or Joseph, was a first-generation immigrant from China, having come as a young boy from Southern China like many other Chinese to the US at the time. He worked for Farmer Sterling as a house boy or a mui tsai or 妹仔, where he labored on his farm and attended to any duties of the home. He later drove a milk truck, enabling a more expansive network of professionals. With such experiences among English-speaking Europeans and Americans, he became successful businessman, running a draying business that shipped goods by his horse-drawn carriage from the nearby San Francisco wharfs to Chinese Quarter merchants. Later he would run a mortuary for the Chinese. He was bilingual in Cantonese and English and able to bridge languages and cultures, affording him a particular type of capital as a professional.

Mary McGladery also immigrated as a young 11-year-old child from mainland China and was believed to be trafficked into a brothel in the Chinese Quarter for the first five months in the country (Martinez-Cola, 2018). Reverend Loomis, a minister to the Presbyterian mission of Chinatown, found the terrified Mary and brought her to the Ladies Protection and Relief Society, a Christian mission for displaced girls. The children's home was run by the relief society, located in a sparsely populated area on Franklin Street between Geary and Post, a historic practice of placing children's homes, and asylums away from the city's centers (Heritage on the Marina, 2020).

The children in the home came from households where difficult circumstances befell parents, but all were White, and Mary was the first Chinese resident. The matron of the society took her on given Reverend Loomis' encouragement and her concern for Mary's frightened state. Much later, Christian missions in San Francisco raided brothels in Chinatown and rescued more children like Mary, but she was among the first (Ngai, 2010).

At the home, Mary was given an Anglo name ascribed to her by an Irish assistant caretaker. Under her care, she was schooled in western customs, including the adoption of Christianity. Because all her housemates and caretakers were White and English speaking, she was fully immersed, linguistically and culturally. Her network within the mission, as a successful convert, enabled a type of social network that differed from the mostly working-class neighborhood of San Francisco's Chinese Quarter.

Neither Mary nor Jeu Dip were formally educated in a school system in the US and at the time there were no mandatory attendance laws. Jeu Dip's experiences as a young houseboy and businessman were his schooling, whereas Mary's were informed by the tutelage within the Lady's Relief Society, an organization and a home regarded as a Christian mission. Religion, its customs, the English language and its accordant middle-class values intersected to create a distinct and newly formed Chinese-American, the new and shared identities of Mary and Jeu Dip (Ngai, 2010).

Mary was 18 years old when she met the 23-year-old Jeu Dip and they courted in English (Ngai, 2010). Mary originally came from Shanghai where the language was Mandarin. She had been immersed in English since the age of 11 and was educated in the mission home. In comparison,

Jeu Dip came from Southern China's Guandzhou province where the main language was Cantonese and the language of most residents of the Chinese Quarter. At the time, it was rare to find someone who identified as a Chinese person having mostly grown up in the US and who had assimilated to most of its customs in language and etiquette and who had also attained a middle-class lifestyle. Mary and Jeu Dip became a unique Chinese-American couple living outside of the Chinese Quarter in a mostly white, middle-class neighborhood.

Mary had grown up away from the Chinese Quarter and although she was of Chinese heritage, the Quarter was not a space where she interfaced or identified. At the time, the Chinese Quarter was regarded as a site of brothels, drunkenness and illegal activities and, given her initial traumatic experiences in Chinatown as a young girl, she did not identify with its hedonic identity. Further, the proportion of Chinese women in Chinatown was one in 20 at the time, given exclusionary immigration practices that privileged the cheap and expendable labor of Chinese men who would be fully invested in their work (Lee, 2015).

Mary and Jeu Dip were married in a ceremony at the First Presbyterian Church in San Francisco with Reverend Otis, a minister within the Chinese mission presiding. Jeu Dip became Joseph and he and Mary adopted the German surname of Tape. The practice of anglicising names was commonplace for immigrants as it enabled their name to carry an astuteness of Westerness and Whiteness, and perhaps create the condition of fuller inclusion and belonging. In print, the Tapes could be like the guests at their wedding ceremony – White and Christian.

The anglicization of Chinese names was a practice supported by the Christian missions, one of which had been responsible for rescuing Mary as a young child. Perhaps intended to smooth interactions between American and Europeans who would have difficulty pronouncing their given Chinese names (Zhao & Biernat, 2017), anglicization was also a means for Christianity to metaphorically baptize them into their faith communities. By demarking lineages, ethnically and linguistically, Mary (Irish) and Tape (German), Mary and Joseph were adopted into the greater Christian community. Yet in appearance, they were racially Asian – the Tapes were Chinese. So, the Western naming convention situated them as well-convened guests that had adopted their customs and practices, yet their full inclusion would invariably be partial as they were ascribed as perpetually different and foreign (Leonardo, 2002).

The Christian missions in San Francisco and beyond, regarded Mary and Joseph Tape as successful converts. Their home became a popular destination for personnel working in the Christian missions to demonstrate how evangelism can lead to a fully assimilated Western family with the virtues of Christianity. A Sonoma County, California publication, called the *Weekly Calistogan* reported on the 'Americanized Chinese' and 'how the celestials on the Pacific Coast are adopting American habits and institutions'.

> John [wrong name used] and Mary courted and were married. John built a neat little house out in the western addition, where in due time, two little Tapes appeared: Mamie and John. It was an American family in custom, costume, and speech, and the mission folk used to take visitors out to the Tapes, and exhibit them as examples of how Caucasian the Mongolian might be made. (Independent Calistogan, 1885: 1)

The Tapes became the idealized and model family, which exemplified the success of Christian evangelism, which had implications not just for converting the Chinese within San Francisco's Chinese Quarter, but the greater global context – bringing Christianity to China. If the mission could accomplish such goals within the US, the hopes for doing so abroad seemed more possible. Such practices of showcasing the Tape family, provide a historical context for the genesis of the model minority stereotype (Wu, 2013): the permeable and cooperative convert.

English has long been a tool for evangelism within Christianity or what scholars reference as a 'missionary language' (Pennycook & Coutand-Marin, 2003: 37). The Christian mission who had rescued Chinese girls from brothels or sites of enslavement used the Bible and other religious texts written in English to draw them into the church.

The Tapes had four children, all of whom were US born. When their eldest, Mamie was 8 years old, the Tapes attempted to enroll her at the nearby Spring Valley School in 1884, the third established public school in San Francisco at the time. Yet her application was denied as the school's administration and the board of education policy for the district cited state education policies that excluded children who had 'filthy or vicious habits, or children with contagious or infectious diseases' (Political Code, § 1667). Demarked as a 'Mongolian' student, Mamie was denied enrollment at Spring Valley, and the Tapes began a legal battle to contest the decision. The Tapes sued the principal of the Spring Valley School, Jennie Hurley, and it prevailed in the California Supreme Court: *Tape v. Hurley* (1885). The Tapes won. Despite this seeming victory of early civil rights within public schools, the success was short lived when Mary reattempted the enrollment of her daughter, Mamie at Spring Valley.

When the Tape family tried to enroll Mamie after the California Supreme Court 1885 ruling in their favor, the Spring Valley administration did not comply. The administration claimed that classrooms were at their maximum of 60 students and that Mamie lacked the appropriate vaccination records. While the school was hustling to create reasons for not enrolling Mamie Tape, the school board was working on its own legal rebuttal, claiming that a free and public education can be availed to all US citizens, but the call for integration was not a requirement and a separate school would suffice. Thus, the California legal code was amended just nine days later to include 'When separate schools are established, Chinese or Mongolian children must not be admitted into any other school'. ('An Act to establish a Political Code relating to public schools,' 1885)

During this battle, Mary Tape took on an active role of resistance. She took to the newspapers to express her indignity of the district's response to her daughter's denied enrollment. Mary invoked her Christian and middle-class identity, writing to the school board in a local newspaper. Mary's writing is drawn verbatim from the *Daily Alta California* in 1885.

> Dear Sirs: I see that you are going to make all sorts of excuses to keep my child out off? the Public schools. Dear sirs, Will you please to tell me! Is it a disgrace to be Born a Chinese? Didn't God make us all!!! What right have you to bar my children out of the schools because she is a Chinese Descend.... Do you call that a Christian act to compel my little children to go so far to a school that is made in purpose for them. My children don't dress like the other Chinese.... Her playmates is all Caucasians ever since she could toddle around. If she is good enough to play with them! Then is she not good enough to be in the same room and studies with them?... It seems no matter how a Chinese may live and dress so long as you know they Chinese. Then they are hated as one. There is not any right or justice for them. (Daily Alta California, 1885)

Mary invokes constructs that lay the historical foundations for what we now reference as the problematic model minority myth (Wu, 2013, 2018). We see how Mary draws upon Christianity, the Western clothing that her children wear and the White, middle-class networks in which she and her children traverse. She reinforces that her children are not 'like the other Chinese' and that they do not behave in Chinese ways, like the children in the Chinese Quarter. By articulating her supposed symbolic capital of Westerneness and Whiteness, she admonishes the school board for racializing her child as fully and unequivocally Chinese, consistent with the language of subtractive exclusion which at the time was 'children of filthy or vicious habits, or children suffering from contagious or infectious diseases' and thus, their exclusion from public schools ('An Act to establish a Political Code relating to public schools,' 1885). Mary boldly acclaims that not all Chinese are the same and that there are differences in class, religion, a symbolic capital which she has supposedly acquired, consistent with the White Anglo Protestant construction of 'pulling yourself up by your bootstraps'. Mary argued that her degree of assimilation was high and merited her child attending her neighborhood school of Spring Valley.

Mary also draws upon her Christianity and calls on the board to act with grace as her daughter has been ascribed with 'disgrace' for merely being Chinese. She also uses a rhetorical device by stating and asking,

'Didn't God make us all'!! By using the evaluative language of sameness, she argues that as a collective group of Christians, they should draw upon such rationalities and admit her daughter to school. Mary targets her attention to Superintendent Moulder. Mary Tape's April 16, 1885 letter continues in her original words.

> You have seen my husband and child. You told him it wasn't Mamie Tape you object to. If it were not Mamie Tape you object to, then why didn't you let her attend the school nearest her home! Instead of first making one pretense. Then another pretense of some kind to keep her out? It seems to me Mr. Moulder [School Superintendent] has a grudge against this eight-year-old Mamie Tape. I know they is no other child I mean Chinese child! care to go to your public Chinese school. May you Mr. Moulder, never be persecuted the way you have persecuted little Mamie Tape. Mamie Tape will never attend any of the Chinese schools of your making! Never!!! I will let the world see sir What justice there is When it is govern by the Race prejudice men! Just because she is of the Chinese decend, not because she don't dress like you because she does. Just because she is decended of Chinese parents I guess she is more of a American then a good many of you that is going to prevent her being Educated.

Mary directly calls out Mr Moulder, the Superintendent of San Francisco Schools as having a personal grudge against her young child for being Chinese and criticizes him for persecuting her daughter, an American citizen. She goes on to confront the entire male, White board stating that they govern by racial prejudice and such behavior does not constitute justice. She declares that Mamie is more American than he and the board. Her appeal to justice for their problematic racial positioning of Mamie draws from the ideals of Christian faith – as believers experience maltreatment and as fellow Christians, the Board should rectify such inequities. She calls for the school board to recognize their flawed logics.

Mary admonishes the school district for not seeing her child as an equal to the other White students who attend Spring Valley. Importantly, Mary points out the race and Christian morals of her family with no mention of she and Joseph's immigration origin. Perhaps inferred in Mary's message is that she has become middle class, Christian, and is thereby redeemed and thus, now an equal, especially her US-born children.

Mary Tape also reinforces that her child will not go to a separate, Chinese school: *'Mamie Tape will never attend any of the Chinese schools of your making! Never!!!'* First, Mary claims that the distance is hefty, which at the time would be a lengthy walk and/or ride in a horse and carriage. Recognizable here is Mary's young beginnings in the Chinese Quarter, where she was trafficked into a brothel, a location that holds traumatic memories. Mary had been rescued and shed that identity in location and positionality and now, her children are subjectivities of exclusion from their public school.

In 1885 the beginning on April 13, 1885, just months after the adopted ruling (with Moulder's meddling amendment) of a separate school, Mamie and her brother, Frank would attend the reopened Chinese Primary School alongside children from the Chinese Quarter. Early photographs of the Tapes demonstrate the class differences among their fellow students. The children from the Chinese Quarter, all boys, and all first-generation immigrants, wore their hair in queues. Mamie and Frank wore western clothing, and their hair was cut and styled in a Victorian manner, consistent with how their parents and local Christian neighborhood were attired.

In the Chinese Primary School, the eldest Tape children began to learn Cantonese, not because it was taught formally in the school, but because it was the main language used among their classmates who lived in the Chinese Quarter. As Ngai (2010) describes, the Tape children acquired Cantonese so they could interact on the playground with their fellow students, demonstrating that English was the majority language of the household.

While the Chinese Primary School began to increase in membership from a mere ten to nearly 100 in just one year, Andrew J. Moulder, the Superintendent who Mary Tape had admonished demonstrated his disdain for the Chinese in a handwritten resolution affirmed by the school board and sent to the building principals on April 1, 1886.

To the Principals:
The Board of Education have adopted the following Preamble and Resolution which you will please communicate to each one of the teachers in your School.

'Whereas in this State there is an earnest and concentrated effort being made by the Caucasians to rid themselves of the Chinese element in our midst, whose presence in our midst is a gigantic evil production of great wrong to laboring men and women of the community and if not checked will directly and injuriously affect the future welfare of at-least 3/4ths of the children now in Public Schools of this City who of necessity must be the coming wage workers and whose welfare it is our duty to protect and advance in every way possible and advance in every way possible and, Whereas the Press, the Labor organizations, our Representatives of Congress and the municipal government of our Cities and Towns are doing all in their power to further the good work and accomplish by peaceful means the desired would, therefore Resolved That it is the sense of this Board that no Principals, Teacher or employee in the Public Schools Department of this City employ, patronize, and or encourage the Chinese in any way, but do all in their power to legally promote their removal from this Coast and to discourage further immigration.'

In these sentiments the Superintendent heartily concurs. They represent the feeling on this subject of the Taxpayers of San Francisco by whose liberality and cheerful contributions our Public Schools are supported.

But independently of this consideration the duty which the teachers owe to the children committed to their charge should prompt them to active efforts to save the rising generation from contamination and pollution by a race reeking with the vices of the Orient, a race that knows neither truth, principle, modesty nor respect for our laws. The moral and physical ruin already wrought to our youth by contact with these people is fearful.

Let us exhaust all peaceful methods to stop its spread.

Sincerely,

Andrew J. Moulder, Supt. and the School Board

(Moulder & San Francisco Common Schools School Board, 1886)

Moulder describes his beliefs about the contamination and pollution of the Chinese, as they conceivably had brought their diseases from afar, consistent with his historic claims that cholera was brought on to the US by foreigners. Moulder invokes his Christianity claiming that the Chinese have no modicum of truth and thus separation of them from the public schools is necessary. While a segregated school, afar from the San Francisco public elementary schools of the time, the growing representation of the Chinese posed a threat to the health, economic and religious aspirations of modernity and a democratic Christian nation. Moulder and the board were emphatic about Chinese exclusion, leading the California Supreme Court law to create the conditions for a separate Chinese Primary School just as the Chinese Exclusion Act of 1882 had taken hold.

Mamie and her brother, Frank attended the Chinese Primary School for several years (present-day Gordon J. Lau Elementary), but as its population grew, the school was to be relocated to an older high school, distant from the Chinese Quarter. As Mary and Frank's younger siblings, Emily and Gertrude were now school aged, the Tapes decided to move across the bay to Berkeley. In Berkeley, all the Tape children could attend a public school that did not have the same exclusionary practices. With the pressure of the case distant as the Tape family no longer resided within their radius, the School Superintendent Moulder rallied California state representatives to continue separate schools for its Mongolian students, a term that would then take on exclusion of multiple Asian communities including Koreans and Japanese who were tracked to the Chinese Primary School. In 1906, the primary school was officially renamed the Oriental School segregating the greater Asian diaspora of San Francisco.

Mamie Tape's US national origin was originally sufficient for the California Supreme Court to rule in the favor of Mamie's admission. But, the local school board, run by Andrew Moulder who undoubtedly used his sway as the former State Superintendent (Cloud, 1952) created the conditions for the California Supreme Court to change the details of its ruling in just a short nine days; a separate school, but not equal in any way given its inadequate staffing, funding and subpar facilities.

Mary Tape was an early feminist, advocating for her children's right to a public education within her neighborhood, largely argued on the citizenship of her children, not her race. The Tapes set the groundwork for *Brown v. Board of Education* (1954) and the case of *Tape v. Hurley* would be cited therein. The US Constitution's Fourteenth Amendment for an equal education would eventually outlaw school segregation based on race (*Brown v. Board of Education*, 1954, 1955) and San Francisco schools would later have to comply with the courts.

Being Asian in the US has always been a contested category, along the continuum of subjugation and valorization (Kim, 1999). The Tapes experienced subjugation and exclusion from schools. In response, Mary Tape attempts to valorize her family by claiming their class, Christianity, the US citizenry of her children, and inferring her physical and ideological affiliation with a mostly White, middle-class neighborhood. But as she valorizes her proximity, she disdains the Chinese Quarter and the Chinese Primary School. Such tensions illuminate the unique in-between space that she and her family occupied in becoming Chinese-Asian Americans.

2 Before Lau, there was Mrs Lau

Lucinda Wong Lee Katz, Kinney Kinmon Lau's Teacher

It was January 1970 and Lucinda Lee unexpectedly became a lead first-grade teacher at Jean Parker Elementary in Chinatown's San Francisco Unified Schools (SFUSD) on Broadway Street between Mason and Powell Streets. Lucinda was a Teacher Corp intern, a newly minted program committed to preparing recent graduates for teaching under the tutelage of a master teacher, along with licensure and graduate courses by night and weekends (Rogers, 2009; Terrar, 2009a). The Teacher Corp program was to provide her with mentoring with a master teacher. But, just before Lucinda's second semester as an intern, the principal said, 'We need you to take this over'. Lucinda Lee was thrust into on-the-job training as her master teacher had taken ill and would not be reporting until the end of the school year. Nearly all her students were newcomers from Hong Kong, Taiwan or Canton, China and the building designed for a few hundred students was over capacity (Figure 2.1). Amidst learning about the principles of teaching during her evening and weekend courses, Lucinda spent part of the school year in a storage room with her students huddled close to her as she taught them all subject areas in English. She shared, 'We found space wherever we could find it'. Within the classroom sat the reserved 8-year-old, Kinney Kinmon Lau, a recent immigrant from Hong Kong, who would soon become the lead plaintiff in *Lau v. Nichols*.

Lucinda Wong (Lee-Katz) was born in 1944 in the Chinese Hospital of San Francisco's Chinatown. Her parents came from Hong Kong and Cantonese was used in their North Beach home and immediate community. Lucinda was the eldest of four children, with two middle sisters and one younger brother. Lucinda recounted her father's ascription of her from a young age sharing, 'It was pretty obvious that my father raised me as though I was a firstborn male'. Her father found that Lucinda possessed leadership qualities and he continued to instill this confidence in his eldest over time.

Figure 2.1 Lucinda Lee teaching her mostly newcomer class of first-grade students in a teacher workroom. At the time, the instruction was in English only.

Fang family San Francisco Examiner photograph archive © The Regents of the University of California, The Bancroft Library, University of California, Berkeley. This work is made available under a Creative Commons Attribution 4.0 license. Full citation from San Francisco Examiner. Wood, J. (1970, January 23) U.S. Funds Urged for Chinatown Schools. The San Francisco Examiner, 3.

Lucinda's North Beach home was just adjacent to Chinatown and down the hill was her elementary school, J. Washington Irving on Broadway (present-day John Yehall Chin Elementary) where she and her siblings attended. In the early 1950s, there was no provision of English as a Second language (ESL) or bilingual programming in SFUSD and Lucinda spent her days in a general education classroom among her mostly Chinese Cantonese peers, also coming from households where only Cantonese was spoken. None of the teachers or staff at Irving were Chinese or Chinese American and the linguistic hierarchy was dictated by the mostly Caucasian and monolingual-English-speaking teaching staff, who did not live in Chinatown. Lucinda recounted her early experiences with her kindergarten teacher.

> Mrs Nelson (pseudonym), my kindergarten teacher, said to me, said to everyone, 'No Chinese here, no Chinese, only English'. And I remember, you know, it was miserable, just even in kindergarten. I had just come from a home where Chinese was the main language for five years. And then I went to Washington Irving Elementary School. And Mrs Nelson was my first teacher. And it was like a disconnect, you know... like what? We can't even speak Chinese at all? And all my friends were Chinese speaking because Washington Irving collared from Chinatown and North Beach. Okay, so, I had implanted in my head that you had to give up your Chinese to learn English. It wasn't true, but that was like the only connection I could make.

As a young 5-year-old, Lucinda constructed her Chinese as an aversion to Mrs Nelson and its use would impede her English and would nationalize her as a Chinese foreigner. Wanting to please her kindergarten teacher, Lucinda learned quickly that the school's medium was always English, and that Cantonese was reserved for home, Chinese school and speaking with other Chinese community members.

Lucinda's parents required her and her siblings to attend Chinese school after school every day. Many of her classmates from Irving joined her.

> So going all the way through American Public Schools, my parents decided that I was going to keep my Chinese language too. So, I went to public school from 8:30 to 3:00 and then come home to change bags. And then I went to Chinese school from 4:00 to 6:00, which was kindergarten through 12th grade.

Lucinda discussed the messaging she got from her parents and then from, Mrs Nelson who had 'long hair, braided and put into two buns on either side of her head'.

> So, the juxtaposition of her saying 'No Chinese here!' and then my parents saying we think Chinese is really important and you need to keep up your schooling was a disconnect when I lived with that. I learned how to code switch. I learned how to linguistically code switch and cycle socially—code switch. So, I knew what I had to do. But it wears on you.

Lucinda expressed the fatigue that comes with traversing different settings with authority figures configured distinctly. Lucinda mitigates the family language policy of Cantonese, reinforced by her family's expectation of attending daily Chinese school and the schools' macro language policy of English only, so Lucinda and classmates can demonstrate their Americanness by speaking only in English.

After her time at Irving, Lucinda Wong went onto Francisco Junior High, where her ascription as the 'eldest son' continued to hold fast as her father campaigned for her to run for leadership roles at her middle school. Lucinda shared, 'So, when I was in the seventh grade, he started painting signs with me'. But, at this interval in time, Lucinda, was rescinding her Wong name and taking on the last name of Lee.

Lucinda's father was a paper son. Paper sons (or daughters), like Lucinda's dad had acquired papers stating that they had a Chinese family member in the US with residency or citizenship. The period of the paper sons and daughters took hold during the Chinese Exclusion Act (1882–1965) but was most prominent in the early 1900s when the economic conditions in Asia were declining and America was prospering (Wang, 2007). Applying for paper son status was a legitimate way to make one's sojourn to the US as the only other method was to be a merchant and only few such permissions were granted annually (Lee, 2015; Takaki, 1998). There were other methods to claim paper son status, including taking on the identity of someone in the US to immigrate to the US.

Mostly men took the risk and paid for these papers to be theoretically unified with their paper family. For residents of San Francisco, adopting this method became even more probable, following the San Francisco's 1906 earthquake and fires, as many legal documents were destroyed in the fires that subsumed the city, including Chinatown. An estimate of 25% of the Chinese population in the US was undocumented hampered by the extremely restrictive immigration policies, namely the Chinese Exclusion Act (Ngai, 1998).

In 1955, Everett Drumright, who served as the US Consul to Hong Kong announced that many Chinese were using this paper son strategy and such fraudulent activities created a collective suspicion that Chinese Communism was infiltrating the West (Lai, 1994). With undue speed, Drumright introduced the 'Confessions Program' collaborating with Immigration and Naturalization Services, relying on self-reporting to move the amnesty proceedings along. Paper sons could now report their borrowed names without threat of deportation and reclaim their family name and maintain their US residency or citizenship. While this policy was advertised as an expedient measure to legalize a large body of Chinese living in the US, only 14,000 elected to do so. The program came with other objectives, stipulations, and thus risks.

Self-reporting of paper sons also included questions about Chinese friends and families who may also have false papers and suspected of spreading a Communist agenda. Self-reporting paper sons were interviewed, and part of the protocol included questions about their friends and families with expectation that paper sons would turn them in. Because the program was founded on suspicion, reporting paper sons were not willing to implicate anyone other than themselves and those not reporting, feared that reporting could lead to permanent deportation and repatriation (Lai, 1994). As many paper sons were now married and had families with US-born children, this was too great a risk to imagine. Further, many would have to share their manufactured immigration status with their immediate family and greater community, a betrayal that many did not want to unveil.

In 1957, around the time that Lucinda was running for student office at Francisco Junior High, her father was one of the 14,000 who participated in an Immigration and Naturalization Services (INS) Confession program, where he reported his paper son status and began the legal process of reclaiming his given family name of Lee. Lucinda had learned from her father that money had been sent for years to his mother in China, but the funds were intercepted by the US government and never arrived. When the cumulative sum returned to him in the US, her father was distressed that his mother had never received the money.

> So, somehow he felt like he was a liar and a cheater just because he came over as a wrong... he could not stand. I remember him, really puzzling

over what to do and he says, I'm going to court today and then he came back. He didn't say anything. If he did say anything, it's out of my memory bank. But, he simply told us that he changed our name. I didn't know how that was going to be reflected in my daily life. And then soon thereafter, maybe a few days later, the principal called me into her office, and she says, 'Lucinda Wong, you are now Lucinda Lee and we have the papers'. So, I had to shift my entire thinking. You know, I ran for the president of Francisco Junior High School, my dad said, 'I'm going to help you paint your posters'. And he said, 'Lucinda Wong for President' and we made about 15 posters, and I put them up in the school and hung them along the hallway. And it was like in the spring when I changed my name to from Wong to Lee. It was so shocking. To have that happen, so not just was I not supposed to speak Chinese, but I was under this cloud of fear that we were here illegally. And then I get my name changed in 8th grade. It was the weirdest thing.

Lucinda shared her ongoing concerns into college after she learned that she was not Wong, but a Lee. Her whole family behaved well, not wanting to draw attention to the authorities and feared knocks on the doors from officials. I wondered if the family language policy of attending Cantonese school faithfully from kindergarten to 12th grade was in part driven by her father's concern about his confession and possible deportation? I connected our father's histories in an email exchange (Table 2.1).

Table 2.1 Email exchange about language preservation (August 31, 2023)

Dear Lucinda: As I was thinking about your family's policy of Cantonese use at home and Cantonese use in Chinese school, and how they wanted you to value your language. I wondered too if this had anything to do with your dad's precarious concern, and yours, about deportation? I say this because when my dad was interned during World War II, he remembered kids going to Japanese school in addition to or in substitution of American/English schools in camp. Why? There were concerns that they would be sent back to Japan: Repatriation. The Issei wanted their U.S.-born Nisei kids who had little to no proficiency in Japanese to keep it up because they foresaw being kicked out of the U.S. Secondly, some Japanese Issei were so upset by their treatment that they could not consider a future in the U.S. for their family and elected return. Over 1300 were repatriated or expatriated (for the Nisei) back to Japan, including those U.S. born. Among all the participants, you were the only one that went to Chinese school K-12! Most stopped after elementary school or 'cut' Chinese school to hang out with friends. And most everyone kept their paper name and did not reclaim their family name. In appreciation, Trish	Hi Trish: I think you nailed it! The worry that all of us might be deported was part of his thinking for learning the home language (other than pride), especially for his first born since my name was changed back to the family name 'Lee' in 1958. I had the longest time and incentive for learning Cantonese. Your description of the over 1300 who applied to be repatriated back to Japan was such a clear reminder of what Asians went through during that time. Thanks for telling this very important story....Asians, 1882 Chinese Exclusion Act, Paper sons and daughters, Commodore Stockton, Jean Parker, *Lau v. Nichols*, Harry's influence and Chinatown Rising...these stories will be forgotten if we don't get them recorded and shared. Thank you, Lucinda

The effort to maintain and develop one's first language is tied up in one's positioning as an immigrant or a child of immigrants and as perilously documented, even Lucinda who was a US citizen. The possible outcome of deportation is so real, that language serves a tool to prepare children for a significant move; and one that could happen briskly. Consider the Lee family's from a language as right orientation (Ruíz, 1984), which posits that one has the freedom to use their first language, which invokes a sense of liberation; yet for Lucinda's family fear and restraint were moderating their interactions. Thus, if there is a language as right and resource, it was done out of a concern for survival of their possible repatriation/expatriation. There is historic precedence in this case, as was for over 1300 repatriated Japanese and Japanese American. For the Chinese Confessions Program, Lucinda's paper son status positioned her family as a possible deportee to China; a country she had never visited.

After graduating from Lowell High School, Lucinda attended San Francisco College (now San Francisco State University) and majored in music and musical arts and became a liberal arts graduate. At the age of 22, Lucinda joined the San Francisco Teacher's Corp, an intensive program designed to qualify teachers post-baccalaureate, given the quickly diversifying demographics of San Francisco, including the influx of immigrants from Southern China, Taiwan and Hong Kong (Low, 1982; Rogers, 2006; Terrar, 2009b). As Lucinda was regarded by her father and the community as a leader, Lucinda was encouraged by Chinatown leadership, and Reverend Harry Chuck from the Cameron House, a youth community center with Presbyterian roots, to apply for the Teacher Corp program.

The Teacher Corp was focused on teaching 'low income and disadvantaged youth' in partnership with local school districts and universities (National Teacher Corps Task Force, 1965). As part of President Lyndon B. Johnson's Great Society Program for social welfare, he embedded these foci within the Higher Education Act of 1965 (U.S. Congress, 1965). Its sponsors, liberal Senators, Gaylord Nelson and Edward Kennedy, advocated for teachers with distinct attributes suited for teaching in urban and rural settings, but also to challenge and innovate traditional teacher preparation programs (Rogers, 2009). Instead of identifying teachers from the typical teacher programs, the Teacher Corp identified 'bright' liberal arts graduates who were more likely to hold to equitably oriented aims, unsettling the goals of traditional programs held within colleges of education. In a conference sponsored by the National Teacher Corp Task force for the recruitment of future teachers, the statement was shared, 'What is our image going to be? Conventional educators or innovators, milque-toast or activists?' (National Teacher Corps Task Force, 1965: 1). Importantly, the National Teacher's Corp was an effort to disrupt the professional training in pre- and in-service education, creating educators who were focused on social welfare and community engagement. Studies of the short-lived National Teacher Corp program (later moved into other legislation) found that Corp teachers created culturally relevant curriculum, including content drawn from their local communities and reached out to local families regularly (Marsh, 1979: 25).

The San Francisco Teacher Corp hired progressive interns, many of whom were people of color, who were placed in schools throughout SFUSD. There were eight leaders who oversaw up to 10 Teacher Corp interns (Low, 1982). Some Teacher Corp interns spent years in the Peace Corp and brought this service-orientation to their work as developing educators (Daniels, 1971). The SFUSD positioned this program with great esteem, placing 40 Teacher Corp interns in their schools. Interns were featured in the *San Francisco Examiner* and other local publications, highlighting their busy schedules of teaching by day, licensure and graduate work by night and weekends, affording little time for family and friends (Drewes, 1969). As many came in as interns and were not classically certified as were their non-Corp colleagues, tensions often emerged from their political and ideological stances, which differed from their other traditionally prepared teaching colleagues.

The aspiration for Teacher Corp interns and teachers was to be placed in communities of racial match, but such was not always possible. Tensions grew thick as Corp intern and teachers pushed for transferring teachers to schools reflective of their racial identification (Wright, 1971). There were appreciably fewer Chinese teachers relative to other racial groups, and thus the number of Corp teachers assigned to Chinatown was not as proportional as hoped.

SFUSD Teacher Corp interns earned $75/day, while simultaneously taking coursework at San Francisco State toward their teacher licensure over a year, followed by a Master's degree. Many were hired full-time in their local SFUSD placements when done. Because most Corp teachers did not come in with degrees in education, this set them apart from their other colleagues who had mixed sentiments about their alternative track to licensure, along with the added attention they received for their willingness and devotion to serving in 'ghetto schools' (Wright, 1971: 3).

Lucinda was among a growing number of Chinese and Chinese American teachers who were gravely underrepresented in SFUSD schools, including Chinatown, where most of the Cantonese speakers resided at the time. Beginning in the 1969-70 school year, Lucinda's Teacher Corp intern placement was Jean Parker Elementary. Jean Parker was the smallest-sized building among the elementaries in Chinatown proper and the building was overcrowded (Wood, 1970). Every child in the school lived in Chinatown proper and all were recent immigrants from Taiwan, Hong Kong or Canton, China, most living in Single Rent Owner (SRO) units with one room per family and a common bathroom and kitchen area. All were young newcomers, including Kinney Kinmon Lau.

Within her crowded classroom, Lucinda Lee got to know her students well, connecting with parents often, a credo invoked within the Teacher Corp program. As her master teacher was out on sick leave in the Spring semester of 1969, Lucinda ran parent-teacher conferences that year and remembered meeting Mrs Lau for the first time.

> I was Kinney's teacher for one year and it was at Jean Parker School and his mother came in and said, 'Miss Lee, can you teach my son math in Chinese?' because I'm bilingual. And I said, 'Actually, the language of instruction is English, so I cannot but I can take him in after school and I can work with him and so forth'. She said, 'No, it won't work that way because he's going to keep getting further and further behind. I want him, I want his class to be able to learn English and learn the other subjects in Chinese'. I said, 'Well, that's not how the system is set up'.

Implemented in 1872 due to increasing concerns about immigrant language use 'infiltrating' the schools, English became the only medium of instruction in the US (Robeledo Montecel & Danini Cortez, 2001). Ninety-five years later in 1967, California Senate Bill 53 was passed allowing for provisions of bilingual education. Sponsored by Governor Ronald Reagan, California politicians and educators were experiencing the rapid influx of migrants from Mexico and Latin American, and using Spanish was seen as a viable method to teach students. The pressure for such provisions did not come from the Cantonese community nested in Chinatown, San Francisco, rather the dominant language group at the time tipped the scale in support of bilingual education. Although this law had passed in California even before Lucinda had begun her teaching at Jean Parker Elementary, she had not yet heard such messaging. Given the history of exclusion of the Chinese from the rest of the city, her own experiences as a child and that schools were not yet racially integrated, knowing about allowances for bilingual education would not have been on Lucinda's radar, and thus her internalization of a continued English-only mandate. The early messaging about the capital of English persisted.

Mrs Lau was steadfast, advocating for instruction to be offered in Cantonese so Kinney would not falter in the subjects that were not English language arts. She returned on multiple occasions, adding more reasons for furnishing Kinney with instruction in Cantonese – a form of bilingual education.

> So, one of the things that Mrs Lau triggered in me in 1968 when I had Kinney was that she said, 'I don't understand why in America, we can't teach Chinese and English at the same time?' …because she's from Hong Kong… and in Hong Kong, British Crown Colony…they could speak

Chinese and English, all intertwined, all the time. So, it was accepted ... and so English, as a second language, was the accepted form because you had to learn English. And nobody said you have to give up Chinese to learn English. *Nobody said that.*

Lucinda detailed how this differed from the English-only doctrine of her kindergarten teacher, Mrs Nelson, and the greater language policy of SFUSD and the state of California at the time where English was the only permissible medium of instruction, a 95-year-old California law instituted in 1872 (Mehlman Petrzela, 2010). Mrs Lau's and Kinney's early bilingual experiences within Hong Kong schools illuminated a different possibility: Schooling could have different language mediums of instruction and impact content and language learning, keeping students on pace with grade-level learning. Given that all of Lucinda's students were newcomers, Mrs Lau opened a new instructional possibility for Lucinda.

Deeply aware of the explicit and de facto language policies of her school and in her new role as an 'intern', she agreed to tutor Kinney after school in Math and she did so in Cantonese. Lucinda's tutoring could have been a finite and kindred moment between teacher and student. But the story of Mrs Lau's advocacy and Kinney's earnest curiosity was shared with her then boyfriend, Norman Katz. His roommate, Larry Katz (no relation), was a young lawyer, keen on civil rights issues. Lucinda shared, 'Norman and Larry were roommates. And Larry worked at Neighborhood Legal Assistance and told... Oh, my God... I told Ed Steinman about this case. So, Ed took it on'. After her conversation with Norman Katz and Larry Katz, Edward Steinman of the Chinatown Neighborhood Legal Assistance League reached out to Lucinda by phone. Lucinda described the tenacity of Mrs Lau and how she felt her son's instructional needs were not being met during the school day. Although Lucinda found her tutoring to be beneficial for Kinney, it did not compensate for the entirety of the school day, where all the instruction was in English. The year was 1970 and the groundings of the Lau case were developing and now in the hands of Edward Steinman, the Chinatown Neighborhood Legal Assistance League (Chapter 8) and activists like Ling-Chi Wang of the Chinese for Affirmative Action (Chapter 7). The *Lau v. Nichols* case would be introduced to the US District Court of Northern California in March of 1970, just as Lucinda was finishing her first year at Jean Parker in first grade.

In the 1970–71 school year, Lucinda was completing her Teacher Corp training and was now eligible to work as a fully certified teacher in SFUSD and did so at Jean Parker. In the 1968–69 school year, two years earlier, SFUSD had applied for and received a Title VII grant to pilot Chinese-Cantonese bilingual education; the first provision of its kind in the public schools of Chinatown (Supplementary Educational Center of San Francisco Unified Schools, 1969). Funded by the then named Bilingual

Education Department at the Department of Health, Education, and Welfare (DHEW), the budget was made available with the earlier passage of the US Bilingual Education Act of 1968. The total funds allotted by DHEW was $50,000 with SFUSD matching with $17,000. Girded by the participatory and service-oriented goals of the Teacher Corp, along with the pecking kindergarten teacher voice of Mrs Nelson, and the language maintenance message of her parents, she saw a Cantonese bilingual education as a method to enjoin children to a fuller repertoire of inclusion, linguistically, culturally, and racially. Lucinda made the move to Commodore Stockton Elementary to become a bilingual teacher in the 1971–72 school year.

At the time, Commodore Stockton was 95.3% Chinese with nearly all children coming from Chinatown proper (San Francisco Unified School District, 1974; Supplementary Educational Center of San Francisco Unified Schools, 1969). The Chinese program which Lucinda often referenced as 'experimental' given its pilot status had matriculated to the second grade and she was to be the teacher. Lucinda had been trained in the primary grades and preferred to be in kindergarten and advocated with her principal to be the bilingual teacher for the earliest grade as it was not yet being furnished. Lucinda remembered her terse conversation with her male, White principal.

> I think we should try and get bilingual-bicultural into kindergarten. I want to volunteer to teach it. And he said, 'There's no way we're going to have bilingual-bicultural last in our school and I'm not giving you kindergarten. You stay at the second grade'.

Lucinda's principal was unsupportive of bilingual education's start at Commodore Stockton and was resolved about keeping it small scale at the time. Undeterred, Lucinda continued to advocate for its inclusion and eventually, bilingual–bicultural at the kindergarten level would be implemented, but long after her tenure at Commodore Stockton. She did find a nesting place for early childhood, bilingual–bicultural education. She shared her push-back to her stubborn principal.

> And I said to him, 'Well, something's going to happen and it may be my leaving the school district', and I did in 1972–73. I went and started a bilingual-bicultural daycare center across the street called the Chinatown Community Children's Center.

The stubborn Commodore Stockton principal was thwarted. Eventually, Commodore Stockton would become a school with a Cantonese and Spanish bilingual–bicultural program, furnished in all grade levels. Bilingual–bicultural education was on the rise and Chinese American teachers like Lucinda were adamant that it was here to stay. The sun was rising for Cantonese-Chinese bilingual education, benefitting future Chinese students, an educational program that had eluded Kinney Lau.

3 Before Lau, There Was School Desegregation and Bilingual Education
Lucinda Lee, Commodore Stockton Chinese Bilingual Teacher and Her Students

Inspired and emboldened by bilingual teaching within a public school, Lucinda Lee transferred to nearby Commodore Stockton Elementary as a second grade bilingual teacher in the Cantonese-Chinese pilot program in the 1971–72 school year. The relatively new Cantonese-Chinese bilingual program had been underway since the Fall of 1969; the only one of its kind in the US. Lucinda saw the possibilities of creating a bilingual education that was not available to Kinney Lau, who was still at Jean Parker, and now a fourth grader. But in the 1971–1972 school year, her first year in the bilingual program at Commodore Stockton, the constituency of mostly Chinese students was about to change as *Johnson v. SFUSD* (1971) prevailed and district wide busing became mandatory. Chinatown, San Francisco was now to be racially integrated as was the rest of SFUSD.

The Cantonese-Chinese bilingual pilot began in the Fall of 1969. The grant was funded by the Title VII grant from the Department of Health, Education and Welfare (DHEW) as authorized under the Elementary and Secondary Education Act's Bilingual Education Act (1968) and came with many resources including dollars for staffing, professional development, consultants, curriculum development inclusive of calligraphy and illustrations used for Cantonese texts (Supplementary Educational Center of San Francisco Unified Schools, 1969: 31). Most of the licensed teaching staff were educators like Lucinda, American-born Chinese who self-described as having good communicative competence in Cantonese, but less so in its written form (Low, 1982). As the Chinese bilingual–bicultural pilot program in part had an aim of language proficiency, the district then identified native speakers of Cantonese, most educated as children and young adults in Hong Kong to serve as teaching assistants (Low, 1982; San Francisco Unified School District, 1974). As many of the children at Commodore Stockton were newcomers from Hong Kong, like Kinney, they benefited from an adult who had a similar and more recent immigration history, familiar with their historic schooling context.

Given that the program was a pilot, only part of the student body received a bilingual education even though most of the school population was Chinese and Cantonese speaking. In short, a first-grade classroom had one to two sections of Chinese bilingual/bicultural, whereas the other two sections did not. Thus, not all native speakers in the building received the bilingual/bicultural model and many did not receive any English as a Second Language (ESL) instruction either, an inequity that would be raised in the early stages of the Lau case.

In that 1971–1972 school year, Lucinda was teaching within a bilingual model and also within a classroom that was racially, linguistically and geographically heterogeneous: an initial attempt at a two-way bilingual program before such naming conventions existed. In looking at the classroom photo composite of Miss Lucinda Lee's room from the 1971–1972 school year, no longer was the portrait homogeneously Asian and Chinese like her 1969–1970 class at nearby Jean Parker, but a collective portrait that resembled the Latine community of the Mission, the Black community of Hunter's Point and the White and Asian faces of Noe Valley. The proportion of Chinese remained high in Lucinda's room as non-Chinese, English-speaking families had to choose into the experimental pilot program. Latino-Spanish speaking families were typically placed in a bilingual/bicultural program in Spanish, meaning the proportion of Latinos in her classroom was lower relative to the Spanish bilingual–bicultural strand at Commodore Stockton. We observe the earliest manifestations of English majority students choosing into a bilingual education, and Chinese and Latino students being placed into it; a long-standing critique about how language programs are conceptualized with greater capital for English majority speakers (Morita-Mullaney & Chesnut, 2022).

Staying Put: The Walkers

Lucinda Lee and I hosted a class reunion for the Cantonese students of her classroom from 1971–1972 school year, the first-year racial integration year across SFUSD. Lucinda had stayed in touch with many of her students and a few enthusiastically agreed to meet the class reunion. We decided it would be best to gather the Cantonese speakers and the English speakers distinctly, capturing their early experiences in Cantonese-Chinese bilingual education.

Linda, Melissa, Jeannie and Theresa, Chinese Americans, were all second graders in 1971 and lived in Chinatown within walking distance to Commodore Stockton. Each of them would walk to school with their siblings or friends except for Melissa, whose mother was always in tow, ensuring that she arrived safely at school. When they arrived at school, they would enter the larger playground with a basketball court on the ground level on Clay Street and play until the principal blew the whistle. Linda shared,

> ... we start playing whatever it could be, jump rope, jacks, whatever it is, until the bell rings and we line up, say the Pledge of Allegiance, and then go into our classrooms.

During the morning gathering time, the Chinese of Chinatown were the only children on the playground, and those that were coming afar by bus were brought in by a different entrance in relative secrecy. Lucinda remembered,

> You know... I was very well prepared by... the central office, that we were going to encounter lots of problems with the busing. So, they trained us how to go out and meet the buses, not let the parents come near us and walk the kids into the school immediately. Now, it wasn't most of you. It was mostly like Medora and Megan and Andre and all of the kids that came in. They were brought in immediately under... almost like guards, and I had to be at the front of the line to see... meet the students and walk them in. And this happened for, like the first couple of months. It was a big deal!

At the main entrance to Commodore Stockton on Washington Street were angry parents opposed to busing. Chinese parents no longer assigned to Commodore Stockton protested their children being bused out and mostly White anti-busing advocates from throughout the city joined them on the picket line. Lucinda's principal wanted the incoming students to be safe from the possible ridicule and anger of the crowd. Lucinda continued describing the procedure for bus arrival.

> He [the principal] basically said when the buses arrive and somehow, they were timed, and I don't recall more than one or two buses, but we would stand there and meet them. And then I don't know who they were, but people held the parents and the crowds back and then the kids would get off the bus, and I ushered them in to the closest door and then through the school down to the classroom... We see these people there, and that was it. I mean, they were anti-busing. They were making a stand. And some of them were parents, but many of them were not.

Anti-busing interest groups attached themselves to the energy of Chinese parents, taking advantage of the political and media attention brought to Chinatown. Interest convergence emerged as the demands of the anti-busing groups could be parlayed with the collective energy of the Chinese of Chinatown (Mintz, 1985).

Linda Chu, a Chinese second grader, shared her memories of her bused classmates, taking a circuitous pathway into the school. She shared,

Linda: Did they actually have to go up to the second, not the playground, that one level up? I remember a lot of students were walking up that way towards that mini yard and said, like there was a basketball court or whatever….?

Lucinda: There was a basketball court. Yeah, we had to walk them in the nearest door, which was very far away from our classroom, and we had to come in and then go down two levels and then walk across to the other school because Commodore Stockton was a very large school. They had the annex and they had the regular. And I recall being, you know, I wasn't afraid of much, but I was afraid that somebody might throw things at us or scream at us because I had to protect the kids coming in. And you can count in the photograph [class picture] how many of those were and some of them came from Hunter's Point, then from Noe Valley and then from the Mission. So, I had like two or three buses that I had to wait for and then we would bring them in.

Jeannie, Theresa and Linda remembered the picketers, but not the purpose of their stance.

Jeannie: The pickets, but I didn't understand what were they doing. I had no idea what they were doing. I remember mom bringing me to school… and just playing and we see all these picketers. I have no idea what they were doing. And I think the teacher didn't explain to us either.

Theresa: …I didn't know anything… anything about… I just thought I saw the kid walking on top and then say, 'Oh, that's interesting', but never thought anything of it.

Linda: I don't remember what was the reason, but you know, we were playing … but I did see the picketers. I just don't know what was the reason behind it. Kids were young!

Jeannie, Theresa, Linda and Melissa were young, 7-year-olds at the time, and they did not know the purpose of the protests. Afterall, they were the walkers and came in via the playground, distant from the entrance where picketers were located. It was not until they were bused to Patrick Henry Elementary in fourth grade, that the construct of busing would become more apparent to them. By then, the protests had subsided and busing was fully implemented within SFUSD. Families could see the full application of the desegregation plan for the duration of their children's elementary schooling at the interval of fourth grade. Thus, families could plan

Walkers and the Curriculum

Lucinda remembered how she managed the classroom during her first year in the experimental bilingual program at Commodore Stockton. During the day, there were three different chunks of time with different teachers and staff supporting students throughout the day, even though she was the lead teacher for all her second-grade students. First, was Chinese Language Arts or the developmental bilingual portion of the day for the native Cantonese speakers including Linda, Melissa, Theresa and Jeannie, which was led by Ms Tai Sui Fong. Ms Tai was a teaching assistant and lived in Chinatown. She was educated in Hong Kong and had some teaching experience. She would pull the Chinese speakers to one part of the room and teach them what would be equivalent to their grade-level curriculum in Cantonese. As nearly all the Chinese students in her classrooms also attended Chinese school after school or on weekends, their skill at Chinese calligraphy writing and reading was higher relative to the non-Chinese students who were bused in. Lucinda described this model as supporting their Chinese literacy.

While Ms Tai taught the Chinese students, Lucinda worked with the English speakers and some American-born Chinese who had higher proficiency in English, using a model developed by the pilot program called Chinese as a Second Language informed by curriculum developed by Gordon Lew (Chapter 4) and Robert Sung,[1] consultants and staff hired on the Title VII grant. Designed for non-native speakers, they worked on oral language and pronunciation of the nine tones and attended to the calligraphy strokes.

While Lucinda remembered the actual blocks of the day and their respective purposes, the students did not remember how they were separated at different times of the day within the bilingual program model. The Chinese students remembered the community that they created with one another and how they looked forward to coming to school to learn more from their new friends, bused in from distant neighborhoods.

Lucinda employed a lot of music, given that it was her major in undergraduate at San Francisco State. She remembered focusing a lot on singing musical jingles, which the students knew well and could sing on demand, either in English or Cantonese. As Lucinda had been a Teacher Corp intern, she held to its principle ideals of teaching a curriculum that was inclusive of students' varied interests and identities in the classroom (Rogers, 2009). The construction of teaching language and content concurrently (e.g. content-based learning) was not yet a developed language teaching concept, so she drew from the identities of her classroom. As the program was a pilot and experimental, this offered autonomy and leeway to figure out the best content and approach for her classroom. Further, this preceded the rigid academic standards that became characteristic of the educational reform of the 1990s and beyond.

For the Chinese students of Chinatown, they remembered the music and the little flutes that they played. Melissa shared, 'I remember the little flutes that we had… and playing them by number'. While Lucinda remembered taking them on a tour to sing at the nearby YWCA, the students mostly remembered their instruments and the formulaic way of reading the numbers and then expressing them through their mini-flutes.

While Lucinda and students shared the memory of flute-playing, the Chinese students mostly remembered the weekly field trips, which were a part of the Title VII grant, which stated.

> The pilot program will provide supplementary funds for transportation, ticket fees, etc., to make possible frequent trips by children in pilot class to cultural events such as plays, concerts, exhibits, etc., with special emphasis on those which have relevance to the culture and history of China and Taiwan (Supplementary Educational Center of San Francisco Unified Schools, 1969: 16)

Linda piped in to share her gratitude for all the field trips.

Linda: But I want to take this opportunity to thank mostly for all your weekly field trips. Oh my god, that was to this day, this is the only class that ever actually had a weekly field trip. And you know, it was just the funnest thing. And when I was talking to Megan, and it's so funny because that's the same thing that she remembered is that weekly field trip and that actually opened up my horizon because the thing is, you know, like we were, I mean, I was an immigrant, so parents don't take you anywhere at all. I mean, so this is like an opportunity to actually be able to go outside Chinatown and actually see things, you know, explore things. That's why I was so touched when we saw that Fairyland, that shoe! Yeah, I still remember today. And it was, you know, you might think is a tiny just reported that to this day, 53 years later, is still very vivid in my memory. You know, so I want to take this opportunity to thank you.

Melissa: I remember we did go to the Fairyland, but I don't know, sometimes it's been such a long time, but I do understand why I like to explore now is because you have opened my horizon, because I like to wander a lot, and explore and just do things that are little different.

Lucinda provided a window into spaces beyond the physical and imagined boundaries of Chinatown. The redlining of Chinese into its Chinatown was historically entrenched. Since the immigration of the Chinese to San Francisco as early as 1848, Chinese were not able to rent or own in places other than Chinatown and nearby North Beach. As such, Chinatown emerged as its own enclave and community, since outside of it was unwelcoming and hostile. Children were often told 'not to cross Broadway' into non-Chinatown areas (Chuck & Chuck, 2019). To describe Lucinda's students as unadventurous, sheltered and protected dismisses how the greater San Francisco community consistently treated them as a suspect class. Yet, under Lucinda's leadership with supportive funding from the Title VII grant, her integrated classroom traveled across Chinatown, San Francisco, and the greater Bay Area, traversing newer spaces.

During the 1971–1972 school year, each classroom was assigned a spot on the wall of the outside playground where they played before entering school. For Room 10M, in the basement of Commodore Stockton, students and groups of students each received a square where they could paint their memories of San Francisco. Linda painted Fairyland and Melissa painted a giraffe from the San Francisco Zoo (Figure 3.1).

The mural from Miss Lee's 10M classroom from the 1971–1972 school year is now painted over. Luckily, Linda Chu's future husband, William Tsui took a snapshot of it and assembled it into a photo album, capturing

Figure 3.1 Melissa Lai, student in Miss Lucinda Lee's second-grade Chinese bilingual–bicultural program painting a mural on Commodore Stockton's walls for Room 10M. Photo represents the first Chinese bilingual second grade classroom during SFUSD's first year of mandatory racial integration and busing (1971–1972 school year)

Figure 3.2 Excerpt of Commodore Stockton mural from Miss Lucinda Lee's 10M classroom. Photographed by William Tsui

many of Linda's school memories. On the bottom left, you can see Linda's painting with the Fairyland shoe, representative of her expanding landscape of the Bay Area (Figure 3.2).

Student constitution

With a blended and integrated classroom, Lucinda created the conditions for students to share the histories of their families, talking about where family members were born and what their parents and grandparents had experienced. As the children came from different parts of the city and had different immigrant or migratory pasts within their families, storytelling generated curiosity, connection, and care in their classroom community.

Melissa remembered her bused-in classmate, Megan Kitagawa, a third-generation Japanese American from Noe Valley who talked about her family's experience of Japanese incarceration during World War II. President Eisenhower issued Executive Order 9066 following the Japanese bombing of Pearl Harbor in Hawaii, leading to the large-scale rounding up of 120,000 Japanese and Japanese Americans into incarceration camps throughout the US. All camps were distant from the Pacific Coast as the Japanese were suspected of consorting with the Japanese enemies. The camps served to isolate and distant Japanese and Japanese Americans from this Pacific axis due to the suspicion of possible infiltration; claims that were never corroborated (Takaki, 1995). Melissa remarked on her own families' dislike of the Japanese, given Japan's historical invasion and occupation of China. But, when Melissa heard Megan's story, her perspective began to change. She remembered,

> I love Megan. One of those things I still remember about her concentration camp… she did a presentation to this day, I still remember… the concentration camp or what she's gone through. And my mom would say, 'Oh, Japanese don't like Chinese', and I say, 'Huh?' I mean, just comments like that. And I, you know, I think about it, but I didn't give that personally. You know, sometimes with the comments, you know, you can say, oh, you know, it kind of affects the way you think, but then you kind of know better, you know, as you go further in your life. And so, everybody's created equal.

Melissa revealed the intra-ethnic and intra-racial tension among differently identifying Asians as her parents conceived the Japanese with great suspicion and disdain. Through school integration, Melissa had contact with children with different histories she had not yet heard, and this contextualized and localized Megan's family's experiences in the US. Her classmate became the connector and changer.

Linda reflected on Melissa's connection about her parent's anti-Japanese beliefs, sharing that such was the same with her father. He had fought in World War II, as a solider for the Hong Kong Army, and a bullet 'passed right through his body'. She recognized the tragedy of war when the opposing side is perpetually the enemy, but how the next generation has an opportunity for restoration. Being with the same classmates at Commodore Stockton and later, at Patrick Henry, their narratives of their parents were being reshaped by the young classmates, like Megan, that they came to know at school. Linda shared,

> I mean, why is you know and then but then we learn, on the other hand and saying that last generation, it's not these people that actually had done any harm to us. Right? You know what I mean, this is the previous generation or whatever… I guess through that kind of understanding, you know, we just kind of like, say, 'No, we can't be biased about this', you know what I mean, you know, or you know, and I think throughout the time that we were there, you know, we hang around with these people for a good six years. Right. So, you know, somehow or other, we built up some kind of rapport, some kind of relationship.

The convergence of busing with a Chinese bilingual education created a distinct opportunity for histories to be unsettled and re-narrated. Melissa and Linda became such catalysts in their own families as Megan's story about her parents and extended Japanese family demonstrated the subjugation; a construct also shared by Chinese families' immigration stories of sojourning to the US. Together, they began building their shared Asian American histories and identities.

Leaving Home: The Bused In

Megan Kitagawa and Medora Payne lived in Noe Valley on the same street, a few doors down from each other, and attended Douglass Elementary, their neighborhood school for kindergarten and first grade. But, for second grade, they were assigned to Commodore Stockton in Chinatown as part of SFUSD's Horseshoe Plan for racial integration.

Megan identified as third-generation Japanese American female and her strongest language was English, but her heritage language was Japanese. She described her family and her greater neighborhood as very progressive. Medora identified as a White female and was monolingual in English and described her parents as being 'very, very liberal'. Megan and Medora traveled by bus daily and it took over 30 minutes to arrive, where Lucinda would meet their bus and escort them through the windy path to Room 10M in the basement. Lucinda recollected her memories of meeting their bus from Noe Valley and swiftly escorting them to their classroom.

Lucinda: ...And so, it was a very tough time. Do you remember Medora when you took the bus and got off the bus on either Washington or Clay? And there were cameras and all kinds of people there watching for the first two or three days?
Medora: Well, it makes me sound like Ruby Bridges.
Lucinda: Yes. It was like Ruby Bridges. It's only here.
Megan: That's so weird because just always in my mind, it's always been a predominantly, you know, Chinese American, you know, Chinese population at that school. There's a Facebook group about ... for Commodore Stockton alumni, and people are posting pictures from the 60s and the 50s and the 70s. And it's pretty much all, you know, Asian faces.

Lucinda expressed the anger of the picketing crowds, and how she and her colleagues practiced a safety procedure for school entry for the bused-in students. Medora and Megan remembered that the Chinese children were on the playground when they arrived and that they would meet them in the classroom, but did not recall the purpose of their alternative entry. Medora associated busing from her historic readings of Ruby Bridges with her own current students at the Fred Korematsu School for Social Justice where she now teaches. She had no idea that she was brought in under such close guard as a second grader. While Medora and Megan's entry did not resemble the federal marshals that accompanied Ruby to school each day in

Louisiana with White parents yelling at her while she walked under close guard, rather, they came in under the supervision of their Chinese teacher in relative secrecy. As middle-class students from the mostly White, liberal community of Noe Valley, they were to be protected by its teachers.

Medora and Megan were regarded as bright and later qualified for the gifted program in their district, but as high-performing students at their former Douglass Elementary, the Chinese program at Commodore Stockton served to enhance their level of challenge by becoming bilingual in a language other than their mother tongue. Further, early developers of the program wanted it to go well and saw how racial integration and bilingual education could co-exist. This idea of language and learner integration was long before the bilingual education field had the programmatic naming convention of two-way or dual language bilingual education (DLBE) in the US (García, 2009; Howard et al., 2018). Further, there was no thought of DLBE gentrification, where more privileged students crowded out the minoritized students (Delavan et al., 2022; Valdez et al., 2014). Busing was mandatory and thus, there was not the construction of selection bias presently critiqued within dual language models (Morita-Mullaney & Chesnut, 2022; Morita-Mullaney et al., 2020) rather, that students were placed in the school to meet desegregation policies. Given its pilot status, Medora and Megan were positioned to be high achieving, thereby making the Chinese pilot program successful and demonstrating the spirit of racial and linguistic integration. Two systems of language and racial integration could be mutual and complementary. The racially integrated constitution of the classroom (although it did not meet formulaic balances) addressed negative liberty or freedom from, and the bilingual program addressed positive liberty – freedom to (Berlin, 1958; Thompson, 2013).

The Bused and the Curriculum

Medora and Megan's Chinese classmates, Linda, Melissa, Jeannie, and Theresa, had been at Commodore Stockton since the 1969–1970 school year, prior to busing and in the first year of the Chinese pilot program. Most received a bilingual program from the onset, and all knew each other as they lived in Chinatown and attended Chinese school after school together. When Medora and Megan came in second grade, they were the newcomers to the Chinatown school, where the curriculum would now differ as they focused part of their day on the development of Cantonese. Lucinda asked them what they remembered about their second-grade year in terms of their language learning. Medora shared,

> I think I had a good feeling about the program. I wouldn't say that, you know, it really, it wasn't like an immersion program like my daughter here in 2020 ... so it's like really, really big. But I appreciated it because one, it had great teachers that were really dedicated and out there and really wanted to do something new and innovative.

Medora reflected on her child's experience outside of SFUSD, where she received an immersion education; schooling with a target language other than English, but designed for native speakers of English, and the blending that she experienced at Commodore Stockton was not the same. Medora also noted the scale in which immersion was building in her local district, relative to the small Chinese pilot program of her youth. Medora concluded by talking about the teachers and how devoted they were to the students and figuring out the innovative bilingual model by doing things differently and creatively. Specifically, Medora referenced Lucinda's emphasis on music, exclaiming, 'I've got my flute' and played the song they collectively performed in her classroom over 50 years ago. Lucinda and Megan marveled that she had saved the flute and was able to describe the method that Lucinda had used in teaching them to read music.

Megan then shared about her feelings about the bilingual program.

> ... I think because it was at the beginning of my education, I didn't really know anything else. I mean, I had two years of, you know, quote 'normal schooling'. And then I came into Chinese bilingual. So, I thought it was just fun...

Megan reflected on her initial schooling in her Noe Valley neighborhood where she attended Douglass Elementary or what she termed as normal school. But, her memories of Commodore Stockton, especially that first year reflected daily fun.

Lucinda also described the program model and how their day was divided, but Medora and Megan remembered learning Cantonese speaking and writing with Miss Lee, but both admitted that their level of proficiency was still minimal. They recognized that there was another teacher in the classroom working with the Chinese students, where their curriculum appeared to be more advanced than theirs, but like their Chinese classmates, they did not remember any other teacher besides Miss Lee.

Content and the Curriculum

Megan and Medora used Gordon Lew's lesson books when working in Miss Lee's small group (Lew, 1965, 1966). Gordon Lew was a native of Hong Kong and worked for the Community College of San Francisco as a Cantonese instructor and was hired by the Chinese pilot program as a consultant (see Chapter 4). His books were designed for young learners and for those developing literacy in Cantonese. Megan had sent me one of her original workbooks authored by Gordon Lew and described how she learned how to read and write in Cantonese and made such associations with English, her first language (Lew, 1965).

> I enjoyed it... I especially enjoyed the writing because when we learned that all these are pictures... because I love to draw. It just made more

> sense... instead of spending like, 'let's do you know, let's write out the word.' ... You know, at heart, it's just letters put together. But for me, just the Chinese writing part, it looks kind of like a heart big. You know, your arms are up big like a man. So, I just was fascinated with the whole pictogram thing.

Megan recalled how Cantonese clicked for her when she conceptualized that pictographs located where the meaning was laden, and not inscripted distinctly in letters and blends, like she had learned in English at Douglass Elementary. As Megan loved to draw, the visual representation resonated strongly with her. As she often toggled in English to Cantonese, she sometimes critiqued what seemed like an overly complicated system to convey the pronoun 'I' in Cantonese.

> Why is it so many strokes to just say, you know, or in English, as one letter, *I*. And then in Chinese it's 1, 2, 3, 4, 5, 6, you know, like 8, 8, or 9. What does the visual represent for? I? It doesn't make any sense.

The furnished curriculum helped her understand that writing was pictographic or logographic system and that each stroke did not necessarily represent a distinct sound as it did in English, rather part of the meaning. She used memorization to pattern the strokes from start to finish when the nuance of the meaning sometimes alluded her.

Yet, for Medora and Megan, the focus on field trips was the most memorable. While their Chinese classmates talked about Fairyland, the zoo and going to Lake Merced outside of Chinatown and San Francisco, Megan and Medora talked about the local trips within Chinatown proper. Megan shared,

> One of my favorite trips, just not even a field trip, was just going out around Chinatown, and she bought a box of cha siu (barbecued pork)... and she fed everybody a piece of cha siu, and I was like, this is the best thing ever and so and so delicious. So, things that we're centered around food were fun. You know, introducing us to like the New Year's foods ... and like moon cakes (in relationship to the Mid-Autumn festival).

For Megan and Medora's Chinese classmates, such food items were familiar to them. They celebrated the New Year within their local Chinatown community and ate cha siu and mooncakes. But, as Megan and Medora were eating these new foods just across the street from Commodore Stockton, they were learning alongside of their Chinese classmates about the meaning of the foods in relationship to Chinese customs. As many of Megan and Medora's classmates were American-born Chinese, they recognized the foods of given seasons and the annual rituals, but not necessarily their historical significance; a primary focus of the pilot Chinese program. Megan and Medora's Chinese classmate, Linda Chu shared about Kong – the day before the official Chinese New Year.

> The red envelope. So yeah... you say the good wishes and then your parents hand you these envelopes, right? But then we heard from school. There's such a thing as *Kong*... and that is actually the night before New Year's it [the envelope] is to put under the kids' pillow ... so this is learned. So, one day I remember way back when we asked our parents.... 'Won't we get some'? And then my dad snickered up, and then he finally begrudgingly handed off one envelope. But again, this kind of stuff is how we pick it up, and not necessarily from home, like Megan said. They might not be actually sharing this kind of culture, because it's all kind of embedded. You know what I mean?

As a result of schooling, and the explicit focus on culture, this differed for students like Linda, for whom the culture was embedded. Distinctly, we see how the Chinese students came to identify with their history in a way that made the enmeshed more visible, offering them an affirmation in their voice, especially in solicitation of extra red envelopes the day before the actual New Year! Importantly, the excavation of this history explained the constructs that undergirded the celebrations within their local Chinatown community. Without a keen focus on the reasons for given foods during certain celebrations, the history may have alluded Chinese students like Linda.

Student Interaction on the Playground

Megan and Medora remembered their interactions on the playground included their new Chinese classmates as they were in the minority, and also from a different community. Megan remembered the games that her Chinese classmates brought to school, none of which was standard school issue. Megan remembered playing jacks, Chinese high jump and plastic linking circles during recess.

> ... we love to play jacks. There is a similar thing where they had these plastic circular, linking, circle rings. There was something to do with that and hand you. So, we learned a lot of kind of like you say—Chinese playground games. Oh! Chinese high jump!

> You know. You take rubber bands and then you string them together. And you make a really, really, really long (stretched rubber bands)... and then you jump over it, and then you raise it, and then you jump over it, and then you raise it, and you you're getting up to like over your head and people will.... you know you have to kind of get your leg up there first when you jump over it. And then there's other variations where you know you could do tricks. You know there's more footwork involved.

Importantly, Megan and Medora played the games of the community, learning about the different rules that were unfamiliar to them. The playground was endlessly and discursively fascinating, not just for the games they would play, but the ways in which the Chinese would describe the identities of one another to Megan and Medora. Megan shared what she learned on the playground.

> Megan: ... that was one thing term we learned. It's cool. What's the difference between FOBs (fresh off the boat) and ABCs (American born Chinese), you learned about that.
> Trish: When did you learn about it from kids or the other kids?
> Megan: Because they would, they would let you know. If you know, if they are FOB or ABC. And I don't think we thought it was a bad thing. It was just, that's the term: FOB and ABC. If you were born here, or if you're not born here.

While this reference was commonly used among their Chinese classmates, Megan recognized that they used this as a marker to explain their origins and regarded as explanatory, but also as a term of endearment.

Bicultural over Bilingual

For the Chinese and the English speakers of Lucinda Lee's racially integrated classroom, students remembered their language instruction, but the bicultural element of the program were the memories that endured. Linda Chu spoke of her Chinese school that she attended in the afternoon as much more rigorous and stricter with someone monitoring the direction of her brush strokes and the way she spoke Cantonese. Linda found that the language teaching was less explicit at Commodore Stockton. The bicultural was the curriculum and the community they co-created in the classroom, on the playground and on their field trips throughout the Bay Area. Lucinda continued to remind me: 'It was bilingual-bicultural with an emphasis on bicultural'. While this in part could be explained by the pilot status of the Chinese bilingual program, it in large part spoke to a grander belief of fostering curiosity and exchange among the children, a relationship that has endured for over 50 years. Sun rising.

Note

(1) Robert Sung, a native of Hong Kong was the curriculum developer for SFUSD's Cantonese pilot program. He worked closely with Cantonese-bilingual staff to create the materials for the program.

4 Before Lau: Personalized Curriculum Writers, not Publishers

Gordon Lew, the Chinese Curriculum Writer

Gordon Lew is a minister, elementary teacher, college professor, Chinese linguist, publisher, and advocate for Chinese language instruction. Originally from Hong Kong, Gordon Lew came to Boston, Massachusetts in 1952 to attend the New England Conservatory of music. He came as a paper son, under the name Lew and united with his 'paper' family in Boston. He did not participate in the paper son's 'confessional program,' like Lucinda's dad did, as he was professionally established as a Lew. Gordon would go on to be one of the lead curriculum creators for the earliest stages of the Cantonese bilingual program in SFUSD.

During his studies in New England, he was drafted into the army and served for two years and then returned to his music studies, graduating from the conservatory in 1959. Gordon then relocated to San Francisco where he participated in the Congregational Church where he served as a youth pastor and began attending Seminary at the Pacific School of Religion. At the time, there was a high demand for bilingual Cantonese-English speakers to serve Chinatown, so Gordon was ordained sooner than his classmates and became a pastor at the Cumberland congregation in Chinatown. 'People liked my preaching' he said. Gordon made the word accessible to the different generations of Cantonese in the city. His connection with the church invariably connected him with the many Chinese after-school programs throughout Chinatown as many were hosted in churches. While serving as an 'interim pastor' while going to seminary, he also took on the role of teaching in the after-school programs or what local families would call 'Chinese school'. He developed curriculum materials that would be engaging to young children, many of whom were American born Chinese or newer immigrants who were not schooled in Hong Kong, Taiwan or Southern China and whose reading and writing in Cantonese was limited. As Chinese children had been mostly educated in US schools in English, and their families were mostly merchants, they used a repertoire of text needed for their jobs, thus their children's exposure to written Chinese was mediated by such circumstances.

While Gordon was serving as a pastor, teaching in an after-school Chinese school, developing Cantonese curriculum for the programs, he also worked for the *Chinese Times,* a paper local to Chinatown, San Francisco. Gordon shared, 'I was all over the place. It was crazy' to explain his many jobs and identities.

The *Chinese Times* was founded in 1924 and was regarded as the 'official voice of the Chinese American Citizens Alliance' (Lai, 1982: 1). The Chinese American Citizen's Alliance was formerly called the Native Sons of the Golden *State*, a fraternal organization developed by American-born Chinese in 1895 to advocate for the political and civil liberties of the Chinese. Yet, its evolution was done in resistance to the all-White and male, Native Sons of the Golden *West* as they actively waged anti-immigration campaigns on the Chinese, Japanese and Mexican community. In 1915, the Chinese Native Sons *State* group, created in resistance, would formally change their name to, the Chinese American Citizens Alliance – the official voice of the *Chinese Times*.

The *Chinese Times* was founded by Walter Lum and designed for the American born Chinese and the Chinese residing in America. The paper was published in Chinese, and for a short period of time between 1957–1959, there was a Chinese broadcast on the local radio stations (Lai, 1982). While the paper was positioned to add on an English version for the growing community of American born Chinese, such did not materialize.

Gordon joined the staff of the *Chinese Times* by invitation of his good friend, the editor who needed a translator. Gordon talked about the teletyper that whirred before him in the busy newsroom. The teletyper was set to receive news from China in the Associated Press format and it was delivered in Chinese. Gordon described how complicated China was at the time and he explained that the editor 'asked me is that that is about to start the Cultural Revolution (in China). So, there were a lot of news. And then also the Vietnam War'. It was Gordon's job to not only decipher the content, but to analyze and write it in a way that was accessible to its Chinese readership who were not originally from Mainland China and were mostly a merchant community. Gordon and his colleagues lamented that there was not a Chinese-English version of a newspaper for the Chinese of the Bay Area, specifically, Chinatown.

To address the need for a bilingual paper, Gordon founded *East West,* a bilingual weekly that was free of charge, with expenses offset by advertisement revenue (Figure 4.1). *East West* was regarded as 'liberal or left-of-center' and had sections in Chinese and others in English and circulated between 1967–1989 (Lai, 2008: 21).

Figure 4.1 *East West*; Chinese-American Journal (circulated in Chinatown from 1967–1989)

As *East West* was founded in 1967 during great civil unrest throughout the world, Gordon wanted the local Chinese to remain connected to the international diaspora of Asia. As he had served in the US military for a short time, he witnessed the impact of US relations with Asia as directly related to the treatment of Asian groups in the US, citing the incarceration of Japanese Americans as an example. He felt great urgency to address the details of US-Asia relationships in *East West* to prevent a repeat of an US-based Asian detention. Gordon shared the intense work he did figuring out US–China relations for *East West* along with his many other jobs, which led this his utter exhaustion. He stated, 'And that was when I was young…. 1960s is really scary'.

The bilingual *East West* weekly's initial pages were in English with Chinese following in the latter pages. Yet, the bilingual paper was not a parallel translation with the exact same content distinctly expressed in each language. *East West* was designed for the second generation, American born Chinese (English) and the first-generation Chinese immigrants (Chinese). Depending on the issue's content, English content could be longer relative to Chinese content. I asked Gordon about the Chinese section intended for the immigrant community. He immediately stated, 'Immigration. You know, how to get your green card… the INS just changed the rules… and the Confessions program'. As many Chinese immigrants of Chinatown had come with aliases or as paper sons, questions ran deep about the purposes and the possible drawbacks of the program. This content was reflected in many of the *East West* weeklies in Cantonese. The English version had more to do with education, employment, and advertisements for Chinese schools at the local churches and community centers.

The significance of *East West,* founded and managed by Gordon reflects the eventual publisher of the curriculum materials used in the Chinese bilingual program. There was an urgency to get curriculum materials into the hands of after-school programs in Chinatown, San Francisco, and the greater Bay Area. By owning the publishing company, *East West*, Gordon was able to produce and disseminate his materials swiftly.

Gordon was a licensed California teacher and wanted very much to work for SFUSD. He was a talented musician, educated in a music conservatory and had the content expertise of music and the teaching capacity as demonstrated from his years teaching in Chinese after-school programs. But he was often overlooked for teaching jobs. Gordon remembered speaking with a San Francisco Supervisor. The supervisor said,

> 'Gordon, you have a Chinese accent'. Of course, I have a Chinese accent [Gordon thought]. And he said that if you have a Russian accent, you have a German accent, I will hire you. You are a graduate of a music conservatory. So very well, good school and you have good marks and all that. But you have Chinese accent. So, we cannot hide. He said that maybe you should go to Siskiyou County (rural county).... But in San Francisco, no. In 1967... the [San Francisco] Unified School district hired me.

Gordon had been born and raised in Hong Kong and came to the US when he began his undergraduate studies. Although his proficiency in English was strong and his capacity to serve as an educator was more than adequate, he experienced direct linguistic discrimination by an elected official, a city Supervisor who had the power to deny him a teaching opportunity. Yet Gordon was unrelenting and continued to apply for music teacher jobs.

Beginning in 1967, just after *East West* was established, Gordon finally became a music teacher in SFUSD and worked at Chinatown's Jean Parker Elementary, teaching students music in the cafeteria in the overcrowded school. Gordon's time did not overlap with Lucinda Lee's at Jean Parker as he left in 1969 to teach in the newly formed Chinese Department at the City College of San Francisco, then under the same employment umbrella of SFUSD.

Gordon had previously done lectures for the City College of San Francisco on Chinese culture, and he was a familiar face to the faculty and administrators. During the interview process, Gordon remembered how the deans gathered faculty, students, teachers and administrators from area schools to offer feedback on the lectures offered by five candidates. Gordon was selected and became a Chinese language and culture professor. Years later he would learn that because he was already an employee of SFUSD, working for the City College involved less paperwork as he was already internal to the system. Yet, Gordon's history of how the schools operated and his deep knowledge of Chinatown's language education within after-school programs, he was well positioned to become an advisor to the Cantonese bilingual pilot program based at Commodore Stockton.

The Chinese Bilingual Pilot grant's secondary objective included the development of curriculum materials in English and Cantonese with intensified language instruction with a specified focus on continually refining and editing the materials used in the experimental program; initially for a group of 25 first graders (Supplementary

Educational Center of San Francisco Unified Schools, 1969: 13). Gordon fulfilled one of the key grant activities 'to utilize fully a number of expert consultants in the field of bilingual education so as to assure for the effective success of the pilot program' (1969: 5). Gordon drew from the materials that he had developed for the after-school programs throughout Chinatown and the greater Bay Area which focused on the writing system of Chinese and deepening students' understanding around cultural celebrations and activities.

Gordon was deeply aware of the language differences between American born Chinese and newly immigrated students from Southern China and Hong Kong. He saw this manifest within his after-school Chinese courses where the students were blended together.

> That's the difficulty. Now, if you go to Chinatown school, even now... You sit there and you know where the difficulties lie. Very simple because the people just came from Hong Kong, they are always the top of the class. They don't even have to learn spoken Chinese because they speak Chinese at home.... But the second and third generations are struggling... so they hate learning Chinese.

Gordon described the immigrant youth as having not only the spoken Cantonese that was native like, but that they were able to read, write and use proper stroke techniques in their calligraphy, which was not the case with American born Chinese students. Gordon continued describing how Chinese parents would often bribe their children to attend after-school Chinese school with the incentive of a dollar. One family offered Gordon the ultimate compliment when a child who was being bribed responded, 'Mom, you don't have to pay me anything. I will go to Gordon Lew's class'. Such stories demonstrate how Gordon brought the students' linguistic resources to light and affirmed their engagement in their own identity work.

Drawn from these experiences in Chinatown's after-school program, Gordon learned that his instruction needed to draw from the varied types of language learners within the pilot program. He used this heuristic to guide the development of reading and writing materials for SFUSD's Chinese Pilot Program.

One of his first publications used by the students in the program was Chinese New Lessons 1 (Lew, 1965). In this green colored workbook, students were introduced to Gordon's format. In the introduction he wrote in English,

> Congratulations! You are now studying Chinese. You may already know that Chinese is the most widely spoken language in the world, due to the fact that China is the most populous nation. Roughly, one out of every 4 persons in the world is Chinese. The Chinese written language is different

from others, as you will see, many of the words are composed of pictures or ideas. As you learn to combine the strokes and the basic work segments together to form new words. We will discover the logic of the ancient Chinese. You'll learn to see things as you saw it. You'll find that much of their wisdom and way of life has a modern tone. A rich culture is therefore, opening to you. We try to present this course in a non-complicated matter. If the lessons are planned to give students a basic vocab with simple sentence patterns and new characters are presented in various exercises which we have discovered to be better a better learning tool than rote memorization. Thus, you will find the lessons packed with exercises, translations, additions, readings, matchings, puzzles. We hope that you find this exciting and challenging, although there are many miles ahead. You are heading in the right direction. Happy learning,

Gordon Lew

(Lew, 1965: i).

Gordon's introduction articulates the history, logic, and values of learning Chinese. Distinctly, he draws out how the origins of Chinese can be seen with a modern tone, encouraging American born Chinese to value the past by making it contemporary. Gordon personalizes and humanizes the language agent in relationship to Chinese and not as a discrete subject area. He ends the introduction by shaping Chinese language learning as a lengthy sojourn.

After the introduction, the beginning pages turned to the language as a logographic, showing pictographs and superimposing the script on top of it to make sense to the students. Further, because calligraphy writing in Chinese involves strokes, knowing where to begin and end a stroke, lift the quill, and place it again on the page in relationship to the previous stroke, was important for the writing to be intelligible and for developing handwriting (Figure 4.2). Directionality of strokes was key. Each stroke had an on order with as many as 22 different steps to produce a logograph; a word or a phrase.

Alongside the print and the pictographs were places to practice repetitively. Each page contained a different concept and was illustrated and described simply. This initial workbook intended for the younger grades

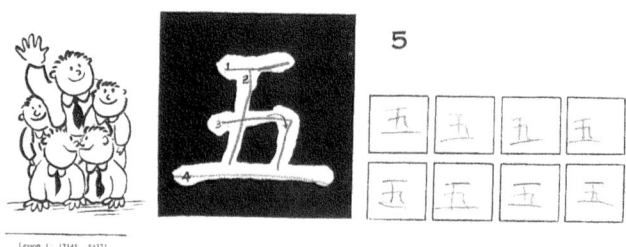

Figure 4.2 Gordon Lew's *Chinese New Lessons 1* (1965: 5)

in the Chinese pilot program was only 44 pages, so it was not overwhelming to an American born Chinese or students for whom Chinese was not their first language. As Gordon said, 'It was engaging'.

The Title VII pilot program had a secondary emphasis on linguistic and cultural affirmation as written in their original grant which stated, 'Further develop and refine each child's knowledge and skill in his native language providing an educational environment that will afford each child a greater awareness and appreciation of his "mother culture and tongue"' (Supplementary Educational Center of San Francisco Unified Schools, 1969: 12).

To this end, Gordon developed six books about Chinese cultural traditions including *The Story of the Red Envelopes, Winter Festival, The Moon Festival is Here, The Story of Ching-Ming, Dragon Boat Festival* and *Preparing for Chinese New Year* (Lew, 1971a, 1971b, 1971c, 1971d, 1971e, 1971f). All six books were published by *East West*, Gordon's publisher in 1971, noting that they were uniquely prepared for the SFUSD's Chinese Bilingual Pilot program.

While these topics could be seen as surface level, they were significant for the American born Chinese students who celebrated a New Year and received red envelopes filled with money from the adults in their lives. Yet many children enjoyed the cash contents but ignored the actual red envelope that held important messages of hope, support, and love from their elders. Students like Linda Chu (Chapter 3) in Lucinda Lee's class appreciated how Gordon's texts made the embedded ritual explanatory and explicit. Portrayed with illustrations and supporting text in English and Chinese, students learned about the genesis and the purpose of the red envelopes. In the opening to the book, *The Story of the Red Envelopes*, the Chinese Bilingual project staff wrote the following (Figure 4.3).

> It is with pleasure that the Chinese Bilingual Program, ESEA Title VII, disseminates this information about a specific custom in the celebration of Chinese New Year. Due to "assimilation", much of the content within this booklet has either been taken for granted or has been forgotten by many within the Chinese community. May this be the beginning of many attempts to bring into focus a very rich heritage – one of America's total heritages.
>
> February, 1971

Mr. Wellington Chew,
  Supervisor
Mr. Al Yuen,
  On-Site Administrator
Mr. Victor Low,
  Acting Project Manager
Mrs. Sophie Lau,
  Chairman of Chinese
  Bilingual Advisory
  Committee

Figure 4.3 *The Story of the Red Envelopes* introduction by Gordon Lew (1971e: 1)

The Chinese bilingual team of SFUSD were close knit and were devoted to stemming the tide of assimilation, which they witnessed as a central part of Chinatown's language shift. While the Title VII grant for the pilot program had much of the language of English language learning and adopting American ideals inscribed in the Bilingual Education Act of 1968, their application differed in that portions focused on 'providing an educational environment that will afford each child a greater awareness and appreciation of his "mother culture and tongue"' (Supplementary Educational Center of San Francisco Unified Schools, 1969: 12).

Gordon demonstrates the value of culture being a part of the daily curriculum and that students see their identities reflected therein. Critiques have persisted that only focusing on celebrations within bilingual programs reinforces a surface-level characteristics of culture, leading its learners and teachers to reinforce an esoteric view of culture, reifying problematic stereotypes. But Gordon's curriculum was localized as he knew that American Chinese youth's understanding of their cultural heritage was nascent. As we learned from Lucinda's students at Commodore Stockton, for the Chinese American students' the explicit amplification about the meaning of the a given ritual provided them with a deeper understanding of their histories as Chinese. The Gordon Lew curriculum was distinctly customized for Chinese students' identities.

5 Before Lau, Chinese Educators Were Assigned Outside of Chinatown
Victor Low, the Bilingual Educator and Administrator

Victor Low was born in San Francisco. He was an ABC – an American-born Chinese. He grew up in a Single Room Occupancy Hotel (SRO) in two rooms with his parents and seven older sisters. While SROs were considered small, crammed and for the 'low income', Victor saw his SRO as being even smaller and more crammed relative to others. 'We were very poor,' he said.

Victor's home was just adjacent to Commodore Stockton Elementary, the YMCA, an area playground and the First Chinese Baptist Church where his family attended and where he is still an active member. As he shared, 'This was my world as a young child'. Victor recalled his outside world being an encapsulated bubble; his Chinatown home. Victor recalled his language learning journey, listening to music on the radio and on his used phonograph. By replaying the songs, he took to paper and pencil, writing down the lyrics, repeatedly reinforcing vocabulary and grammatical patterns. 'It helped me learn English'.

Victor attended Commodore Stockton Elementary where 99% of the students were Chinese and the one African American girl, who was endlessly harassed. The families of Chinatown in the 1940s were a mixture of US born with most parents being immigrants. Victor and his family were residentially isolated and access to housing outside Chinatown at the time was not possible. Thus, their interactions among racially and linguistically different communities was rare, in part describing why the one Black girl was 'taunted and jeered' on the playground and the White teachers did little to intervene. After all, the White teachers did not reside in Chinatown proper, driving in by morning and driving out by afternoon to their White communities throughout San Francisco. Victor described one of his White elementary teachers applying her lipstick just moments before dismissal and promptly leaving Chinatown at the final bell.

All of Victor's teachers were White and mostly female, but one year he was to have Miss Elizabeth Hall, a Chinese-American teacher (Low, 1999a). Victor shared,

> When I heard that she was to be my teacher in the Fall, I couldn't sleep in the summertime. I couldn't sleep! I couldn't wait to have this Chinese teacher! …And when she acted like *them*… and not like *us*. Yeah, I was disappointed.

Victor realized how Miss Hall had assimilated in speech, mannerisms, and disposition to be like the other White teachers in the school who dawned white gloves and caps in the 1940s. His aspiration for racial and linguistic affiliation with his Chinese teacher and class community was thwarted.

Miss Hall was born in 1911 in San Francisco to her newly immigrated family from China. Her parents came as the Ho family, but immigration papers documented the name of Hall, and thus, the family name stuck. Elizabeth was supposed to attend the Oriental School of SFUSD, just like Mamie and Frank Tape from 1885. Elizabeth received an exception and attended the Pacific Heights School, where her family lived (Knight, 2013).

Miss Hall graduated from the Polytechnic High School of SFUSD and in 1931 received a scholarship to attend UC Berkeley. She later transferred to San Francisco State to receive her elementary teaching credential, consistent with the movement of elementary licensure to state universities. Upon graduation, Miss Hall was not able to secure a teaching job within SFUSD, and went on to serve in a variety of private schools, tutoring, while working on her Master's degree. In 1941, 10 years later, she was finally hired at Commodore Stockton Elementary. During her 10-year attempt, SFUSD had an arbitrary hiring quota of three Chinese teachers (Low, 1982; Wong, 1977). Despite the hiring practice of only three Chinese teachers, Miss Elizabeth Hall went on to serve the SFUSD as the first Chinese American principal. She led in area Chinatown schools, including Sarah B. Cooper, John Hancock and ultimately Spring Valley Elementary School, the site of the Mamie Tapes denied enrollment attempt in 1885. It was indeed an ironic full circle.

As a fourth grader at Commodore Stockton, Victor Low wanted a teacher that was 'like him'. Victor now recognizes that Miss Hall likely had to 'shape up or ship out', especially given the restrictive quota for Chinese teachers, which she tenderly had to mitigate and guard. But Victor recognized early on the value and significance of cultural and linguistic identity and affiliation, something that would guide his burgeoning commitment as a future bilingual educator in SFUSD.

After his elementary years at Commodore Stockton, Victor matriculated to Francisco Junior High School, adjacent to Chinatown in nearby North Beach area of the city. Like his elementary school, many of his classmates were ABCs, but he began to recognize the increasing immigration of families from southern China and Hong Kong to Chinatown. Along with his peers, they called the newest Chinese residents, FOBs, or Fresh off the Boat families. The FOB middle schoolers did not follow his ABC course schedule at Francisco and were isolated in Americanization classes. While such courses did focus explicitly on survival English and American history, the classes also had the aim of extracting their Chinese and acculturating them into American ideals. Such segregation was not limited to just school as it manifested in community basketball, Victor's favorite sport. Serving as a referee between an ABC and an FOB team during his days at Francisco, he was cornered in a building one evening by the FOB team, because he had made a call in favor of Team ABC.

> And I thought, I called it the way I see it. OK. And I guess they didn't like it. The FOBs didn't like what I did. So, after school, they waited for me so back... so, after school, four or five of them followed me and they stopped me. They pushed me inside a lobby and they were ready to hit me, and they were waiting for Dai Go (gang leader of the FOBs). I mean, this is the leader .... but the guy said, 'Let him go'. So, I said, 'What was that all about?' I had no idea what that was all about.

Victor clearly identified as an ABC, and he is not sure why the Dai Go gang leader of the FOBs saw fit to relieve him from a beating. While Victor could not name this rationale at the time, it was another early indication of his bilingual teacher identity of intermediary and interlocutor.

Victor continued to see the tensions between the ABCs of the US and the FOBs of Hong Kong and Southern China that were indicative of systemic segregation of students across lines of language, and immigration recency, particularly when he got to high school. He continued sharing, '...All of the FOBs went to Galileo and the ABCs went to Lowell and George Washington and Lincoln and whatever... so just this stratification... of division'. As Victor attended school long before language provisions were in place for identified-English learners, school placement was a mechanism for exclusionary and categorical tracking (Morita-Mullaney et al., 2020; Umansky, 2016).

During his years in high school at George Washington, on the foggy side of San Francisco in the Outer Richmond district between 1952 to 1955, he followed his Chinese classmates via the muni bus to school (Low, 1999b). When Victor arrived at his large high school, drawn from communities throughout the city, he was in 'culture shock' as he saw the racial differences in bold relief. His encapsulated bubble of Chinatown was unsettled. 'I had never seen so many Whites and Blacks in my life!' Victor exclaimed. He described his days at Commodore Stockton and Francisco

Junior High as a space of mostly Chinese, where they were the student leaders and participants in every extra-curricular activity. Now, they were blended, and Victor began to see the racial and income differences across student communities. In his band class, Victor compared his metal clarinet on loan to that of the first chair, who had a wooden clarinet which he owned. His fellow clarinetist also took private lessons.

In the Fall following high school graduation, Victor, having grown up at the Chinatown YMCA where many of his activities were structured and timed, he did a 'radical' thing, working at a summer camp in the Northern California mountains with young, White boys. Victor was amazed at the free-flowing nature of activities and the seeming lack of structure. He also was immersed in a speech community that differed than his variety of English and this came to the fore when one of his younger campers critiqued his pronunciation of 'Walter', the name of the camp director's son. Victor referred to him as Water. Victor shared, 'I never heard that medial L'. Victor was beginning to realize how he was ascribed as having a Chinatown accent.

Such racial, linguistic, and socioeconomic differences became even more visceral when he enrolled at San Francisco State for his undergraduate degree to become a teacher.

> So, when I went to State College, which is another experience talked about being seen... feeling—being a minority. I mean, there were only two tables of us, right? I got it. I'm a minority. I never knew that.

Sensing this profound difference as a minoritized student was further reinforced when he was told by the school of education that he had a 'Chinatown accent' and would need to receive speech services.

> And I didn't know I had a Chinatown accent because I went through school, public school from kindergarten to high school. And so, I said, 'Well, how do I, how do I get rid of this Chinatown accent?' So, I just already took some speech classes. OK, so I took it not once, now, I took it three times before I could go into the School of Education and twice before I could student teach and a third time before I could graduate by that time... It scarred me. OK. I was afraid to see anybody. I was afraid to open my mouth...

Linguistically segregated to Chinatown, and around many of his ABC peers in junior and high school, his days at the state college demonstrated the further stratification he had described earlier on in relationship to FOBs. Now, Victor was experiencing the stratification, but it was not interracial or interethnic, rather his Chineseness against the institution's Whiteness. His variety of English was not regarded as standard and certainly, not White.

Drawing from these formative experiences of linguicism, Victor reflected on his anticipation around his student teaching placement.

You know, so it took me a long time to figure that out. So, getting into teaching ... when all those kinds of experiences. I was hoping and praying that when they assigned me to be a student teacher, I finally realized that my accent and my Chinatown background and my poor educational background in Chinatown did not equip me to teach White kids. So, I prayed to God and whoever else did, I will not be assigned to an all-White school.

Victor went onto describe that his concerns were nested in the historic Chinese exclusion era and how such sentiments of subjugation became imposed. Victor continued, sharing how placement in an all-White school could position him. He stated, 'Putting me there would expose my inadequacies and may even jeopardize my employment'.

Victor, having attended area Chinatown schools until high school, had little to no interaction with White students in his K-12 education. Such residential and school isolation, along with the linguicism mapped to him by his teacher education program, he was concerned about his positioning at an all-White campus, where he would have to speak and behave like his White colleagues and families. Victor sensed the need to 'shape up' like Miss Hall, his fourth-grade Chinese American teacher.

Victor's hope materialized when he was placed at Hunter's Point Elementary School in SFUSD for his student teaching with Mr Fitzgerald, a White teacher. Most of his 34 sixth-grade students were Black. Victor recalled the banter he had with the children who had not interacted with a Chinese teacher before as they jokingly asked about 'his laundry'. He found such statements to be in jest and saw it as a method of connectivity and affiliation. Hunter's Point would later become the site where David Johnson, an African American father would work with the National Association for the Advancement of Colored People (NAACP) to forge a class action lawsuit again SFUSD on behalf of his daughter, Patricia for segregated schools; far more likely in the Hunter's Point community.

When Victor graduated with his elementary teaching license, he served briefly in the Army, but during his six months of service, he continued to think about 'the nightmare about being sent to an all-White school'. Victor applied to SFUSD, expressing his desire to be placed in a non-White school. He was placed in the Mission district at Marshall Elementary with a mostly Latino and Spanish speaking student constituency. In 1966 during his tenure at Marshall, a California state law was passed that required all sixth graders to take a foreign language. Victor found himself back at school taking Spanish courses at San Francisco State, spending his own salary to fund it.

The drive to introduce foreign languages to the classroom was indicative of the growing space program in Russia. When Russia launched its sputnik in 1957, politicians quickly pointed to a faulty US educational system as it had not produced a high caliber of students. The Citizen's Advisory Committee on Education was assembled in 1960 (Stone, 1966). The advisory committee created 825 bills, half of which were passed, one being the Fisher Act or the Licensing and Certificated Personnel Act of 1961, moving toward an explicit focus on content and diminishing the value of teaching methodology. Foreign language became a big emphasis influenced by the demands of university liberal arts departments who claimed the need for more expertise in the foreign languages (Coons *et al.*, 1960; Tierney *et al.*, 2011).

The Fisher Act provided an imminent timeline for the implementation of foreign language in schools. The subjects to be taught in elementary and secondary school, included instruction in foreign language by 1965, and beginning no later than grade 6 (Tierney *et al.*, 2011: 33).

Victor took Spanish classes at San Francisco State as the impending deadline of 1965 was upon him. He reflected on his language learning experience, detailing how his bilingualism in English and Cantonese set stage for an easier acquisition of Spanish.

> I also learned something else too… because I'm bilingual it's easier to pick up a certain language for some reason… I may be more used to it.

While his sixth-grade colleagues struggled to acquire Spanish or French, Victor found it formulaic and attainable.

Although the Fisher Act did not specify what languages should be taught in sixth grade, SFUSD landed on Spanish and French as the languages their sixth graders would learn. Victor remembered his initial reaction to teaching Spanish to his mostly Latino classroom. 'I was teaching Spanish to Spanish speaking kids. That's how stupid it was, right? These kids know more than me!' While this was Victor's first reaction to teaching Spanish to students who were more proficient than him, he found that this shaped how he included culturally relevant content into his teaching, shaping a unique form of linguistic responsiveness and engagement. He continued,

> …they were the new arrivals. They loved it [Spanish] because I was speaking the language. I didn't know much, but I knew enough. And you know, with the phonograph, you sing songs and whatever, right?

Victor again observed how one's native language is woven into identity and how it created a connection for his newcomer students. Drawing from his love of music, which he regarded as an early English teaching tool for him, he employed his strategies of self with his immigrant classroom. This time, Spanish was a part of the teaching straying from his personal and historic emphasis on English learning.

Victor next became an English as a Second Language (ESL) teacher at Jean Parker Elementary. Assigned to a set of 12 newcomers from Hong Kong, he spent his days on the school stage teaching basic, survival English to his students. Victor did not 'pull' the children out of their grade-level classroom, rather, he worked with them in a stand-alone class for the entire year, with the plan to integrate them into a grade-level classroom at year's end. The model was indeed an early-exit model. At the time, there was no ESL or Bilingual department at SFUSD, so Victor created his own resources, drawing from scant district resources and speaking with the growing number of Chinese educators throughout SFUSD. As Victor shared the native language of Cantonese with his students, Victor remembered how he, 'code meshed' across Cantonese and English with his students.

Victor was at Jean Parker during a time that the quota for a count of three Chinese teachers was lifted and as the number of Chinese students was growing. Harkening back to his 'Chinatown accent', he witnessed Gordon Lew's (Chapter 4) difficulty in accessing the SFUSD system because he was Hong Kong born and had an even 'stronger FOB Chinatown accent'. Victor, an ABC had gotten into the system following graduation from his elementary education degree, but Gordon, ten years his senior and an FOB struggled to secure a job in SFUSD and Victor believed it was due to linguistic racism. 'His accent was too strong', yet none of this was reflected in official hiring policies, rather constructed locally, demonstrating early push back by White administrators on the racial and linguistic affiliation that could empower Chinese students. Ultimately, Gordon prevailed, becoming a music teacher, where he taught adjacent to Victor's stage in the cafeteria. Over the years, they became best friends; a friendship that persists today.

In the 1967–1968 school year, Victor applied for leadership in the National Teacher Corp with SFUSD. As discussed in Chapter 2 with Lucinda Lee, Kinney's teacher, the Corp program was intended to bring new energy and fervor to the teaching profession and unsettle the traditional preparation that Victor had acquired at nearby San Francisco State's School of Education. While the interns were to be the new, liberal arts graduates with no formal teacher preparation, the team leads, like Victor needed successful teaching experiences and come highly recommended by their principals.

The city was divided into eight Teacher Corp teams and Victor had Chinatown, supervising eight interns, six of whom were Chinese; two FOBs and four ABCs and one Latino and one White intern. He described his intern team, of which Lucinda was a part as the best team among the eight. His other team leader colleagues were often overwhelmed and discouraged as their Corp interns treated them poorly. He reminisced,

The interns who think they own the world! They questioned... I guess, their knowledge. They questioned, their methodology. They questioned, whatever, you know? These team leads have been at it for 10, 20 years, right? So, it's not like they don't know anything. But here comes these interns... who thinks, God's creation or whatever...

Victor's description of the rebellious interns was captured in the *San Francisco Examiner* where some interns refused to participate in the Pledge of Allegiance during morning assemblies on the playground (Wood, 1969). The headline read, '5 Teachers Refuse to Salute Flag', going on to detail that it was a 'matter of conscience' that they objected to the pledge (1969: 1). The SFUSD involved their lawyers to investigate the matter, but because interns were supported by the federally funded Teacher Corp project, they were technically not SFUSD employees.

Victor felt quietly fortunate as his interns were energetic, open-minded, and willing to be mentored. He shared, 'So, I didn't have that problem at all. If anything, I think I earned their respect. So... because of my experience at Marshall coming up with this, I call it creative units to make it more relevant'. Victor had long created instructional units that were drawn from his student's experiences. At Marshall Elementary in the Mission, he learned Spanish and used music to connect with his students. At Jean Parker, he created units germane to their new community in Chinatown, and used Cantonese so students could quickly engage. As the Bay Area Rapid Transit (BART) was being developed, he used the construction sites to detail the civic realities of the students' local communities within SFUSD. His interns welcomed his mentorship, as evidenced by Lucinda Lee's frequent field trips and other colleagues just starting their teaching careers.

> I thought we were a good team... There was no strain in relationships. We were interested.... I thought we were interested in education. In fact, Roland Lim did his own unit only on Chinese-Americans history. He taught a unit at Jean Parker with the kids.

Victor's pedagogy about culturally inclusive education aligned with the open-minded and progressive oriented agenda of the National Teacher Corp. Given that all his interns were guaranteed jobs when they completed the program, he was thrilled that a new type of teacher would be working in Chinatown schools. During his tenure as the teacher lead in the Corp, based out of Jean Parker Elementary, he kept a close eye on the largest school in Chinatown nearby, Commodore Stockton Elementary – his former elementary school. In 1969, the district had written and received a competitive US Department of Education Title VII grant to pilot a Chinese bilingual program, and he was intrigued (Supplementary Educational Center of San Francisco Unified Schools, 1969). Gordon Lew (Chapter 4), his friend and Jean Parker colleague, was already working as a consultant to develop curriculum for the bilingual program. As the National Teacher Corp program was short lived, lasting only two years with two cohorts of teachers, when the position of District Project Manager of Title VII was opened, Victor formally entered the world of bilingual education.

His new office was located at the old Commerce High School in a dilapidated gymnasium next to the official central office. Like his stage experience at Jean Parker Elementary, he was hosted in a cubicle among other meso-level administrators charged with leading programs throughout SFUSD. Among his cubemates was Robert Sung[1], a native of Hong Kong and a hired staff person who developed most of the biliteracy resources for the Chinese Pilot program. Victor regarded Robert as speaking an elegant and native-like form of Cantonese as he was from the sophisticated Hong Kong. Robert became his linguistic mentor, mediating his Chinatown variety of Cantonese with the more formal one of Hong Kong. Victor and Robert figured out a linguistic exchange.

> … but he was the one I befriended because in my wanting to re-educate myself, I told Robert. I said, 'Well, Robert, I help you with your English and you help me with reading, writing and every day before work began'. You know, I helped him, and he helped me.

As Victor oversaw the implementation of the Title VII pilot program at Commodore Stockton, he continued to disparage his Cantonese, continually seeking out 're-education'. As he was now leading a bilingual language program, he was driven to be more acquainted with Cantonese in all its forms. Importantly, Victor regarded Robert as his linguistic ambassador, whereas Gordon Lew (Chapter 4) was his cultural mentor. These colliding events of bilingual education, desegregation and funding opportunities created the conditions for Victor realizing and reclaiming his Cantonese language identity which had been devalued over his formative and early adult years.

The Title VII program that Victor assisted was made possible by the authorized *Bilingual Education Act (BEA) of 1968* under the Elementary and Secondary Education Act. The BEA's authorization fell within President Lyndon Johnson agenda for social progress. While Johnson did not explicitly support bilingual education, he did see this as part of meeting the larger agenda of his Great Society Program, which galvanized the short-lived National Teacher Corp program.

Scholars have critiqued the initial BEA as largely being symbolic with inadequate resources, structure, and requirements (Crawford, 2002; Escamilla, 2018; Moore, 2021). The scale of the bilingual program was small with only 76 projects serving 27,000 students in the first year of funding in 1969 and no specificity about language allocation, program objectives, other than providing an education that would connect and affirm bilingual students with their native language. For SFUSD, the target was 25 students in one bilingual classroom (Supplementary Educational Center of San Francisco Unified Schools, 1969).

As shared in Chapter 2, the Chinese Bilingual Pilot Project was Title VII funded for $50,000 with $17,000 of support coming from SFUSD itself (Supplementary Educational Center of San Francisco Unified Schools, 1969). The budget was simple and straightforward and described on one page. Staff accounted for $31,565 of the budget with an additional $17,000 from SFUSD to hire a one bilingual teacher, a paraprofessional, a curriculum writer (Robert Sung), a clerk typist and a variety of consultants, one of whom was Gordon Lew. General operating expenses included a copy machine, a film strip projector, two language Masters, two listening centers, a phonograph, screen, slide projector, two tape recorders and a typewriter (Supplementary Educational Center of San Francisco Unified Schools, 1969: 31). Later a calligrapher would be hired to assist with the development of written texts as the program matriculated into the upper grades. Although the program was slated to begin at Jean Parker, a familiar location to Victor, it began at Commodore Stockton, due in part to its larger facility and the greater number of Chinese pupils (Interview, Victor Low, May 1, 2023).

The main objective of the Chinese pilot program was detailed in the grant application stating,

> The primary objective of the bilingual pilot program is to develop an experimental class, in which curriculum and materials may be developed for 25 first grade children from the target area that will afford them special and intensified instruction in English and Cantonese so that at the end of a one year period of time, the children will display certain language skills... (Supplementary Educational Center of San Francisco Unified Schools, 1969: 11)

Activities to meet the objective included understanding simple 'social' questions in English and Cantonese and that there would be parallel proficiency in both languages.

SFUSD's small ESL program leadership had committed to studying different bilingual programs throughout the country and visited such locations as McAllen and Edinburg, Texas, New York City, Miami Dade, and San Diego, California who had developing bilingual programs. While the models provided a useful reference point, all of them were for Spanish-speaking students and there were no commensurate models nor resources in Cantonese. Thus, a significant emphasis within the grant application was for the development of Cantonese materials. Importantly, these resources were not acquired by a large-scale publisher, rather developed by a well-organized group of Chinese educators after school and being printed in nearby printing presses in Chinatown. The curriculum was historicized and localized for the Cantonese-Chinese of Chinatown.

Victor continued in his leadership of the Cantonese program in Chinatown but became more involved in the overall leadership of the district's growing bilingual programs in many other languages which he said kept 'coming and coming'. The interest, need and advocacy within varied linguistic communities was present throughout San Francisco and bilingual education was experiencing an intense surge. The sun was still rising.

Note

(1) Robert Sung, a native of Hong Kong was the curriculum developer for SFUSD's Cantonese pilot program. He worked closely with Cantonese-bilingual staff to create the materials for the program. He is now deceased.

6 Before Lau, Collective Advocacy Had Many Tentacles
The Association of Chinese Teachers (TACT)

The quota system of three Chinese teachers within SFUSD had faded with time and more Chinese and Chinese American teachers were hired in the district following World War II. By 1959 a greater representation of Chinese teachers was evident throughout the city with a total of 71 Chinese identifying teachers (Low, 1982: 147). This growing set of Chinese educators in the 1940s and 1950s was a combination of those trained as teachers and those that could not find professional jobs in their given fields and ended up in teaching. The Chinese continued to experience hiring discrimination and teaching became a professional means to earn a living (Low, 1982).

The Immigration and Naturalization Act of 1965 alleviated a long history of Asian exclusion heeding to legal immigration to the US. In SFUSD, the number of Chinese students ballooned. Most Chinese were newcomers and the demand for language services was high. The profession of English as a Second Language (ESL) skyrocketed and many American born Chinese and Chinese residents were hired to serve in these capacities. In and around 1965, about 75% of Chinese teachers were assigned to Francisco Junior High, the site of the newly immigrated children from Hong Kong and Southern China and a feeder school from Chinatown (Low, 1982: 153). Many became de facto ESL teachers as they had some language proficiency to facilitate the newcomer's integration. Attending to the growth in the local community of Chinese students along with the incline in Chinese teachers hired, a professional organization was founded – a space to support Chinese educators and the growing Chinese community.

Association of Chinese Teachers, namely ACT was founded in 1969 by Chinese and Chinese American teachers of SFUSD, many of whom were newer ESL teachers at the time. The founders included

Rosemary Chan, Ruby Hong, Ted Wong, Phil Lum, Roger Tom and Sandra Gin (TACT, 1999). Later, in 1971, five of the founders developed articles of incorporation, changing their name officially to The Association of Chinese Teachers (TACT). TACT was regarded as a catchier term and as John Lum, TACT's initial newsletter editor described it '… some of us felt that our newsletter would often be anything but tactful. So, out of a sense of mischief, we stuck with the word "TACT"' (TACT, 1999: 11).

TACT was described as a non-profit and volunteer organization. Its original articles of incorporation in 1970 did not specify anything 'Chinese' about its focus, other than its organizational name (Wong *et al.*, 1970). TACT conducted some of its activities at the First Chinese Baptist Church, just a block from Commodore Stockton Elementary, a site where many of its founders were members (Chuck, 1971).

Following their official incorporation, a founding group of eight Chinese educators created TACT's goals:

- To pursue those aims that would produce educational excellence in our community.
- To participate in the educational policymaking of our community.
- To participate actively in making known the educational needs of our community to the school district and to legislative bodies.
- To promote liaison and cooperation between the educational policy-making organizations in our community.
- To promote professional growth and development of educators in our community.

(TACT, 1984: 4)

TACT described themselves as committed to educational quality through advocacy, collaboration, professional development, and policy transformation between school and community.

TACT's meticulous archives documented the active role of its membership with state and district policy, inclusive of such activities as letter writing, testifying in front of the school board, board of supervisors and/or the California state legislature. In the Fall of 1970, just following TACT's official incorporation, they participated in an active letter writing campaign asking their California representatives to repeal the Emergency Detention Act of 1950 (U.S. Congress, 1950). Also referenced as the McCarren Act, the policy was developed by the House Committee on Un-American Activities, asserting that any suspect of Communist activities could be detained. The Emergency Detention Act was developed shortly following the then lawful incarceration of Japanese Americans during World War II in the 1940s with an argument for such policies to persist should a national emergency necessitate its enforcement (Izumi,

2005; Okamura *et al.*, 1974). The Act persisted for 20 years beyond its 1950 implementation, and TACT participated actively in its repeal as it had an immediate impact on the newcomer Chinese families who were positioned as potential loyalists to the Communist party. Such thinking was reminiscent of the suspicion imbued with the Confession Program for paper sons, where those suspected of Chinese-Communist aspirations could be identified and deported, a circuitous strategy of entrapment that reduced the number of confessors from self-reporting. The goal of the Emergency Detention Act had a similar agenda. Andrea Lai, the Corresponding Secretary, wrote a letter on behalf of TACT articulating its problematic impact to the Chinese of San Francisco. She received a response from Robert K. Boyer, special assistant to US representative, Congressman Mailliard.

> Your letter will be brought to the Congressman's attention upon his return, and I am sure that he will appreciate our courtesy in taking the time to convey your interest in the matter. Thank you for writing. (Boyer, 1970)

In the end, the Detention Act was repealed due in large part to the Japanese American community who articulated the deleterious impact of war hysteria resulting in unlawful detention and incarceration (Okamura *et al.*, 1974; U.S. Congress, 1971). As many of the Chinese American educators of TACT had parents and family members who were paper sons and daughters, committing to the Confessions program meant the possibility of detention or, worse yet, deportation. The fear of deportation or repatriation was vivid for TACT members as their family members had experienced a long history of exclusion beginning with the Chinese Exclusion Act, delimiting the type and volume of immigration from Asia. The new generation of American born Chinese in charge of TACT could now advocate for the harms of the past to be foregrounded and remedied.

TACT also participated in the solicitation of bilingual education funds through the California legislature, to amplify the federal Title VII funding and district funding they received in 1969 for the pilot program based at Commodore Stockton Elementary. California Senator George Moscone, a civil progressivist for the African American, Asian, Hispanic and the LBGTQ community wrote a letter to TACT following their inquiry about Senate Bill 1252, which provided funds for a pilot of bilingual education for SFUSD's non-English speaking community, and while it prevailed, it was unfunded (Moscone, 1970).

In addition to TACT's statewide push on policy, TACT's advocacy from within their district was thoughtful and strategic. TACT's focus on adequate staffing within ESL programing, along with adequately trained staff was a primary force in the early years of TACT. Beverly Ng, a TACT member and an ESL teacher wrote an internal letter to Larry Lui of TACT's ESL Advisory committee updating him on the staffing crisis at her school. Ng went on to ask for concentration sites throughout the city to address the high influx of Chinese immigrants, all newcomers. Beverly wrote to TACT's ESL advisory committee, requesting two certificated ESL teachers to travel between two campuses and four instructional aides to be stationary at four schools (Ng, 1971).

Focus on the secondary level was also pervasive as student numbers were ballooning with content area teachers overwhelmed and unequipped instructionally. The English department chair and the ESL chair at Marina Junior High wrote a letter in March of 1971 to Dr. Thomas Shaheen, SFUSD's Superintendent. The letter was sent in anticipation of busing and that the district fell short of considering the language needs and rights of the Chinese community at Marina and beyond. Geralyn Guerin, English Department Chair and Judith Mohler, ESL Department Chair at Marina wrote,

> At Marina, of course, we are primarily interested in the language problems of the Chinese-speaking students, who for many years have constituted a large part of our school population. You must be aware that this district has failed to provide many of its Chinese-speaking students, both native-born and foreign-born, with adequate command of the English language. (Guerin & Mohler, 1971)

Geralyn and Judith represent language as a problem with great urgency and need, and localized to their school alone (Guerin & Mohler, 1971). Notes handwritten on the letter by TACT members demonstrate that their letter was used in district-level meetings to bring the language rights of the Chinese to the fore. Wellington Chew, the Chinese ESL director at the time handwrote a note to Larry Lui, the lead of TACT's ESL/Bilingual committee, stating, 'This letter is germane to the topic of Wednesday night' (Guerin & Mohler, 1971: 1).

While the topic of racial equity and language rights was part of district conversations in advance of busing, the messaging continued when mandatory busing was implemented in September 1971. The TACT ESL/Bilingual Committee met in the Fall of 1971, focusing on Francisco, Marina and Roosevelt junior highs, illustrating key concerns related to staffing, identification of students, collaboration with the zoning office for desegregation, district ESL/bilingual office and the Chinese bilingual program (TACT, 1971). The most pressing content articulated in the meeting notes addressed the policy intersection between racial desegregation and language program provisions.

Mandatory busing had begun in September 1971, just a month earlier and the district was centering its decisions around satisfying the aims of the Horseshoe Plan for racial desegregation with over 300 yellow buses moving elementary children across the city to their newly assigned schools.

This complicated and new matrix of student assignment made the provision of language services secondary, and TACT was vocal about such oversights. The October 4, 1971, ESL/Bilingual Committee meeting notes describe the tensions.

- There is a need for a closer working relationship the Spanish Bilingual Program since there is a need for Spanish bilingual teachers in Chinatown and Chinese bilingual teachers in the Mission.
- There is a need to place Chinese teachers in the Mission district schools <u>before</u> the next racial count.
- Through emergency funds (ESAP), hopefully more personnel can be hired. (TACT, 1971).

TACT identified their district's practice of race as a main organizing construct, superseding the construction of language (Crump, 2014; Flores & Rosa, 2015; Morita-Mullaney, 2018; Thompson, 2013) and that the Chinese were 'unimpressible' and in a sense, less countable (Low, 1982). As the *Johnson v. SFUSD* (1971) as implemented within the Horseshoe Plan was in force in its first year, TACT reacted to the district's assumption that the Mission District only had Spanish speakers and Chinatown only had Chinese speakers, when busing blended the racial and linguistic constituencies. As no de jure language policies were yet in force in California, only relying on the local construction of need, the ESL profession had emerged in reaction to the sudden immigration from Asia, following the Immigration and Nationalization Act of 1965. Because ESL or language services were effectuated as a *de facto* policy and had the earnest commitment of Chinese American ESL Teachers and supported by the newly incorporated TACT, energy was poking at the fissures in the official policy of racial integration.

The Emergency School Assistance Program (ESAP, 1970) or what TACT referenced as emergency funds in their October 1971 letter reflects funds appropriated for desegregation with the objective of reducing racial isolation (U.S. Congress, 1970). Authorized by the Department of Health, Education and Welfare (HEW) (the name of the US Department of Education at the time), districts could solicit funds from the federal agency for programming related to reducing racial isolation. As TACT had early knowledge of possible funds, they were prepared to ask the district for language and multicultural programming specific to the Chinese community, demonstrating TACT's early clarity in language planning and policy. Letters, meeting notes and newsletters of 1971–1972 reflect the early concerns over racial integration and language rights and TACT trying to reconcile how the two could co-exist and critiquing SFUSD administration's oversights.

TACT's early beginnings were affiliated with the North Beach Chinatown Council, where social issues were identified, discussed and action taken for resolution (Lai, 1982). In February 1969, a meeting was called by the Education Committee of the North Beach Council, inviting families and Robert Jenkins, SFUSD's Superintendent. Hosted at Commodore Stockton Elementary, 400 Chinese students and families attended the scheduled two-hour meeting. Social activist and chairperson of the forming Chinese for Affirmative Action, Ling-Chi Wang moderated the session beginning with 'Language and cultural barriers are keeping thousands of Chinese and Spanish speaking children from getting their education in the city' (San Francisco Chronicle, 1969: 2). Superintendent Jenkins responded, stating that everyone in the country was in crisis, but that San Francisco was best positioned to solve the problem, saying, 'We're determined to move strongly forward in bilingual education' (1969: 2). Jenkins went on to detail the federal funding that was available to support bilingual education, but the crowd wanted immediate solutions. A student from Galileo spoke about the lack of textbooks, critiquing the investment in the band program over curricular materials for the Chinese. The meeting came to a climax when a cherry bomb exploded under Superintendent Jenkins' chair and he and his administrative team made a quick exit. Outside the building were more protesters and Jenkin's car was undrivable as the air in his tires were let out. Editorials in the *San Francisco Examiner* framed the Chinese as a vocal and unappreciative minority group. One anonymous constituent complained in the editorial section.

> The entire Chinese community should not have to bear the onus of the poor behavior of this small minority. Yet it ill behooves voluntary migrants to, as it were, blame their language handicaps on the host country and demand that the better life be handed to them on a spoon. (Anonymous, 1969: 30)

The anonymous author went onto to discuss the high cost of ESL programming and how the 'instructed' should be appreciative of the services they receive and such behavior of harassing the Superintendent lacked decorum (1969: 30).

Just two weeks later on March 12, 1969, another emergency meeting just for Chinese teachers and Superintendent Jenkins was summoned by the Education Committee of the North Beach Chinatown Council. The 40 Chinese teachers attending expressed their concerns over being 'kept in the dark' on programming for ESL or bilingual with some thinking the programs were the same (East West, 1969). As many of the Chinese teachers were teaching outside of Chinatown proper, they were unfamiliar with the pilot bilingual program that was in its planning stages at Commodore Stockton Elementary and how it differed from an ESL program model. The early beginnings of TACT in collaboration with North Beach Chinatown Council revealed the early tensions between teaching methodologies: ESL or bilingual?

Many of the TACT teachers identified as American born Chinese and had grown up without any real language services in a sink or swim model in the public schools. Some younger TACT members worked as ESL teachers in SFUSD and saw the move toward bilingual education as a threat to their continued tenure in SFUSD (Ling-Chi Wang, Interview, February 13, 2023). Some American born Chinese teachers who constructed themselves as only 'kitchen Cantonese speakers' were concerned that their ESL role would become a bilingual one and their limited skills in teaching reading and writing would be revealed. Some members simply did not understand the programmatic differences and wanted clarification. Historically, SFUSD had not hired Chinese teachers in great density until 1953 given the immigrant influx, so having their ESL program model put into question, disrupted their notion of tenure for a coveted teaching job that had historically excluded the Chinese.

In June 1969, TACT leadership invited Wellington Chew, a Chinese American, and the District Supervisor of the developing Chinese Bilingual School at Commodore Stockton to answer outstanding questions about the scaling of bilingual education. The TACT ESL/Bilingual Committee reported to Chew that there was general teacher dissatisfaction with bilingual education. Chew was clearly incensed by TACT's assertions and their line of questioning, responding,

> 'I didn't leave an important dinner,' Chew maintained 'in order to be asked loaded questions.' He threatened to leave if the audience did not restrain itself from asking 'hostile' questions about Chew's bilingual program. (Lum, 1969: 2)

This interaction reveals the early tensions between TACT, which was more ESL leaning at the time, in large part driven by TACT teachers' historic experiences as Chinese children in Chinatown schools and their own positions as ESL teachers. Many worked at Francisco Junior High where nearly 75% of the Chinese teachers were hired in the late 1950s after a long stint of a three Chinese teacher quota (Low, 1982; Wong, 1977). Tensions would persist with Wellington, as TACT continued to push for the expansion of ESL programming throughout the city (Chinese for Affirmative Action (CAA), 1972; Guerin & Mohler, 1971).

In 1970, TACT's founders and leaders gathered their membership to discuss their ideological differences and misunderstandings across language program models hosting the *ESL/Bilingual/Bicultural: Dreams and Priorities* conference (Figure 6.1). The conference was not only attended by TACT members, but also leaders of the community and the local churches with community activist, Ling-Chi Wang and James Chuck, Pastor of the First Chinese Baptist Church. An important take away was that bilingual education was not a remedial program and had the potential to scaffold newcomer students into English, while maintaining their cultural identities and thus, the use of the term 'bicultural.' A result of this gathering was meeting with high school principal, Samuel Gompers who ran a remedial and continuation high school. He and his faculty were

Figure 6.1 The Association of Chinese Teacher's Conference on *ESL/Bilingual/Bicultural: Dreams and Priorities* (1970). Pictured left to right Wellington Chew, William Wu, James Chuck, Antoinette Metcalf, Ling-Chi Wang, Dennis Wong, Phillip Choy, Hannah Surh, Michael Kittredge, Ben Tom and John Lum

frustrated that well-performing students from China and Hong Kong were problematically positioned as low achieving solely based on their English proficiency. Using their native language allowed students to express their brilliance more fully, while reaffirming their cultural identities (TACT, 1984, 1999).

As understanding grew around bilingual education, the tensions lessened and energy was devoted to adequate and appropriate representation of Chinese and Chinese American educators given the historic exclusion of its students, like Mamie Tape and the three-Chinese-teacher quota. TACT actively interacted with the Chinese Bilingual Director, Wellington Chew (pictured in Figure 6.1) and requested meetings and wrote letters to Associate Superintendents and the Superintendent about hiring practices. In 1970, when Wellington took a leave of absence, TACT recommended six candidates and asserted their preference for Miss Barbara Gee who was a TACT founder, had a Master's degree in English as a Second Language, but lacked the administrative credential (Lum, 1970). The district included TACT and community members in the selection process, but ultimately the district dismissed their feedback and selected another candidate. Even faculty at the University of California at Berkeley who were preparing future teachers criticized the districts' rejection of the top three candidates recommended by the selection committee (Walton *et al.*, 1971). A method for critiquing and pushing back on district behaviors who rejected or dismissed TACT's feedback was via their TACT newsletter. Enter Yu Scum and Yu Rat.

John Lum, the younger brother of TACT's first president, Phil Lum became the first TACT newsletter editor in 1969. Using his wit, humor and creativity, John created the fictitious characters of Yu Scum because it rhymed with Lum, and Yu Rat because he was born in the year of the rat (Lum, 2004). John Lum and the next newsletter editor, Jones Wong, used Yu Scum and Yu Rat to present the perspective of TACT and the sentiments of its Chinese educators. Many of Yu Scum and Yu Rat's commentary was related to staffing and working conditions. In 1971, Yu

> **A FRUSTRATING TIME WAS HAD BY ALL
> (CHINESE, THAT IS)**
> by Yu Rat   (September 1971)
>
> Summer vacation has come and gone, and Yu Scum has yet to be bused out of Chinatown. In truth, Yu has not had a very restful summer because he has been sulking over some unpleasant happenings, to wit:
> - An Asian American not named as Bilingual Director
> - Leo Lowe's lost to the SFUSD (we wish him well)
> - the reappointment of Galileo's principal
> - the shabby treatment of Chinese educators at Galileo
>
> There's more but Yu is trying to recuperate.

Figure 6.2 TACT Newsletter from 1971 and 1973, featured Yu Rat and Yu Scum who used satire to articulate their concerns about administrative decision making within SFUSD

Rat (a.k.a. Jones Wong) wrote about summer vacation critiquing the appointment of the new Bilingual Director who was not Asian American, the inconsistent provision of leave requests and how Leo Lowe was not granted leave, yet was granted to a White educator (Figure 6.2). With sarcasm, the article ends with 'There's more but Yu is trying to recuperate' (YuRat & Jones, 1971).

Soon, central office administrators, most of whom were White, began to ask, 'Who are Yu Rat and Yu Scum?', believing they were bonafide Chinese educators of resistance. Brilliantly, Yu Rat and Yu Scum represented the TACT collective of Chinese educators who could speak freely in such prose, while avoiding individual scrutiny. Aside from the collective alias of resistance, many TACT members met with leadership, board members and superintendents to ensure that the needs of the Chinese community and its educators were being addressed. Persistent resolve for visibility and equity was central.

TACT was formed in 1969 right as Chinese bilingual education was being adopted and the role of Chinese bilingual supervisor was created. Yet, senior administrative roles alluded many, even those with the appropriate credentials. TACT was also created the year that the Chinese Bilingual Pilot was launched at Commodore Stockton in 1969, but most of the city schools were employing a version of ESL, and not all Chinese students were receiving such provisions. Jennifer Horne, an ESL teacher at Roosevelt Junior High and later the TACT president, advocated for more ESL staffing, given the growing newcomer community of Chinese students. She was the only Chinese educator in her building and became involved in TACT to directly address such inadequacies for Chinese immigrant families.

TACT also was at the forefront of the mandatory busing that began in the 1971–1972 school year, continually advocating for coordination between language programming and school assignment personnel, so that the linguistic needs of identified-Els (English learners), specifically those newly immigrated from China and Hong Kong would not be forgotten.

But ESL and bilingual education was not the only focus of TACT's early, pre-Lau years. TACT advocated for the hiring of more Chinese educators, fuller participation in hiring practices, and equal treatment of its teachers. TACT also committed to building the awareness of the non-Chinese school community who continued to describe Chinese students as suffering from language problems, mapping such negative ascriptions onto its Chinese educators. While TACT's membership had a good representation of the Chinese teachers employed by SFUSD, some Chinese educators were a party of one at their schools, oftentimes serving in communities where there were few to no Chinese students.

In TACT's pre-Lau years, they employed the strategies of affirmative action for educators and language rights for students and families to adjudicate language programming for the Chinese community. Yet such intersections were constructed to be in conflict as the public and key district and board officials conceived these as self-serving. If the district was to invest in hiring more Chinese educators and/or leaders, then the demands for language rights would increase. Additionally, because mandatory racial integration was in its initial years and Superintendent, Dr Thomas Shaheen, was a pro-busing and student integration advocate, having racial and linguistic integration work in tandem presented as having contrary aims, potentially devaluing the aim of racial integration. TACT's initial years show their fervent advocacy for connection, discussion and visibility. Chinatown was not the small enclave of exclusion, where the sequestered Chinese Primary School and Oriental School once sat, rather a sun rising and one troubling the waters of what full inclusion meant.

7 Before Lau, Community Agencies at the Core
Ling-Chi Wang and the Chinese for Affirmative Action (CAA)

L. Ling-Chi Wang was born in mainland China and grew up in Southern China's Xiamen region and later in Hong Kong given the impoverished conditions of China's war with Japan. He remembered the famine brought on by wartime, eating one bowl of rice porridge a day and miraculously recovering from what he believed was malaria when he was 11 years old. His mom and three other siblings would later flee to Hong Kong, the plight of many in Southern China given the Chinese communist troops moving southward. He spent his elementary and secondary years in Hong Kong where his parents described him as a mediocre to poor student, disinterested in the content of the classroom and more inclined to read area papers on politics. His parents were devout Christians and through this network Ling-Chi attended Hope College, a Dutch Reform school in Holland, Michigan where he majored in music. Later he would enter Princeton Seminary, but during this time he became increasingly interested in Semitic languages and moved his scholarly pursuits to the University of Chicago. In the heart of Chicago, he saw the social upheaval of the 1960s. Coupled with the social conditions of the city and his early readings of Antonio Gramsci, Ling-Chi was drawn into critical scholarship and how it was embodied within social activism. After his first year, he went to San Francisco for summer break with his then girlfriend, Linda, also a student in Chicago. While in San Francisco for break, Linda's hometown, he saw another urban portrait and the plight of the Chinese and Chinese American youth of San Francisco. He was drawn into this diaspora of Asian America and transferred to UC Berkeley for his PhD.

While a graduate student at UC Berkeley, he continued his work in San Francisco youth agencies, working with Chinese American and Chinese immigrant gangs in collaboration with the area YMCA and YWCA who had similar initiatives. While local law enforcement and at times, the Six Companies (the Chinatown governance) regarded the youth's behavior as the fault of the child, Ling-Chi saw how it was endemic of poor housing, under or unemployment, and accessible instruction within schooling.

He wanted to bring together all the stakeholders of Chinatown to systemically address these social inequities.

The Chinese for Affirmative Action (CAA) was co-founded in 1969 by Dr Ling-Chi Wang, Alice Barkley, Buddy Tate Choy, Germaine Wong, and Lillian Sing (Chan, 2007). The CAA filled a significant role in the civil rights movement of and for the Chinese in San Francisco as employment, and representational disparities were flagrant. To this end, CAA was founded with three goals. First, CAA addressed employment discrimination that dismissed the Chinese as being unqualified or unsuitable for area jobs. Employers often cited language barriers and the small Chinese physical stature that would make them incapable of hardcore labor. Secondly, was representation in the media, specifically radio and TV and that workers looked like the Chinese community and that programming was designed for the growing community of Chinese. Lastly, was the needs of the newcomer Chinese in Chinatown and throughout SFUSD whose linguistic needs were addressed inconsistently and inadequately throughout the city.

In 1969 when CAA was first formed, it was one of a few social service agencies with an activist agenda for the rising community of Chinese Americans (Chuck & Chuck, 2019). CAA's main agenda of advocacy and resistance stood in contrast to the long history of the Chinese Consolidated Benevolent Association, more commonly referenced as the Chinese Six Companies. The Chinese Six Companies maintained their connectivity to their homeland, often referencing Chinatown's residents as *Huaqiao* or more aptly, sojourners. Literally translated *huaqiao* means someone of Chinese ethnicity living on non-Chinese soil, but the nuance of a *huaqiao* is best understood as someone maintaining strong ties and roots to their home country and province of China (Wang, 1969, 2007). Representing the six main provinces in the Canton region, the Six Companies original pursuit upon its founding was to foster this continued connectivity, sending resources from the US back to their home villages. They also made arrangements for the retired, infirmed or deceased to be returned to the ancestral lands, a job that Joseph Tape mediated at his Chinatown funeral home (Chapter 1). The patriarchal governance worked with Chinatown companies to pay dues, which in turn would move between China and the US to foster this continual connectivity, both in resources, services, and allegiance to their Southern Chinese homeland. While this structure made sense to the Six Companies founding in 1882, as most of Chinatown's residents were male and unmarried, this was not the case for the transforming Chinatown. Now, there was a growing representation of young Chinese Americans who were civically minded, melding the histories of their families with the locality of their new homes. The formation of CAA represents a significant shift among the power players in Chinatown proper.

Ling-Chi discussed how he and CAA strategized approaches to reach the above aims. One was through the courts and another through the media. His first big job in his new role at CAA was to address the exclusionary practices within the construction industry.

Chinatown sits just adjacent to the financial district and with an 853-foot tall TransAmerica Pyramid building and a 27-floor hotel, both designed in a pyramid type shape. In the late 1960s and early 1970s, buildings were being renovated and erected to meet the growing demand for real estate in the financial district. The Justice Enterprise company had purchased the Old Justice Hall on Kearny Street, just south of Chinatown's Portsmouth Square (Nolan, 1967). Justice Enterprises contracted with Cahill Construction to create a mega-skyscraper-hotel of 27 floors. Before construction began, CAA worked with Justice Enterprise and Cahill Construction to guarantee a proportional representation of Chinese workers on the site. Given its adjacency to Chinatown, where there was an available workforce, the ask seemed reasonable. Further, Chinatown with its buildings no taller than three to four floors, thought the mega 27-floor hotel was to host a large Chinese Cultural Center with the new facility devoted to Chinese curation. Ling-Chi remembered the genesis moment, crystalizing CAA's vision.

> … before the construction began, you know, myself and several people met with the developer… they break ground. And so, we did not know, but we wanted an affirmative action program at all levels. And they [Cahill Construction] always say, 'Yea, sure. We will hire them.' And so, about a year, more than a year into the construction and it was about reaching the top and I decided to take a census about the hiring record, and I was shocked because of the 220 employees who have been working on that building, only four were Chinese… actually, Asian… Of the four, only one is a journeyman and the other three are apprentices.

Ling-Chi quickly took the area paper, Gordon Lew's *East West* to write an article, alerting the community of their lack of representation on the payrolls of the construction company. Coupled with Chinatown and Ling-Chi's disdain about the company's blatant disregard for their previous agreement, he called on the Human Rights Commission to mitigate the company's discriminatory hiring practices.

> By then they were so upset, we were prepared to ask about anything. So, we want the hotel to be at least 80% Asian. Top management, all the way to chambermaids…And incredibly… For the first 2–4 years, you know, you had a head of personnel, a head chef…

While Ling-Chi regarded the hiring practices of Asians as a success for the Chinatown community, as they now had consistent employment with fair wages, he still harbored the disappointment of the Chinese community that thought the building was exclusively for the Chinese Cultural Center, not a profit-making Holiday Inn hotel. CAA and the Chinese Cultural Center negotiated with the Holiday Inn management to lease the third floor through the year 2025 to host the Center for the cost of $1 a year, a somewhat bitter pill to swallow. The Center was now a renter beholden to the larger shell of the hotel that encapsulated them.

Part of the hotel was a bridge designed by a guest artist from China with a price tag of $600,000 (San Francisco Examiner, 1968a). Right outside the third floor doors of the hotel/Cultural Center is a bridge that goes over Kearny Street to Chinatown's Portsmouth Square; a supposed metaphor for connecting the Center with the Chinatown community. Yet, such symbolism was critiqued. The bridge was really meant as a fast pathway for hotel tourists to readily access Chinatown and not the other way around (Burks, 1971). Ling-Chi also problematized the bridge as it cast a shadow over Portsmouth Square and was money poorly spent when Chinatown needed adequate healthcare, housing and employment.

When the construction project concluded, the hotel held the keys to the iron gates that led to the bridge, the gates were seldom open, viscerally separating Chinatown from the Center with no thoroughfare between hotel, Chinese Cultural Center, and the Chinese community. If you are a resident, visitor, tourist, teacher or researcher in Chinatown, San Francisco, visit the bridge and observe. The gates are presently locked. But not for long. The 'bridge to nowhere' is due for demolition in 2025 (Whiting, 2021).

Ling-Chi and CAA's efforts with the investor and builder to add a Chinese construction crew to their team of 220 explains the discrimination in the workforce in the late 1960s. Many Chinese were excluded from rigorous journeyman training programs, constructed as having inadequate language skills or lacking the physicality for such roles. Yet, this exclusion was part of a longer history of subjugation. Many Chinese adults at the time were paper sons, daughters, or grandchildren, and thus, presenting oneself formally to a union appeared daunting or risky at best and many were permanent residents, not citizens. Further, committing to five years of training as a journeyman at a lower wage was a long-term endeavor. With no visible Chinese journeymen on the job, aspirations to pursue such work seemed improbable.

The Human Rights Commission was a regular resource that Ling-Chi used while at CAA, but he also moved to the level of the courts as he did in the case of *Mow Sun Wong v Hampton* (1977). CAA took issue with San Francisco's civil services, specifically with discriminatory hiring in the police and fire department. In 1971, US citizenship was required to work for the force. Ling-Chi shared,

> We sue the chairman of the Federal Civil Service Commission on the grounds that the commission discriminated against the Chinese....

Federal civil service at that time requires citizenship. And of course, a vast number of Chinese are non-citizens. They may have permanent residency, but not citizenship.

Lack of US citizenship also served as a proxy to infer that officers must speak a standard variety of English and not one accented or shaped by their local speech communities. Ling-Chi stated, 'because we basically contend that the people who do not speak English effectively are denied police service'. Ling-Chi elucidated how national origin, considered a protected class under the Civil Rights Act of 1964 and standard English proficiency intersect and give way to circuitous exclusion. In short, national origin and standard English proficiency must performatively show up as pristinely integrated. More simply, civil servants needed to look and behave like the Tapes did in the 1880s (Chapter 1).

By excluding the Chinese permanent residents as potential civil servants, the Commission was dismissing a valuable resource that could communicate with the Chinese-speaking community, reducing costs to the force. Such policies were shaped by the history of exclusion and while schooling and housing was now more open to the Chinese, viable employment continued to allude them. Ling-Chi worked with area lawyers, but quickly expanded his strategies. 'I decided that I am no longer going to go by litigation, because litigation takes too long'.

In addition to the citizenship requirement, the civil service also required that personnel be taller than 5 feet 7 inches. This summarily dismissed many of the Chinese candidates whose height often fell below the mark. Ling-Chi remembered Fred Lau, a third-generation Chinese American from Chinatown, and his dream to join the police force.

> He was a high school student, graduating from high school, getting ready and his lifetime ambition is to be a policeman. But he's about half an inch shy... And on the front page of Chronicle is that picture of Fred Lau hanging himself upside down from the ceiling and lifting weights to stretch himself on that last half of inch.

Instead of taking Fred's story to the courts, Ling-Chi ensured that his narrative appeared in multiple media venues including the new newsletter for CAA. Fred's accomplishments were highlighted, specifically his high marks on written exams during police training (Washington, 1970). Ling-Chi giggled at the seeming arbitrariness of Fred's exclusion based on 'less than an inch', but his laughs gave way to frustration as it took a media campaign and working with another Commission to bring Fred into consideration.

Ling-Chi connected Fred's story to Herb Caen's editorial in the San Francisco Chronicle about the San Francisco fire department. Ling-Chi recalled,

> You know, cities... like great cities like Tokyo, Shanghai and Hong Kong all have high rises. And if the Chinese are not qualified to be firemen, then those buildings have already burned down to the ground.

From the varied sources including the *San Francisco Chronicle and Examiner*, the CAA newsletters and other written exchanges between CAA and the San Francisco Civil Service Commission, Fred's Americanness was amplified to demonstrate his high degree of assimilability. He was a 'third generation' Chinese American and he 'performed well on his written exams' relative to some of his non-Chinese classmates, three-quarters of whom flunked (Washington, 1970: 18). Yet, the orchestration of such narratives demonstrate how national origin and language are creatively mixed to prove Fred's adequacy. He is distant from the real national origin of his grandparents and thus, more likely to be American-like and thereby, less Chinese speaking and more-English speaking since he outperformed many of his peers on exams. Furthermore, Fred is really trying to meet the height requirement, demonstrating his commitment to present policies. He presents as cooperative. Distance from national origin and native language equals high performance and support of present policies. Unlike Mamie Tape's case in 1885, where the mother exclaimed the Americanness of her daughter when she was excluded from Spring Valley, the mom did this on her own accord. With Fred, we see the CAA, the press and advocacy efforts asserting similar strategies of Americanness. Importantly, we observe how the narrative of Mary Tape are adopted by supporters in Fred's case.

Alongside of CAA's effort with the Civil Service Commission and the City of San Francisco, the arbitrary height requirement was lifted and Fred Lau joined the police force alongside four other Chinese Americans who were previously admitted at the 5 feet, 7 inches height requirement (Figures 7.1 and 7.2). Fred and Chinese American officers made up just four of the 8,200 police workforce.

Figure 7.1 Job announcement with height requirement for the San Francisco Police Department (San Francisco Chronicle, 1971a)

Figure 7.2 Fred Lau stretching himself toward the mandatory height requirement for the San Francisco police force (Washington, 1970: 1)

Ling-Chi and CAA used another strategy when the 1970 Census began its collection in 1969. Historically, census collection involved door to door visits to account for number of people in the residence along with their demographic backgrounds. In 1970, the Census declared that the process would be changing.

> In 1969, we try to stop the 1970 census. Because the census, this is the first time in American history, you know, that's our country's… constitutionally mandated census every 10 years… and first time in history that it was going to be done by mail. Given the way of the housing conditions, you know, they had these huge single room hotel rooms and only one address! And if the answer is the basis for mailing out the census form, we know the Chinese community. Massive undercount.

Residents would be sent a survey to be filled out and returned via mail (U.S. Census Bureau, 1973). Senior Census administrators claimed that it would create a more efficient and direct collection, reducing the cost to its taxpayers as there would be less need for on-site collectors (U.S. Census Bureau, 1973). Yet, what the Census did not consider was that each distinct address may be occupied by multiple families and not just a nuclear unit.

Many of the Chinese in Chinatown lived in SROs; Single Rental Occupancy households. SROs were a single room for a family with a common kitchen and restroom used by hundreds of residents, much like the one that Victor Low lived in (Chapter 5). Nearly all SROs in Chinatown had one address for the hundreds of people that occupied a building, meaning only one survey would account for 20 plus families. In some cases, addresses were unfindable. Ling-Chi and CAA contested this practice, turning to the media, the courts, and the US Commission of Commerce to address its exclusionary practice: the Chinese would be grossly undercounted, reducing much needed resources for Chinatown.

CAA collaborated with the San Francisco Neighborhood Legal Assistance Foundation to sue the US Census, taking on the US Census Director, Vincent Barbarra for the discriminatory practice (San Francisco Examiner, 1970). Lawyer Edward Steinman (who you will meet in Chapter 8 and the lead plaintiff lawyer for *Lau v. Nichols*) of the legal assistance office filed an injunction on behalf of two elderly Chinese men of poverty, Lee Quon and Silk Wing Work. The injunction detailed the improbability of Quon and Work being counted within the census given their residency in an SRO and that they did not speak or read English. The injunction directed the Census to change its methods to have trained and bilingual census takers go to the SROs and that the questionnaire be furnished in Chinese. The injunction also contested the need for census takers to be US citizens. A readily available and suitable Chinese-bilingual workforce was in Chinatown, but many were permanent residents, not US citizens.

The 1970 Census had been stripped down between the 1960 and 1970 census with the aim of making it more straight forward and less invasive as was critiqued during the 1960 census taking. Yet, with its simplified format, the US census did not account for the poor and segregated housing in Chinatown and how survey by mail would be problematic.

Most survey items were forced items with boxes to check. When it came to language, the census asked '17. What language, other than English, was spoken in this person's home when he was a child?' The prepopulated languages included French, German and Spanish with an Other box (e) to write in other languages. For race, the questionnaire stated asked, '4. Color or race: White, Negro or Black, Indian (Amer.) *Print tribe* _____, Japanese, Chinese, Filipino, Hawaiian, Korean, Other – *Print race* _____ '. Notably, the five main Asian racial subgroups were not differentiated as they are presently (e.g. East Asians, Pacific Islanders, etc.). The 1970 census demonstrates how race and ethnicity operate in tandem to racialize the Chinese and other Asian and Pacific Islander groups in a distinct way. The use of Japanese, Chinese, Filipino, Hawaiian, Korean as a color or a race constructs them as an ethnic group, not a racial category. As an ethnic group, the Chinese are framed as having mere cultural differences (Leeman, 2004). When there are just simple 'cultural differences', this is regarded as temporary, because eventually the ethnic enclave will assimilate and change over time. Given this ethnic status, the census differentiating or adapting for collection was unnecessary as Asians were cast as a swiftly assimilating ethnic group. Thus, offering the census in English would be suitable. This ethnic casting 'typically cleaves groups based on religion, language and nativity' (Hattam, 2007), a claim that cannot be fully made with such a diverse Asian diaspora.

For the growing Hispanic community the 1970 census survey was available in Spanish (US Commission of Civil Rights, 1974). Although Hispanic or Spanish-speaking was not denoted as a race in the 1970 census, the option of a bilingual survey was available to them, demonstrating how racializing and languaging the Hispanic community operated differently at the time.

Leeman (2004) distinguishes between ethnic groups and racial groups, arguing that the census has a long history of using these terms to construct minoritized groups. The term 'race' constructs racial groups as immutable, unchanging and, thereby, potentially dangerous, and suspicious (Leeman, 2004: 508). In the 1970 census, we see how the distinct category of Chinese makes them an ethnic group, not a racial group, and there are seeming benefits because they are not ascribed as dangerous, yet we do see the construction of their invisibility, lack of value and their 'unimpressibility' (Low, 1982: 24; San Francisco Examiner, 1970; Van Horne, 1970).

In addition to the Chinese being constructed as unimpressible and invisible during the 1970 Census, Ling-Chi connected voting rights in relationship to language rights stating, 'This is before a ballot initiative and, also there will be no census education. No bilingual ballot'. An important revision to the Voting Rights Act of 1965 would soon be forthcoming that would change the landscape of governmental agencies to furnish content in languages other than English to increase access to varied parts of the US system (Hsu Chen, 2012). If affordances of multilingualism were to be considered for the census and voting, then schools should also follow suit: Enter CAA's role in bilingual education.

CAA's involvement in bilingual education took hold when they began to collaborate with The Association of Chinese Teachers (TACT) and area principals to address the language rights of their newly arriving student community from Southern China and Hong Kong. Initially, TACT opposed the programmatic model of bilingual education as articulated in Chapter 6. In addition to his ongoing discussions of resistance with TACT, Ling-Chi would strategically talk with Chinese parents at Commodore Stockton, to solicit interest and engagement in bilingual education. The White, male principal who was bilingual education adverse with Lucinda Lee, critiqued Ling-Chi's recruitment. Ling-Chi shared,

> ... I would be talking to parents in the schoolyard about bilingual education and passing out leaflets. [Principal] would come out and said, 'Get out of here! If I see you again on this school site, I'm going to call the police and have you arrested!'

Despite the principal's threats and his opposition to bilingual education, the Title VII Chinese Bilingual pilot would eventually begin as a strand in grade 1 in the Fall of 1969 under the principal's reluctant leadership.

Ling-Chi demonstrates the varied approaches he and CAA took to develop and demand language rights for the Chinese students and families of San Francisco: the federal commissions of employment; the civil commissions for civil servants; and the schools' provision of a bilingual education and of course, the courts (e.g. *Wong v Hampton* and *Lau v. Nichols*). Ling-Chi shared his ideological grounding around the provision of bilingual education in this exchange.

> Commodore Stockton was the largest elementary school in San Francisco. Over 1,000 students! So, Jean Parker and Commodore Stockton both had about 98 percent Chinese and none of them getting any help in any way. And that's what really got me fired up... trying to figure out, on the one hand, we have to fight the school board, but on the other hand, we have to offer an alternative. Because I think that the sink or swim method is inhumane. Cruel to children. Cruel to their own self-image. You know, I mean, I'm inferior because every time I speak Cantonese in school, I get fined by teachers. You know, a penny, every time you speak, you get fined a penny. I mean that kind of oppression just to me is unthinkable. You made the children ashamed of themselves and they lose their self-confidence.

Ling-Chi identified that without a formal policy enforcing a language program, the teachers would be the final arbiters of language policy, creating and managing restrictive and harmful conditions at the site of the classroom (Menken & García, 2010). Ling-Chi with CAA would go onto to be instrumental in the recruitment of the *Lau. v. Nichols* plaintiffs and the language rights of the Chinese, collaborating with legal aid lawyer, Edward Steinman on the development of the case. Ling-Chi argued for the case to be centered on the Chinese amidst immense political pressure for the case to be Latine-facing (Art, Research, and Curriculum Associates, 1994).

8 Before Lau, a 'Reggie' Found a Way

Edward Steinman, J.D., the Lau Lawyer

Edward Steinman grew up in Chicago, Illinois in a Jewish household where he often heard Yiddish among his extended family and within the neighborhood. After high school, he stayed close to home and attended Northwestern University for his undergraduate degree and graduated when he was 20 years old. Right after graduation, he relocated to California to study law at Stanford University and never left California. At Stanford, Ed strongly identified as a civil rights activist and aspired to such a vocation during and after his studies. Upon his graduation in 1968, the Reginald Heber Smith Fellowship program was just in its second year, placing new lawyers into communities of poverty, working in legal aid offices.

The philosophical and the structural support for Ed's legal fellowship was inspired by Heber-Smith's 1919 report, *Justice and the Poor*, detailing the history of legal aid (Smith & Carnegie Foundation for the Advancement of Teaching, 1919). In 1920, the American Bar Association (ABA) heeded Smith's call and advocated for legal aid resources to be developed throughout the country to address the needs of the poor. Yet most legal aid never took their clients to court, owing in part to limited resources (Houseman & Perle, 2007). The National Association for the Advanced of Colored People (NAACP) and the American Civil Liberties Union (ACLU) later became involved in the 1960s and in cooperation with the Ford Foundation, legal aid offices were set up within the communities of the poor where services were more readily accessible (Houseman & Perle, 2007).

In 1964 the Economic Opportunity Act (EOA) was passed by Congress and was the catalyst for the development of President Lyndon B. Johnson's War on Poverty (Johnson, 1964). The Office for Economic Opportunity was formed and for the first time, federal monies were devoted to the poor and extended beyond local and national foundations to support community action agencies, (CAAs—not to be confused with the Chinese for Affirmative Action) where the dollars distributed did not have legal counseling as part of their activities. Local community action agencies often critiqued the seeming agenda of legal counsel, more focused on grander and large-scale issues, versus the uniqueness of each community (Houseman & Perle, 2007:

7). In coordination with the ABA and EOC offices, various committees were formed and guidelines on the provision of legal aid services was articulated. The outcome permitted legal aid lawyers to pursue cases on behalf of community action agency clients, that may or may not have been consistent with the goals of a given agency (2007: 9). Thus, we observe a potentially centralized agenda apart from community action agencies that may have overshadowed or dismissed the local needs of a specific community.

An outcome of the EOC office and its supporting legislation was the Reginald Heber Smith Fellowship. The fellowships were initially housed and administered at Georgetown University's law school, but eventually moved to Howard University's law school as it had a dual aim of recruiting minoritized lawyers into the fold (Georgetown University Law School, 2009). The program lasted for 18 years, beginning in 1967 and concluding in 1985. The fellowship is regarded as the only national fellowship to 'support and deploy social justice attorneys' (Consortium for the National Equal Justice Library, 2018: e1). Ed was the second class of Reggies to be placed in community action agencies or what he referenced as legal aid offices in September of 1969.

Ed remembered his 'Reggie days' as a young-24-year-old at the legal aid office in Chinatown North Beach Office as we did a walking tour throughout Chinatown, retracing his steps as a young lawyer. We stopped at 755 Commercial Street, located on a hill leading into the heart of Chinatown. Standing in front of the iron gate to the entrance, he shared,

> The Chinatown North Beach Office was opened in 1966 and until 1970, it was a hole in a wall… the older Chinese thought the office was haunted, which may be why a lot of people wouldn't go.

Ed went on to describe the structure of the legal aid offices throughout San Francisco.

> In those days, they had five neighborhood offices and a central office where the class action was …. The big stuff was at Market… you had one in Hunters Point, which was Black. In those days, Western Addition was Black. Then you had Mission, which is where Lau should have really been… You had Chinatown and you had one south of Market.

Reggies were placed in one of the five offices among civil rights attorneys. While Ed considered all locations, he was most interested in Chinatown as the office was serving a distinctive community of recently immigrated Chinese and employment discrimination was high. Ed had also heard that the office was disorganized, and he wanted to support Chinatown during his short, two-year placement.

Ed: The office was a joke.
Trish: Why was Chinatown the joke office?

Ed: Because it was Chinatown! You know, who are these people? You know, they're all immigrants! No one speaks English. They don't want to get involved. You know, they don't like, they keep to themselves.... And clearly, the Black and Latino offices were where the action was at, but they didn't bring class actions. The class actions were brought by downtown.

Ed went on to discuss the 'smart guys' at the downtown office who had the intellect and the resources to pursue larger scale class action suits. He referenced *Serrano v Priest* (1971), a California case that sought to equalize funding across public school districts. School districts were mostly funded by local property tax revenues, making the per pupil expenditure disparate across communities. Although Serrano originated in Los Angeles county, not San Francisco, it had far reaching implications for San Francisco proper given its long history of segregation in schools and housing. Again, we see the influence of the legal aid offices having a broader agenda for legal rights of its diverse populace versus ones distinctly localized.

Ed recalled the many sweatshops that dotted the landscape of Chinatown. He arbitrated frequent wage disputes, especially among women. Aside from his collaborative work on suing the US Census with activist, Ling-Chi from the Chinese for Affirmative Action (Chapter 7), most of his work was on individual cases. He would regularly meet with women to discuss the types of disputes they had with the employers, including long hours with little or restricted compensation, and language barriers that employers outwardly refused to mitigate. He shared, 'So, I was probably seeing ten people a day and 40 people a week'.

He named off several companies, including *Fritzi of California*, high-quality women's clothing, but with reasonable prices and now regarded as collectable vintage wares. *Fritzi* was founded by Jewish holocaust survivors and Ed was surprised to learn that there were wage disputes toward Jewish immigrant owners and their treatment of the Chinese immigrant workforce. Ed recalls that Mrs Lau came to his office regarding a wage dispute at *Fritzi* and this in part mediated the Laus' selection as the lead plaintiffs. This story was augmented from what Lucinda Lee had shared with me, so I shared Lucinda's recollection of Mrs Lau.

Trish: According to Lucinda there was some sort of connection between you and her boyfriend/fiancée at the time because she was Lucinda Lee at the time and she was Kinney's teacher. And it was her on, her mom, Kinney's mom, they came to her and said, 'Will you teach me in Cantonese?' My son is falling behind in math. And so, what she ended up doing is ... Mrs Lau was so persistent, you know, because Lucinda said, 'I can't. The medium of instruction is English'. It is really sink or swim. And the mom was not satisfied with that, so Mrs Lau persisted. And finally, Lucinda relented and said, 'I'll do it after school'.

While Ed critiqued his recollection of this exchange, it is important to know that all his original documents from Lau that he meticulously saved in boxes had been burned in a fire at his mother-in-law's home, theorized to have started from a toaster. While the official record is available for reading, his narrative notes from his meetings with plaintiff families for the Lau case were gone. Thus, the retelling of stories preserves and restores our collective memories, an important endeavor in narrating historical research.

Ed then began to describe how he visited the plaintiffs for the Lau case.

> **Trish:** So, you went to their homes and you and what was that like for you?
>
> **Ed:** None of them lived in those, you know those SROs. They did not live there but, they lived in. Usually, they were... my memory was in multiple families, two three families living together... No more than three or four blocks away.

Ed's plaintiffs for *Lau v. Nichols* came from mostly nearby apartments. The apartments in Chinatown were intended for single family occupancy, but ultimately, more than one family stayed in a unit and the quarters were cramped. Ed continued, 'You know, obviously...I had done civil rights. I've worked in the South, so I was not surprised when I saw. Terribly sad. Just amazing people living there...'.

Ed and secretary/interpreter, Denise Lee would visit families in their homes. It was just a short walk from their Commercial Street office, and they would journey there in the late evening hours when families were more likely to be at home. He remembered,

> And I compiled this list of people. And then what I wound up having was that I put together like a matrix of different grades of American born, not American born. What the family did. There were different schools... and somehow chose them the names got permission.

Through Denise Lee, the interpreter, Ed would explain the nature of the case, which had been conceptualized with Lucinda Lee Katz and Norman Katz (no relation), Lucinda's fiancé's roommate and Ling-Chi Wang of the Chinese for Affirmative Action. Ed created a brief description of the need for language services for their children attending schools since none were receiving 'special instruction'.

The first set of plaintiffs came from six families with the Sun and Yee family having two children each named in the case (Table 8.1). Most of the plaintiffs came from Jean Parker Elementary, representing grades 1–3 where Lucinda began as a Teacher Corp intern (Chapter 2), where Victor Low (Chapter 5) had taught English as a Second Language (ESL), and Gordon Lew (Chapter 4) had been the music teacher. There was one student from Commodore Stockton Elementary, where Lucinda

Table 8.1 Chinese plaintiffs with no language provisions

Child	Mother	Father	Age	Grade	School	Neighborhood
Wailey Tom	Choi Kam Tom	Father	6	1	Commodore Stockton	Chinatown
Kinney Kimmon Lau	Kai Wai Lam	Father	6	1	Jean Parker	Chinatown
David Sun	Julia Sun	Father	7	1	Jean Parker	Chinatown
Judy Sun	Julia Sun	Father	8	2	Jean Parker	Chinatown
Karen Yee	Fung Yee Yee	Father	8	2	Jean Parker	Chinatown
Joan Yee	Fung Yee Yee	Father	9	3	Jean Parker	Chinatown
David Leong	mother	Yeu Bew Leong	14	7	Marina Junior High	Chinatown
Karen Chiu	Moy Hor Chiu	Father	11	6	Marshall Junior High	Mission
Paullette Cheung	mother	Kun Cheung	14	8	Roosevelt Junior High	Central Richmond

would later teach in their Chinese Bilingual program. The older students were at Marina, Marshall, and Roosevelt Junior Highs. These plaintiffs received no special instruction and were in a sink or swim language model, languishing in general education classrooms. While Commodore Stockton did have a Chinese pilot bilingual program, the program was quite small, and Wailey Tom was not in a bilingual classroom. Other children, mostly at Jean Parker did not have a bilingual program as the pilot was only located at Commodore Stockton Elementary.

The second set of plaintiffs was smaller with two families and represented children who were not taught by persons who spoke their native language, thereby rendering them to no language services or an ESL program model (Table 8.2). None of these students resided in the Chinatown neighborhoods where there was a Chinese pilot bilingual program based at Commodore Stockton Elementary. Thus, their default model was nothing or ESL instruction. The Cheung family uniquely had children that were in both sets of plaintiffs.

As I plotted the addresses onto the map, they all were apartments that were overcrowded. Four of the families lived in Chinatown proper in a narrow corridor of four blocks, not far from 755 Commercial where the legal clinic was. But three families fell outside of Chinatown proper. Two lived in the Mission district, and another lived near Central Richmond district, close to Ed's home in the Haight-Ashbury. I began to see the logic of Ed's matrix. First, there was an intentional mix of ages and grades, a minimum of two elementaries and three junior highs. He also

Table 8.2 Chinese plaintiffs with no bilingual teacher

Child	Gender	Mother	Father	Age	Grade	School	Neighborhood
Kit Ling Lee	female	mother	Henry Lee	6	2	Marshall Annex	Mission
Stanley Cheung*	male	mother	Kun Cheung	9	3	Lafayette	Central Richmond
Sai Chong Lee	male	mother	Henry Lee	11	6	Marshall	Mission
Sai Ho Lee	male	mother	Henry Lee	8	3	Marshall	Mission

*Sibling in first set of plaintiffs.

identified two families outside of Chinatown to demonstrate how the Chinese were spread throughout the city.

Ed remembered the documents families had to sign to agree to be plaintiffs.

> I remember going at night and having to explain to they had to sign. We had to sign two documents. One documented to agree to be the plaintiff. We agree that Ed Steinman represents you as a plaintiff and the other on causes of harm.

While the interpreter supplied the explanation in Cantonese to the families, the two written documents that families signed were in English. To account for this, Denise signed an affidavit stating the process used with families. She attested to being the secretary and de facto interpreter for the Chinatown Office of the Neighborhood Legal Assistance Foundation and that she can 'speak and comprehend the both the English language and Chinese languages, including Cantonese and its various dialects' *Kinney Kinmon Lau et al. v. Alan H. Nichols* (1970: 38-39). Thereafter, Denise attested she 'translated the complaint herein from English to the Chinese dialect – which is the native language of Guardians ad Litem...' (1970a: 38) and then the naming of the families with Mrs Kam Wai Lau listed first.

Families signed the first document attesting that Ed Steinman would represent them and the second form claimed that their public education was harmful to their children based on specific claims. Notably, because Ed was filing a class action suit, he had to detail the 'causes of actions' within the filing. In total, there were seven causes of action with each pointing to a variety of laws and educational codes being violated.

 Constitution and California Constitution Violations

(1) **Educational deprivation:** Plaintiffs have a right to an education under the Fifth, the Ninth and the Fourteenth Amendment of the US

Constitution and under the California Constitution in Section 5 and within the California education code § 1051, 1054, 5011, 5012, 5015, 5652 and 12101 and lack of language provisions for first set of plaintiffs and lack of bilingual programming for second set of plaintiffs is educational deprivation.

(2) **Unequal availability of needed resources:** SFUSD Defendants are furnishing an inferior education to the plaintiffs and thus violating the Equal Protection Clause of the Fourteenth Amendment of the Constitution of the United States and by Article I, Sections 11 and 21, and Article IV, Section 25 of the constitution of the State of California. Furnishing access to a school is insufficient and cannot be argued as the same for all.

(3) **Unequal distribution of needed resources is arbitrary:** SFUSD provision and placement of language services is not based on any criterion and therefore is arbitrary and violates the Equal Protection Clause of the Fourteenth Amendment of the Constitution of the United States and by Article I, Sections 11 and 21, and by Article IV, Section 25 of the Constitution of the State of California.

US Constitution Violation

(4) **Lack of protection from discrimination:** Defendants have an affirmative duty to serve the needs of the Chinese-speaking community and failure to do so constitutes discrimination based on national origin and Chinese ethnicity and thus violates Section 601 of the Civil Rights Act of 1964 (codified in 42 u.s.c. § 2000d).

California Educational Code Violation

(5) **Poor to no provision of compensatory programming that are remedial or preventative in nature:** Defendants have failed to meet the needs of first and second set of plaintiffs and violates the California Education Code§ 6457, to the severe detriment of the plaintiffs and all others similarly situated.

(6) **Lack of staffing and programmatic infrastructure retracts from English achievement:** Given that the medium of instruction is English and outcomes are measured in English, defendants have discriminated by not providing specialized staff for both sets of plaintiffs and violates Article II, Section 11 and Article IV, Section 24, of the Constitution of the State of California, of California Education Code§§ 71, 5766, 5770, 5779, 6060, 6450, 6499.200, 6750, 8551 (a), 8571 (a), 8573, 12820 and of California Code of Civil Procedure§§ 185, 198 (2) (3).

California Educational Code Violation

(7) **Failure to implement programs that best fit needs and interest of students.** The defendants have made no measurable attempt to furnish bilingual instruction to students and thus violate California Education Code§§ 71, 5766, 6457, 13187.6. (*Kinney Kinmon Lau et al. v. Alan H. Nichols*, 1970).

The argument that Ed put forth on behalf of the plaintiffs with the US District Court of the Northern District of California to Judge Lloyd H Burke demonstrated a denial of their Fifth, Ninth and Fourteenth Amendments within the US constitution alongside violation within the California constitution and various California educational codes, documented in 59 pages and filed on March 25, 1970 (Wong, 1970b). Just a short few months later, on May 26, 1970, Edward D. Goldman, Associate Superintendent of Instruction responded on behalf of the board in an 'affidavit in opposition to motion for preliminary injunction and in support of motion to dismiss' (*Kinney Kinmon Lau et al. v. Alan H. Nichols et al.*, 1970: 1).

The motion to dismiss expressed the awareness and the dutiful concern of SFUSD about the plight of the Chinese community and that they had already taken affirmative steps to rectify the provision of ESL and bilingual education for them both in dollars and infrastructure, including bilingual education provisions in English and Spanish, support of the Chinese Education Center for Newcomers and the imminent hiring of a Supervisor of Chinese bilingual education (1970a: 2).

The motion for a class action suit was denied and the defendants, and the district was not found to have violated any laws. Federal district judge, Lloyd H Burke of the US District Court of the Northern District of California conferred the dismissal in a four-page document.

> This Court fully recognizes that the Chinese-speaking students involved in this action have special needs, specifically the need to have special instruction in English. To provide such special instruction would be a desirable and commendable approach to take. Yet, this Court cannot say that such an approach is legally required. On the contrary, plaintiffs herein seek relief for a special need – which they allege is necessary if their rights to an education and equal educational opportunities are to be received – that does not constitute right that would create a duty on defendants' part to act *(Kinney Kinmon Lau et al., plaintiffs v. Alan H. Nichols et al., defendants, Order, 1970)*.

Herein, Burke recognizes the plaintiffs' identification of a special need, and it would be laudable if the district acted on a given approach. Yet, Burke stops at altruism, stating that the district does not have a legal obligation to do so. Burke's decision precedes the implementation of the Individuals with Disabilities Act (IDEA) in 1975 or Public Law 94-142, which made a special need the burden of the district to address and remedy. This is not to say that the Chinese plaintiffs had a disability but demonstrates the early legal foundations that a free and public education is sufficient, and a special need is immaterial and that when Lau prevailed in 1974, it set precedent for what constitutes a special need.

The dismissal language became even more explicit in its reference to bilingual education. On page 2 of the document, Burke recognizes the 'demonstrable efforts' that the district has made to enhance bilingual education provisions (e.g. hiring of bilingual leadership and enhancement of bilingual funds), but its effectiveness is not within the jurisdiction of the courts to evaluate and enforce.

Burke stated that Chinese speaking students had a free and public education just like that of other SFUSD students, satisfying their rights for an equal education. Burke continued,

> Although this Court and both parties recognize that a bilingual approach to educating Chinese-speaking students is both a desirable and effective method, though not the only one, plaintiffs have no right to a bilingual education. Again, this Court is in no position to mandate that such instruction must be given by bilingual Chinese-speaking teachers; though desirable, there is no legal basis to require it (*Kinney Kinmon Lau et al. plaintiffs v. Alan H. Nichols et al., defendants, Order, 1970* p. 3).

The argument suggests that no intentional harm has been done and that access to a free and public education is adequate. Burke's dismissal essentially decentralizes the decision to the district, creating the conditions for ideologies and beliefs of the district administration to arbitrate their decision making (Menken, 2008).

If the plaintiffs' and Ed ended with Burke's dismissal, the outcome may have been a small scaling of Chinese bilingual with the new leadership positions intact. In thinking about my historic district work as a bilingual administrator, I imagined the court's ruling of no district obligation to provide a bilingual education would come as a welcome relief to senior administrators, and internal funding would gradually be reduced, leading to even more regress over time. But, for Ed and the plaintiffs, an appeal was in the works.

Once the initial case was dismissed within the US District Court of the Northern District of California, it was appealed, which Ed attended to officially and in quick order, beginning with documenting the poverty of the plaintiffs. He shared,

> They had to sign they were poor. If you bring the case in forma pauperis, in the form of poverty, then there's no expenses, clearly for them, and no expenses for me. All the discovery is paid for…

Ed appealed the ruling on October 2, 1970 to the Ninth Circuit Court of Appeals. The 68-page document contained nine pages of a table of contents, another 59 pages of argument and three pages of supporting appendices. The argument was thorough in that it referenced 43 court cases at the state and federal level that addressed equal rights, the description of a special need and the burden of the district to provide relief to their students with special instructional needs. Additionally, the Fifth, Ninth and Fourteenth amendments of the US Constitution were cited along with five supporting Articles from the California constitution to support the appeal. Another four US federal statutes, one federal rule of procedure, one code of federal regulation and, lastly, 29 items from the California Education code added evidence to demonstrate SFUSD's neglect of the Chinese speaking students (*Kinney Kinmon Lau et al. v. Alan H. Nichols et al.*, 1971).

In addition to citing legal statute, both state and federal, Ed also drew from SFUSD's own Title VII documents for the Chinese Bilingual Pilot to demonstrate the rationale for Chinese bilingual education. 'When [Chinese-speaking] youngsters are placed in grade levels according to their age and are expected to compete with their English-speaking peers, they are frustrated by their inability to understand the regular class work' (Supplementary Educational Center of San Francisco Unified Schools, 1969: 3a). At the time of the October 1970 filing, Commodore Stockton Elementary (where Lucinda Lee would soon teach and where Gordon Lew was preparing Chinese curriculum) was into its second year of the program, but still had a small imprint on the number of Chinese speaking students being taught by a bilingual teacher.

Ed also drew upon an internal SFUSD report on bilingual education prepared under the leadership of Superintendent Robert Jenkins done a few years earlier, which claimed that a bilingual education could be made available should four criterion exist (Jenkins, 1967).

(1) The presence of suitable groupings of students in sufficient numbers to make a class of those with the same native language, of the same grade level, and ready to take the same subject.
(2) The availability of curriculum materials.
(3) The availability of bilingual teachers of the grade level of subject in question.
(4) The possibility of suitable scheduling arrangements in the school schedule (Jenkins, 1967: 3).

Ed's appeal states that such criteria have been met and SFUSD must proceed affirmatively to rectify the harm upon its Chinese speaking students.

In the appeal, Ed's focus is on personnel and not on a specific bilingual program model. Bilingual education as furnished by schools was still in its infancy, and so this idealized model was aspirational. Ed's specificity throughout the document about specialized staff was concrete and measurable. Ed continues using the reference of 'bilingual teachers' representing the agency and expertise of the Chinese community of greater San Francisco. Further detailed in the appeal is that 'the School District can only satisfy its duties to these youngsters by providing special instruction in English taught by bilingual teachers' (*Kinney Kinmon Lau et al. v. Alan H. Nichols et al.*, 1971: 29–30) and 'The 1964 Civil Rights Act requires the school district to provide non-English-speaking Chinese children with special bilingual instruction in English' (Steinman, 1970a: 39). Observably, there is no statement about a program model, nor that the aim is biliteracy. Rather, the pathway is access by way of a bilingual teacher.

Much of the appeal also contains content on special education and how the Chinese students in the suit have a special need that is not visibly recognizable, yet a need that differs from students with physically recognizable disabilities, also discussed with Judge Lloyd Burke during oral arguments at the courts on May 12, 1970 (*Before Hon. Lloyd H. Burke, Judge in Kinney Kinmon Lau, etc., et al., Plaintiffs v. Alan H. Nichols, etc., et al., Defendants, Oral Arguments*, 1970: 7). Ed cited the 1966 work, the *Invisible Minority,* a report prepared by the National Education Association on the teaching of Spanish to Spanish speakers, demonstrating how the Chinese speakers of SFUSD were similarly situated as invisible (National Education Association, 1966). Ed recognized the precedent and power of special education, a strategy often invoked by bilingual leaders to conjoin narratives with special education to galvanize the needs and rights of bilingual learners (Morita-Mullaney, 2014a).

Following the filing of the appeal in October of 1970, the defendants asked for extended time to present their case, which was granted. On December of 1970, the appellees (defendants) under the leadership of city attorney, Thomas O'Connor prepared a 24-page Brief of Appellees by O'Connor and his Assistant Attorney, Raymond D. Williamson. They asserted four main arguments: (1) Appellants are being provided with a public education as required by California law; (2) appellants are not denied equal protection under federal law nor have their civil rights been violated; (3) the school district has submitted a proper plan and has qualified several schools under the compensatory education program; and (4) a class action suit is not proper here (O'Connor & Williamson, 1970b). For the proper plan under the compensatory education program, O'Connor and Williamson referenced the Chinese Bilingual Pilot Program citing New York and SFUSD as the two recipients of Chinese bilingual funding from Title VII and that funds had increased from $50,000 to $198,000, demonstrating adequacy (1970b: 9).

What the defendants fail to incorporate is the future casting and impact of busing that was just nine months away (September 1971). Chinese students from Chinatown would be sent throughout the city, where bilingual provisions were not established nor in development, later an expressed concern by Chinese teachers (Chapter 7). Such would be articulated in Ed's 31-page response to defendants served to defendants and the US Ninth Circuit Court of Appeals on January 4, 1971.

> It is beyond argument that defendants have failed to meet the requirements of this 'Comprehensive Plan'. The figures are clear and stark. The paucity and total ineffectiveness of the School District's small efforts are revealed both in its admission that nearly 2,000

non-English-speaking Chinese students received no special help in English in 1969–70 and in its budgetary cutback in 1970–1971 for such help (Steinman, 1971b: 22).

Ed continues to return to the figures and numbers, pointing out that services are not located in every single school where many Chinese children attend. Chinese students were more likely than Spanish speaking students to be without any type of language provision (e.g. ESL) and even more likely to be taught by a monolingual-English speaking teacher with no specialized instruction. Harkening back to the time when SFUSD had a quota of only three Chinese teachers, the reputational and cumulative impact was foreclosing on Chinese students' language rights for a bilingual teacher.

Ultimately, the US Ninth Circuit Court of Appeals denied the class action suit for the Chinese, stating that the burden of the proof furnished by the defendants (the district) was adequate and there was no institutional wrongdoing nor oversight by SFUSD. The Equal protection clause within the Fourteenth Amendment of the US constitution had not adequately been proven as a public education was affording them access to compulsory schooling. Irving Hill, United States District Judge in the Ninth Circuit Court of Appeals wrote the following statement upon the denial of amends for the Chinese plaintiffs.

> To ascribe some fault to a grade school child because of his 'failing to learn the English language' seems both callous and inaccurate. If anyone can be blamed for the language deficiencies of these children, it is their parents and not the children themselves. Even if the parents can be faulted (and in many cases they cannot, since they themselves are newly arrived in a strange land and in their struggle for survival may have had neither the time nor opportunity to study any English), it is one of the keystones of our culture and our law that the sins of the fathers are not to be visited upon the children. (*Appeal and dissent*, 1973: 9)

Ed expressed his shock at the outcome. 'It's the fault of the child and the parents! Unbelievable!' Judge Hill based his arguments on the Fourteenth Amendment in the US Constitution, for which he asserts the plaintiffs had not proven as they were attending school and receiving the same education as other SFUSD students. The fault rests with the parents as they are committing the 'sins of the father' upon their children for not teaching them in English, manufacturing the conditions for their school struggles.

With any appealed case at the federal circuit level that fails, it may move onto the Supreme Court for review. Ed shared that the Supreme Court during the early 1970s only heard 80 cases a year, and the likelihood of Lau making it to a hearing was low. Yet, a serendipitous set of events and conversations placed Lau on the docket. In 1973 Ed flew into Washington, DC a full week in advance of the hearing, but Thomas

O'Connor, the attorney for the city of San Francisco flew in cavalierly the night before oral arguments. Ed was prepared.

During oral arguments on December 10, 1973, Edward Steinman was joined by Assistant Attorney General for the Civil Rights Division, John Stanley Pottinger. Ed argued for the constitutional violation of the Fourteenth Amendment and Pottinger argued the case on violations of the Civil Rights Act of 1964 (*Lau v. Nichols Oral Arguments*, 1973). Ed began detailing the undue harm experienced by the 1800 Chinese and how this presented as a constitutional exclusion of an equal opportunity to an education, but Justice Warren E. Berger asked if the same could be applied to five Portuguese students.

> **Warren Berger:** But you say, the constitutional right is the same right?
> **Ed:** I mean that there was the effective exclusion which of course to the factual question which has to be dealt within the case.
> **Warren Berger:** But if they cannot speak English, there is a constitutional obligation on the Government to teach them English. That's your point, isn't it?
> **Ed:** If the Government is going to have –
> **Warren Berger:** Well, just—that's a yes or a no? I don't mean to press you unduly, but that's a yes or a no, isn't it?
> **Ed:** The answer is yes, that we have a system of education.

The conversation shifted quickly, and arguments moved onto Pottinger who argued the violation of the Civil Rights Act of 1964.

> **Stanley Pottinger:** It has construed the meaning of Title VI in a national origin discrimination memorandum relevant to this case by stating that where inability to speak and understand the English language excludes national origin minority group children from the effective participation in the educational program offered by the school district, the school district must take affirmative steps to rectify the language deficiency.

Later in oral arguments Pottinger stated,

> **Stanley Pottinger:** In other words, Title VI is not coterminous with Fourteenth Amendment because it was enacted not only pursuant to that amendment, but pursuant to the welfare clause and hence as it is by the necessary in proper clause.

The use of the phrase, 'not coterminous', meaning the Fourteenth Amendment and the Civil Rights Act were not regarded as congruous or adjacent would have an impact on the final ruling for Lau in 1974. This was not the intended argument of Ed and Pottinger, but rather how it was interpreted among the Supreme Court Justices. In review of these documents Ed continued to share, 'This is bad law' wishing he had used a different legal strategy with the courts. Ed's retrospection about Lau's outcome for language rights will come to light in Section 2 of this volume.

9 Before Lau, An Idealistic Lawyer and Public Servant is Appointed to the School Board

Alan Nichols, J.D., School Board President

Alan Nichols was born on February 14, 1930 in Palo Alto, California, adjacent to Stanford University where he attended for his undergraduate and law degrees. Following his undergraduate he worked in the active infantry in the US Army for five years, serving in Korea and earning the rank of First Lieutenant with a commendation medal with four clusters. Upon his return, he enrolled in Stanford's law school, also Edward Steinman's alma mater, graduating in 1955 with his juris doctorate. While at Stanford, he was on the Editorial Board of the *Stanford Law Review*. He went on to live in San Francisco and serve as a lawyer in various firms and in private practice for 50 years focusing on business, banking, finance, and non-profits. Alan also is a writer of various genres, including his trained profession of law, poems, fiction, and autobiographical work. In the early 1960s he began publishing poetry based on his observations of his train and bus commute to work in the Financial District (Hammond, 1965). As he was aspiring to numerous political offices, he established the pen name of Alan Hammond, so he could adopt a poetic persona and remain anonymous to the greater political community of San Francisco. Within the legal profession much of what has happened with California water rights and laws can be attributed to Alan and his lawyer colleague, Harold Rogers (Rogers & Nichols, 1967). Harold would later become his partner in the firm, Nichols and Rogers. Alan was civically engaged, serving on numerous boards and running for political offices, including the San Francisco Board of Supervisors and his service to the SFUSD school board from 1967–1971, where his name became indelibly ingrained into the fabric of *Lau v. Nichols*.

I met Alan by way of informal introduction from Ed Steinman who shared that he lived in a retirement home near by Dad's home, where I would knock on his door in 2019 to introduce myself. Outside Alan's retirement community, on the 11th floor, was a landscape map of the Silk Road, entitled 'Cycling the Silk Road' with pictures of him on his bicycle. An active explorer, he would travel throughout China and Outer Mongolia, but such adventures followed Lau (Nichols, 1991). We begin with getting to know Alan Nichols, lawyer, father, spouse, politician, Republican, poet and, later, as an explorer.

At the age of 33, Alan pursued for the second time a position on the San Francisco's Board of Supervisors, a governing body for the city and county of San Francisco. The Board of Supervisors focused on ordinances and policies that impact transportation, housing, commercial properties, provision of health and social services and education. Thus, their role has always had a powerful influence on the school board of SFUSD and vice versa. In his 1963 bid for San Francisco Supervisor, he shared his stance.

> 'The future of the community depends on emphasizing neighborhood and family life,' Nichols said. 'In planning freeways or public housing, the neighborhood and the people affected should be taken into account. They should have a say about what is going to affect them'. Nichols would establish a liaison section to act as a middleman between city hall and the public. He wants to cut the red tape individuals and groups now face when dealing with city government. (San Francisco Examiner, 1963: 16)

Alan's focus on making policy quickly actionable and less bureaucratic became a staple in his leadership on the SFUSD school board from 1967–1970. At the time, the seven-person school board was done by mayoral appointment at regular four-year intervals or when a vacancy occurred. Such was the case in 1967. Alan remembered, 'I was actually appointed by a democratic ....' referencing Mayor John Francis Shelley who was the first Democratic Mayor to be elected in San Francisco in 50 years, significant as it also collided with changing policies related to political parties and voting rights.

In those days, Alan described how party politics worked in California. 'We had cross filing. You can file in both the Republicans and the Democrats and Republicans were always getting elected by the Democrats'. Alan described this process as somewhat strategic to become elected, but also as a means of suiting a more Republican leaning caucus. Cross-filing is sometimes referenced as electoral fusion and aims to reduce competition in a general election, by filing across multiple party lines (McHenry, 1946). This practice in California largely benefitted Republican candidates and in 1959 when the Democrats took control over the California Congress and Pat Brown became the governor, the practice was critiqued. The year 1959 marked a time in San Francisco's history where the political leanings were beginning to shift.

In January 1967, Alan was appointed by Mayor John F. Shelley to the SFUSD school board to fulfill a vacant three-year term. He served on the

Curriculum Committee, as Vice Chair of the board and eventually became School board president in 1970 (San Francisco Unified Schools: Office of the Superintendent, 1970), just as the Lau case was being prepared and filed in the US District Court of the Northern District of California.

In his role on the Curriculum Committee, Alan planned for a long-term approach with activities and outcomes with an opportunity to identify timelines, to demonstrate the long-term nature of educational goal making. As a prelude to his proposal entitled 'Proposal for a Master Plan for Excellence for San Francisco School System', he wrote:

> The purpose of the enclosed plan is solely as a basis of discussion for the Board of Education and its Curricula Committee in cooperation with other groups, teachers, staff, and interested persons who might desire to participate in the creation of such a plan. It as such appears merely a draft of one proposal for such a plan. (Nichols, 1967: i)

In his proposal Alan detailed objectives with descriptive rationale with three adjacent columns for identifying dates for completion: (1) start study; (2) approve plan; and (3) start program. Under Part C of the document called, 'Changes, Flexibility, Diversity, Requirements', he addressed racial and linguistic diversity.

> Any students must recognize the diversified approach necessary to solve educational problems in San Francisco, including the differences in neighborhoods and areas, educational background of the parents, particular racial and lingual problems and diverse cultural backgrounds. Nevertheless, high quality must be the objective in every class and in every neighborhood especially in the elementary schools. (Nichols, 1967: 4)

Alan, having spent most of his professional career in San Francisco and where his wife taught and his children attended SFUSD, he was knowledgeable about the different communities throughout the city. His children were in elementary school during his time on the board and during a time that the district was attempting to racially integrate the schools on their own accord as under court order. Desegregation is the bulk of what Alan discussed and he described the racial integration plan that the board crafted and approved that would begin with just six schools and then another six, gradually implementing an overall racial integration plan for the elementary schools. It would take 12 years to implement district-wide. Alan was referencing the San Francisco Advisory Committee's Educational Equality/Quality Plan (Weiner, 1972). He remembered the complexity that other larger cities with a huge student population had with integration and he hoped that SFUSD could do better.

> …you know, if you think of New York or Chicago, Los Angeles, you know, other major cities have a they had big school districts in which integration was an absolute impossibility and they couldn't do anything…

but San Francisco, with maybe 75,000, 80,000 elementary students, we came up with a program or an integration plan, because the courts were requiring it.

He remembered federal judge for the US District Court for the Northern District of California, Stanley Alexander Weigel, appointed by Robert Kennedy in 1962, a liberal appointee who was pro-integration. Alan described the plan.

> ... the school board adopted an integration plan, and it started out with the Richmond district. And the Richmond district is where that's kind of a core of outer Chinese and Asian, mostly Chinese ... we integrated six elementary schools and we did that. We adopted a plan to integrate, or maybe every year or every two years. I think was every year we were going to adopt six schools and integrate them, using busing and using all kind of things... and it and we would have integrated the entire school system in 12 years, including.... We weren't going do anything with the high schools and the junior high and that for all a real hullabaloo was going on and the federal government came in and gave us a whole lot of money. So, we had a lot of extra teachers and we had school thing because the whole idea, the whole underlying plan was to keep, to avoid white flight, what they call those people look like people were trying to get out of town. They were all leaving. And so, I remember [Diane] Feinstein, who is on the Board of Supervisors. She called me and she said, if you carry out this integration, this is like in the summer before we start out the integration, we were busing six schools, six elementary schools, getting a lot of publicity. And she said, you know, you you'll destroy the education system if you do this. And the Supervisor [Feinstein] called Alioto [Democratic Mayor].

Alan reflects the reluctance of even the most liberal of politicians and officials to support integration by means of forced busing. SFSUD Superintendent, Robert Jenkins stated after conducting public forums throughout the city on forced busing claimed that 'No racial group here really seemed to want large scale busing' (Gilmore, 1968: 16) and 'it's too emotional an issue' (AsianWeek, 1988). Alan also remembered a conversation with Mayor Alioto and Supervisor, Diane Feinstein the summer before the small-scale, Equality/Quality Plan was to go into effect.

> I told them both. I said, well, then you're going have to appoint a new school board because we're all riding the buses on Monday! And you know, people are going to burn it down and all this stuff. Anyway, ... nothing like that happened. We had all these extra resources. Every elementary school knew to be an educator. And we had, there were three or four to six extra teachers above the normal teachers.

Alan and his fellow board members responsible for the Equality/Quality Plan rode the buses with no incident. Alan resolved that its small-scale reduced transportation costs, and it could be gradually done over 12 years. In the San Francisco Examiner, he shared,

> ... the adoption of any specific plan or program will be subject to specific assurances of the availability of additional resources to assure increased quality of education for all students involved and not to decrease resources available to target and other schools. (Gilmore, 1968: 16)

Much like his initial years on the Curriculum Committee, where he found study, along with family and community input critical, he followed the same vision for the Educational Equity/Quality Plan. We also see Alan's careful crafting that investment needed to be made into integrated schools to furnish them with the resources needed to make integration and busing successful.

Alan remembered the focus on the Richmond district of San Francisco for the integration plan for 1968–1970. Richmond was home to a mostly White constituency, but also a growing number of Chinese with greater economic resources, relative to Chinatown. By moving students within a small cluster area, the district could start small to scale bigger. Interestingly, by tapping into the seeming safe and promising diversity of the Chinese allowed for such actions to be taken.

> Trish: So that was the place that you focused on. Why did you start there? [Richmond district].
> Alan: The Chinese. Because to sell.... The whole idea that your kids, your white kids are going to do better because of the standards are going to be higher. And you've got parental support of kids and going to school and getting there and being there and all that stuff.

Alan sheds light on how Asian and Asian Americans have long been subjugated while simultaneously being valorized. In reflecting back on the Tape family from the 1880s, nearly a 100 years earlier, they were valorized by the area Christian churches and missions as being the idealized converts, both in doctrine and Victorian mannerisms (Independent Calistogan, 1885). Yet, they were subjugated as the school system rendered them to a separate, but woefully inadequate and segregated Chinatown school. In the case of the Chinese living in the Richmond district in 1968, we see the schools simultaneously rendering them as instruments or subjects of the 12-year integration plan, while valorizing them as high performing. As the Chinese are living outside of Chinatown, seemingly integrated like the Tape family, they become the additive subjectivities of racial desegregation tinkering.

While Alan remembered the two-year plan that ultimately was questioned by the federal courts and National Association for the Advanced of Colored People (NAACP), he went on to describe his plan for racial integration that extended beyond San Francisco County to the entire Bay Area of California. 'I also advocated at that they integrated the Bay Area to prevent the White flight. So, if you went to Palo Alto or you went to Fremont or somewhere, you're integrating the whole area'.

Alan shared that he had written a brief about this comprehensive integration plan, proposing it on a much larger scale, because White flight could be prevented if the conditions would be the same throughout the greater Bay Area, even though he was regularly told by anti-busing advocates that he was trying to slow down decision making (Wood, 1971). He modeled this after other larger cities whose board members he met at the Council of Great City Schools' Conference, a convening group for urban schools' administrators and school board members across the US (Usdan, 2006). Alan shared,

> But we were part of the big city school districts. We had, you know, regular meetings of the school boards, of the various school boards of the major school districts in America. And of course, this was one of the great big, huge issues, integration, and all that.

Other cities had scaled it beyond one singular district. If everything in relative adjacency was integrated, then the phenomena of White flight would be far less likely. Alan recalled his interaction with US District Court, Judge Weigel.

> ...But, but you integrate the entire Bay Area and then you're going to get some kind of balance. You won't get any balance... and that's exactly what happened. All the whites left. And, you know. And so, the school district was never balanced. It was their idea of having the same population of balance of school kids as there were in the community.

Alan and the various district and community groups that had formulated the small-scale plan in the Richmond district were critiqued as the plan was too incremental. The National Association for the Advanced of Colored People (NAACP) wanted more substantive and immediate efforts to address racial segregation in schools, most profoundly experienced by the Black community. Thus, a suit was filed: *Johnson v. SFUSD* (1971).

Eventually, the two year plan with a long-term 12-year aim of full district racial integration was denied by the courts, galvanized by the filing of *Johnson v. SFUSD* (1971). David Johnson, the primary plaintiff was a father whose daughter, Patricia, an African American student was attending an elementary school where 75% of its students were Black, constituting de jure segregation. This lawsuit, filed in the US District Court for the Northern District of California, just like the one that Edward Steinman had originally filed the Lau lawsuit, is where the Johnson family and plaintiffs began, albeit a year later than Steinman. Drawing from *Brown v. Board of Education* (1953, 1954), the plaintiffs argued that in SFUSD 80% of Black children were attending 29 segregated schools, disavowing the foundations of Brown grounded in the Civil Rights Act of 1964 and the Fourteenth Amendment of the US Constitution.

As the US District Court of the Northern District of California proceeded with its fuller implementation of mandatory busing, Alan also recognized the political exploitability of the Chinese and he shared his disdain on how city politicians used them to support their anti-busing stance.

> And as a matter of fact, there are several politicians. One of them was kind of became a well-known state senator. He made his reputation by appealing to the Chinese community and saying that they shouldn't be integrated. And the Chinese politically, were not that active in those particular times. But that made him active and so they were … they're very exploitable as a political force.

Alan recognized the mixed immigration status of the Chinatown community. There was a growing presence of American born Chinese adults who were becoming a voting force, one that politicians began to recognize and strategize to their advantage. Anti-busing was a mechanism to do so. After Alan had described the instrumental use of the Chinese in the Richmond district to create a slow and incremental method for integrating schools to satisfy the courts, I also witnessed his emotion as he described the resistance of Chinatown to busing, which contrasted with the Richmond district.

> Now you're doing this and you know, you're complying with what you're supposed to have to do and the court orders and all that stuff. But that's no excuse because everything is so highly emotional now. At the same time actually, this is kind of relevant to the Lau, because the Chinese community was among the anti-integration group. That was the worst. They were worse than the whites. I mean, that's when I would say we get 5,000 Chinese into that high school [Commerce High School]. When we were talking about what we're going to do about that part of San Francisco, something that was related, and then all the politicians who were making their careers off of getting the Chinese vote, which he never could get otherwise…

Notably, Alan recognizes the interest convergence of San Francisco politicians waging their elections on the platform of anti-busing, along with the Chinese of Chinatown's disagreement with busing. With their shared agreement, there was a chance of political election, and for the Chinese of Chinatown – no busing. Yet, interest convergence operates within an unequal power relationship, where the politicians are the ultimate benefactors, on the subjectivities of the Chinese dissent to busing. Here we observe the subjugation of the Chinese for votes and the valorization of the Chinese for being a minoritized group of color that was anti-busing. The Chinese could work in tandem with the White community opposing busing. This complexity demonstrates the racial triangulation theory that Asians operate in relative comparison to Whites and Blacks, where they are either civically ostracized and excluded and/or included should it meet the aims of the majority (Kim, 1999). We see how the Chinese community becomes the adjacent community of subjugation to postpone or cancel busing altogether.

I invited Alan to say more about the Chinese of Chinatown opposing busing, since it had gone favorably in the Richmond district just two years earlier.

> The fact is, their children, who they depended on for education, they were very much more, you know, that much more oriented towards education. And there's no way if you were involved in education that you couldn't conclude that the education of your kids was going to be destroyed with integration.

Alan theorizes that when such abrupt changes are made without input, study, and method, then the outcome is dissent. Also, Alan recognizes the closed nature of the Chinatown community and how immigrant parents wanted their US-born children to have opportunities outside of Chinatown. Alan also recognizes that the segregation of the Chinese in Chinatown is historic, and the schools that they knew and trusted were one of the few places in the city where they were accepted and taught from a welcoming community. He understood their perspective and disdained the political opportunists that used them strategically.

I asked Alan to identify how busing and Lau were interrelated. He returned to his Equality/Quality Plan and the success they had in educating the Chinese of Richmond district because their level of integration with English majority White students which created the conditions for interaction and thus, English language development.

> You reminded me... is the kids who didn't want to go out there. But the kids that did go out there, picked up English very quickly. In fact, I remember reading a paper for some teacher or something. That was how fast at West Portal [Elementary] where my kids were. How fast a kid who shows up there, how fast they learned English. You know, in the yard at lunch, all those aspects.

Alan articulated how integration across lines of race and poverty could positively impact the English language acquisition of Chinese students and used his first-hand experience of his own children in their Forest Hills neighborhood. Racial integration at the site of the schools contributed to English language development, whereas in Chinatown, the linguistic landscape was homogeneous, lessening the opportunities for multilingual interaction. Alan demonstrates how both civil rights agendas for racial and linguistic equality can operate in tandem. Integration leads to opportunities for English language learning, albeit not a bilingual education.

When the *Lau v. Nichols* resolution came to the School Board in 1970, when Alan was serving as President, he recalled the discussion that ensued with the Board. Most of his fellow board members sided with the school district, believing that it was not incumbent upon the school district to go above and beyond the current language plan. Also, because the federal courts were closely monitoring their progress with integration and busing, that was the primary focus for the board at the time. Alan shared, 'When I was on the board, there was 76 cases lodged against me'. Lau was just one of the 76 that 'became famous after I left' demonstrating the lengthy nature of cases that ascend in the courts to the Supreme Court, a strategy that Ling-Chi Wang (Chapter 7) used sparingly.

Alan understood the logic in the plaintiff's case, that 'the same education did not constitute an equal education'. He remembered,

> I think the thing that surprised me was that I was named the defendant, and it was this very specific resolution. There was the before school board passed some kind of a resolution and that I had my vote on that was consistent with what the plaintiff wanted… A majority voted against the resolution. In other words, against the policy that was eventually done by the Supreme Court.

During Alan's short tenure on the school board, he had been named in one that stood out to him, given its later success in the Supreme Court, but also because of its specificity, which would later manifest into the Lau consent decree for SFUSD following Lau's passage. Here again, we see Nichols' support of the Chinese community and the Lau family for the provisions of language education.

After Nichol's three-year term, the newly elected mayor, Mayor Alioto was receiving consistent pressure from interest groups to stop busing or propose a more conservative plan while fighting the federal courts. Mayor Alioto decided to go in a more conservative direction, identifying more anti-busing board members (San Francisco Chronicle, 1971b: 4).

As readers interested in language education, we may have thought of Alan Nichols as a staunch oppositionist to Lau and its logics. Yet, Alan, a thoughtful intellectual, writer and researcher, was committed to drawing on multiple perspectives to draw his conclusions on the Lau case. He saw how racial and linguistic integration could yield additive benefits for the greater San Francisco community. In anticipation of not being reappointed to the school board, the *San Francisco Examiner* captured his outgoing wishes. 'Nichols has suggested he be replaced with a Chinese-American and Alioto is known to have been interviewing many' (Cone, 1971: 1). In the end, Alan's words were taken to heart, and George Y. Chinn became the first Chinese-American school board member in SFUSD, appointed by Mayor Alioto in January 1971. The sun was rising.

10 Before Lau, There Was School Desegregation and Mandatory Busing
Enter the Freedom Schools of Chinatown

After many years of trying to mitigate their own redistricting, busing for SFUSD was made mandatory by the US District Court for the Northern District of California. The federal courts denied SFUSD's earlier low-key efforts, insisting on a larger scale model consistent with the *Brown v. Board of Education* (1954, 1955) case, and galvanized by the San Francisco NAACP's organization of the *Johnson v. SFUSD* (1971) case. David Johnson was an African American father who pushed for integration as his child, Patricia, was attending a predominantly African American school, demonstrating how Blacks were most likely to be in segregated schooling relative to other groups of color, a de jure method of segregation.

The Horseshoe Plan for busing was implemented drawing from seven distinct zones with each zone having a catchment area or one of proximity. From each zone, the students would be a walker to their neighborhood school for primary grades (K-3) and then be bused to a school outside their zone for intermediate grades (4–6) or vice versa. In short, a student was not to be double bused, rather experience busing one time during their elementary grades (Weigel, 1971). While this was the policy, in practice Black and Latino students were more likely to be double bused away from their local community, placing greater travel times to and from their assigned schools for the entirety of their elementary years to satisfy desegregation objectives (Quinn, 2020; Wright, 1971).

For Chinatown, under the Horseshoe Plan, students in the primary grades were bused in from three outside areas throughout the city to Commodore Stockton Elementary. Students came from Hunter's Point schools, a predominantly Black community and was seven miles away and a nearly 45-minute drive by bus. Next, was Noe Valley, mostly populated by White and Asian middle-class families and was five miles away and 30-minute drive by bus. Lastly, the Latino community from the Mission

District, which was three miles away with a 25-minute bus ride. Meanwhile, most Chinatown residents with students in the primary grades (K-3) were the walkers to Commodore Stockton. Some Chinatown children who historically had attended Chinatown schools like Jean Parker and Commodore Stockton were now being bused to south of Market Street or the Mission District, a 20-minute bus ride (Lum, 1978: 10). Many being bused out to Market or Mission were newer immigrants and were scared to send their children outside of the Chinatown community where provisions of interpretation were not guarantees (Tom, 1978). Some went as far as Treasure Island, a navy base located nearly six miles away and over an hour to arrive by school bus (East West, 1971a). The lead up to the mandatory SFUSD busing was fraught with contention from the Chinese community with many opposed to their children being bused out of Chinatown. Furthermore, the Chinese of Chinatown were accustomed to governing their own community since the larger institution of the city had long excluded them from resources and opportunities.

The Citizen's Advisory Council (CAC) of SFUSD was established in 1969, charged with identifying a desegregation plan with the intent of wide community input. The US district courts afforded SFUSD some autonomy in establishing their own plan with advisement from the CAC and SFUSD. But in 1971, District Judge Stanley Weigel of the US Federal District Court for the Northern District of California assessed these incremental moves as insufficient and ordered mandatory busing. Benjamin Tom, a Chinese American teacher was one of 10 Asian Americans who joined the CAC in the Spring of 1971 following the mandatory order, reviewing the possible desegregation plans and making recommendations for integration that would incorporate the needs of the Chinese and Asian American community (Tom, 1978). The CAC discussed a variety of different possibilities, with wide disagreement among participants, but landed on the Horseshoe Plan which reached the satisfactory scale for the courts. Further, for Ben Tom, the Horseshoe Plan considered provisions for bilingual education and special education services and that such would be implemented once school assignments were made (Citizen's Advisory Committee, 1971). Benjamin Tom remembered,

> Among the Chinese members, I suppose that I was the most outspoken or visible because I was immediately labelled a 'pro-buser' and a 'traitor to our community' by the more vociferous and conservative segment of the Chinese community. The attempts of CAC to elicit some reasonable discussion on our suggestions met with mostly abuse and accusations. We were unable to explain to those Chinese against desegregation that the recommended 'Horseshoe Plan' was the best compromise we could reach among the communities represented on the CAC. (Tom, 1978: 91)

Ben Tom references some Chinese of Chinatown and greater San Francisco who considered him to be traitorous as he believed in the aims of racial integration. Even before mandatory busing, he had advocated for an integrated school for his own children to attend Sherman School versus his assigned Spring Valley school, wanting his children to be around children of different racial backgrounds. His supportive stance of integration a-priori of it being mandatory demonstrates the growing consciousness of American born Chinese, who were willing to stand up to the long-standing governance of the Six Companies in Chinatown, and those wanting to protect the insularity of Chinatown: a social construction established due to its long history of exclusion.

Although Ben Tom represented part of the Chinese diaspora of San Francisco supporting busing, other more conservative Chinese groups did not agree. A group called Concerned Chinese Parents stacked board meetings, often held in auditoriums to accommodate the large crowds. The Concerned Chinese Parent group's rationale for their opposition to busing included:

(1) no benefits from the bilingual education already furnished in their community (e.g. Commodore Stockton);
(2) participation in Chinese School after school would be curtailed due to transport times back to Chinatown;
(3) emergencies would restrict parents from reaching their children quickly;
(4) lack of provision of interpreters and translators at their new schools would inhibit communication; and
(5) animosity between Chinese and non-Chinese children would lead to fights. (Lum, 1978: 62)

The San Francisco press picked up on the racial animosity that would ensue and that their bilingual programming would be compromised, yet still describing the Chinese as the most uncooperative toward the goals of school integration (Ellsworth Jones, 1971). The narrative of locality, the adequate provision of English as a Second Language (ESL) or bilingual education and historic segregation was not described, portraits that were more evident in the local Chinatown papers of *East West* and the *China Times*. *East West* articulated the long exclusion of Chinese opinion in any matters related to schooling writing about three speakers attending a CAC meeting in Spring of 1971 before mandatory busing launched.

Harold Fong, Chairman of the San Francisco Lodge of the Chinese American Citizens Alliance and Chinese parents, Stanley Gee and LB Lum expressed their concerns to the CAC, captured in *East West*, a circulating Chinese newspaper in English and Chinese.

Harold Fong:	None of the eight plans are acceptable and compatible to the needs of Chinatown. You must come up with a better plan because Chinatown has unique socio-economic language and cultural problems.
Stanley Gee:	You've never talked to us to find out what we feel. You just show us maps.
L.B. Lum:	If she's traveling an hour to school and an hour back, there's no way for her to go to Chinese school to get that education. (East West, 1971b: 1)

These captured voices demonstrate SFUSD's hasty attempt to include the Chinese community in discussions about busing are situated in a long history of exclusion. In opposition to busing, a Chinese group asked the Ninth Circuit Court of Appeals to uphold the mandatory busing arguing that for the Chinese, it did not satisfy the burden of de jure segregation. Enter *Guey Heung Lee et al. v. Johnson* (1971).

Guey Heung Lee, Yinig Ngoi Toy and Foon Sit Yee were plaintiffs against the Johnson case for racial desegregation, claiming that the focus of the *Johnson v. SFUSD* case was founded on a Black–White construction and the Chinese were not to includable members in the case's description. Further, Guey, Yinig and Foon described the importance of maintaining their present schools, most in Chinatown to preserve their cultural and linguistic heritage and that affordances for Chinese bilingual education were only available in Chinatown. Further, Chinese students to be bused would not return in time to attend Chinese schools, putting the schools at risk for closure. Finally, they claimed that the use of race in formulating school assignments was unlawful, reinforcing the ideals of many White anti-busing advocates like the Liberty Lobby.

Guey, Yinig and Foon presented themselves as speaking for all Chinese of San Francisco (*New York Times*, 1971), not recognizing a small, but growing contingent of Chinese American educators like Benjamin Tom and Lucinda Lee, Chinese Americans who proclaimed desegregation's merits. Guey, Yinig and Foon's request for a stay to put the mandatory busing on hold was denied at the Ninth Circuit Court of Appeals. As the case advanced through the Ninth Circuit Court of Appeals to the Supreme Court, Justice William O'Douglass contested bilingual education as a reason for stopping desegregation, stating,

> Bilingual classes are not proscribed. They may be provided in any manner which does not create, maintain or foster segregation. 'There is no prohibition of courses teaching the cultural background and heritages of various racial and ethnic groups. While such courses may have particular appeal to members of the particular racial or ethnic group whose background and heritage is being studied, it would seem to be highly desirable

that this understanding be shared with those of other racial and ethnic backgrounds. 339 F. Supp., at 1322. (United States Ninth District Court of Appeals, 1971: 404)

Supreme Court Justice William Douglass recognizes that while cultural preservation is of value, this should be experienced by the entire student constituency of SFUSD and not limited to the Chinese alone. But the statement about 'bi-lingual classes are not proscribed' recognizes that such logics are a device to maintain racial segregation. Clearly, we see the amplification of racial constructions over those that are linguistic. Unity is created through racially integrated classrooms and schools, but language is not central to that cultural preservation. Justice William O Douglass continued,

> Brown v. Board of Education was not written for Blacks alone. It rests on the Equal Protection Clause of the Fourteenth Amendment, one of the first beneficiaries of which were the Chinese people of San Francisco. See Yick Wo v. Hopkins, 118 U.S. 356. The theme of our school desegregation cases extends to all [404 U.S. 1215, 1217] racial minorities treated invidiously by a State or any of its agencies. (United States Ninth District Court of Appeals, 1971: 404)

In reference to the *Yick Wo v. Hopkins* case (1886), Judge Douglass recognizes that a law on its face value may appear to be impartial, but in its enforcement may unduly marginalize a given group. In 1886, laundries in San Francisco were mainly run by the Chinese (89%) and were not approved for permits and had to pay fines. Thus, in its administration, laundry permits privileged White-owned laundries over the mostly wooden ones run by the Chinese. Being exempt from the busing decree for only the Chinese was denied by the Supreme Court, citing a case that had historically ruled in favor of the laundry merchants of Chinatown. Importantly, Judge Douglass cites a case between White and Chinese launders and their disparate treatment in enforcement. In the busing case, Douglass argues that busing administered to one group of color and not to the other would constitute an unequal enforcement.

The Horseshoe Plan for Desegregation Becomes Mandatory: The Chinese are Missing

On September 13, 1971, the 48,000 elementary students in SFUSD were assigned to their new schools with 25,000 of them slated to attend schools outside their neighborhood. One hundred and thirty buses were prepared across the city to transport them. Students were to meet at their neighborhood school and be transported to up to 97 different new elementary schools (Moskowitz, 1971). On day one of busing, many of those buses were sparsely populated and at Commodore Stockton Elementary for outgoing students. The protesters were out, those from the local neighborhoods, many of whom were a part of WALK: We All Love Kids, an anti-busing parent group (Moskowitz, 1971: 8).

The opposition to busing was measurably louder at Commodore Stockton, the largest school in Chinatown where Lucinda Lee was teaching. The *New York Times* lead article on busing read,

> The heaviest boycott was by students who formerly attended Commodore Stockton School, which is in this city's Chinatown. The Chinese have been the most vociferous opponents of the busing plan, which was ordered by a Federal court. (Turner, 1971: 18)

During the first week of busing, 600 students, nearly all Chinese, were to report to Commodore Stockton to be bused to their new schools, but only 29 children showed up with many buses departing, empty (Ellsworth Jones, 1971). At nearby Jean Parker, Lucinda's former school, Principal Virginia Wales described the nearly empty buses that departed her school for their new schools relative to the fuller buses that were incoming to Jean Parker Elementary. Principal Wales shared, 'Chinatown is still resisting' (Ellsworth Jones, 1971: 9). Wales' description of the totality of Chinatown resisting busing along with the *New York Times'* article of the 'Chinese' being the 'most vociferous' collectively ascribed the Chinese as unrelenting and uncooperative in complying with the mandatory busing policy. The Chinese were nationally portrayed as the tenacious resistors to racial integration.

Yet, in speaking with community leaders and activists within Chinatown, the messaging about busing was confusing. Different Chinese newspapers including *East West* and *China Times* all portrayed the busing requirement differently. The *China Times,* written in Chinese, had a readership of immigrant families, whereas *East West* was bilingual, drawing in the immigrant and American born Chinese with content differing across the two papers (Lai, 1982). But families were also getting information from their family associations, and the Chinese Benevolent Association, also known as the Six Companies, sources that some Chinese born residents trusted over the official messaging of SFUSD (Lai, 2004). In opposition to busing, Chinatown began its own schools, the Freedom Schools of Chinatown, opening their doors in 1971 just as mandatory busing had begun under order of the district federal courts.

 ## The Freedom Schools of Chinatown

The original founding and naming of Freedom Schools came out of Prince Edward County, Virginia in opposition to racial integration. The all-White school board voted on closure of all public schools rather than racially integrate as dictated by federal courts, closures lasting from

1959–1964 (Titus, 2011). Teacher volunteers and activists from throughout the US committed to teaching, working in homes, churches, and community spaces to furnish schooling to Black children, while a private system was created for White students.

The Freedom Schools of Chinatown were not named because of the history of segregation in the US, rather is an 'ironic twist' about seeking freedom from a system that had long excluded the Chinese (Lai, 2004; Lum, 1978: 57). In 1885, Superintendent Andrew Moulder of the San Francisco Common Schools and previously the Superintendent of Schools for the state of California said of Mamie Tape's segregated Chinese Primary School: 'Without such separate education action, I have every reason to believe that some of our classes will be inundated by Mongolians. Trouble will follow' (Evening Bulletin, 1885: 2). Funding for the Chinese Primary School and later the Oriental School, received appreciably less funding relative to the well-resourced White schools, like the Spring Valley School Mamie Tape attempted to attend (Low, 1982; Ngai, 2010). Just prior to desegregation's beginnings in SFUSD, committees within the SFUSD used the idea of 'local racial concentration' or 'ethnic enclaves' to rationalize the history of segregated schooling, a term used throughout the US to excuse communities from federal mandates for integration (Lum, 1975; Quinn, 2020).

Following the denied stay in the *Guey Heung Lee v. Johnson* (1971) case to stop busing for Chinese pupils, Chinatown organized themselves very quickly, creating a sophisticated governance structure for the Freedom Schools. They claimed the name of San Francisco Chinese for Education Committee. The leadership was shared by the Chinese Chamber of Commerce, the Six Companies, San Francisco Chinese Parent's Committee and Chinese American Citizen's Alliance. Operational staff included coordinators and co-coordinators, Superintendents and Principals. Also included were public relations personnel who would serve as points of contact with the SFUSD.

The Freedom Schools opened in the Fall of 1971 with 1,465 Chinese students, representing 24% of SFUSD's former Chinese pupils. The schools had four core purposes including a quality education; fostering and preserving Chinese culture; interrelating school and community life; and encouraging parental engagement. They were enrolled in one of three Freedom School systems; called Telesis, Nob Hill and North Beach (Lum, 1975, 1978). The Freedom School's launch made a front page of the *San Francisco Examiner* with the title, 'Parent's Boycott: Chinatown Plans "Freedom School"' (San Francisco Examiner, 1971: 1) (Figure 10.1).

The three Freedom School systems interpreted the aim of 'quality education' differently. The Telesis system had curriculum and instructional goals that included a history of the Chinese in the US and a more immediate history of Chinese Americans. To augment their minimal budget, they formally requested funds from SFUSD to support the schools. North Beach with only one school, also sought support from SFUSD, but

Figure 10.1 Nam Kue 'Freedom School' was one of several Freedom School locations in Chinatown (*San Francisco Examiner*, September 20, 1971).

requested that they be recognized as an autonomous school by the district and was adamant about the cessation of busing. The Six Companies were steadfast in their opposition to busing and 'organized a community-wide meeting with parents, students and communities and decided to form an anti-busing committee chaired by CCBA president, Mr. Wong' (Consolidated Chinese Benevolant Association, 1971). But, the Six Companies also had a more politically motivated agenda largely informing the name and the idea of the Freedom Schools.

The Six Companies' school, who directly oversaw the Nob Hill school, had a primary agenda of promoting a pro-Nationalist-China alliance, which was not wholly representative of the newer residents of Chinatown. In an effort to demonstrate this international alliance between China and the US and to reduce Chinese hysteria in the US, the Six Companies held a Double Ten Parade in October of 1971. They compelled all Freedom Schools to attend under threat of lost funding. Families, students and teachers were to bring signs that bore the words, 'Anti-Busing parents Support Nationalist China' (Lum, 1978: 68). Yet in the end, very few attended, and the parade was a bust.

Lum (1975, 1978) details how the failure of the parade also shed light on the changing constituency of the Chinese in San Francisco. Newer residents from Southern China and Hong Kong did not have the same allegiances with the Republic of China. Furthermore, the parade revealed the reduced influence of the Six Companies, and that the new Chinese were drawing from other systems and networks, which differed from the needs of the Chinese preceding 1965.

Although the Freedom schools attempted to coordinate together, disagreements ensued over what curriculum to include. Staffing issues were pervasive with teachers only making $10 a day relative to the $32 being made by SFUSD substitutes (Lum, 1978: 67). Despite all their many fundraisers (East West, 1971c: 1), after just one year of operating the Freedom Schools, the Telesis system closed. Gradually, parents began sending their children to their assigned schools and other negotiations were changing the SFUSD student assignment system. Specifically a Temporary Assignment Permit (TAP) enabled families to choose a school other than their assigned one (San Francisco Unified Schools, 2020). After just two years, the Freedom Schools closed their doors for good.

Johnson v. SFUSD (1971) alongside of *Brown v. Board of Education* (1954, 1955) claimed that segregated schooling was unethical in that racially minoritized children may feel a sense of inferiority or maltreatment and that the courts had a legal obligation to address such inequities through racial integration (Thompson, 2013). By equalizing the treatment of all students through integrated schooling, then such inferiorities would potentially be remediated. Drawing from Isaiah Berlin's (1958) tenets, he argued that liberty is either negative or positive with negative connoting *freedom from,* whereas positive liberty is *freedom to or toward*. Through busing, Black students would not feel inferior and have freedom from such sentiments.

Thompson's (2013) comprehensive analysis of Brown and Lau reveal that within racial desegregation the premise of negative liberty took hold, but in Lau, positive liberty or *freedom to* was the construction of the courts. *Lau v. Nichols* posited that equality is satisfied when there is differential treatment of groups depending on their needs. With Lau, the need was language provisions so Chinese youth could more easily access content and learning.

In the case of *Guey Heung Lee v. Johnson* (1971), the plaintiffs argued for positive liberty and for the specialized treatment of the Chinese, and that positive liberty could not co-exist with the structures and practices of racial integration (negative liberty). The request by the plaintiffs was not negative liberty alongside positive liberty, rather negative liberty for some and positive liberty for others, presenting an inequitable resolution to the courts, driving the Freedom Schools to operate outside the public schools. In the next chapter we meet the students of Lucinda Lee following the implementation of racial desegregation alongside the earliest provisions of a Cantonese bilingual education. The sun was rising along the landscape.

Section 2
After Lau: The Sunrising Quickly

11 After Lau: Remedies and More Remedies
The Lau Consent Decrees

On January 21, 1974, the Supreme Court ruled in favor of the Chinese plaintiffs finding that SFUSD failed to remedy the language needs of its Chinese students; a violation of the Civil Rights Act of 1964. The Supreme Court overturned the earlier decisions of the lower courts, the US District Court of the Northern District of California and the Ninth Circuit Court of Appeals who found that SFUSD had sufficiently addressed the needs of its Chinese students and that there was no violation of the Fourteenth Amendment for an equal education. The Supreme Court agreed on that count with the lower courts but proclaimed that there was a violation of the Civil Rights Act of 1964. Supreme Court Judge, William Douglass who had overturned the stay for busing in the *Guey Heung Lee et al. v. Johnson* (1971) for the Chinese, stating that bilingual education was not pro-scribed, now shared his opinion from the court on the *Lau v. Nichols* case.

 Supreme Court Judge, William Douglass wrote:

> Under these state-imposed standards there is no equality of treatment merely by providing students with the same facilities, textbooks, teachers, and curriculum; for students who do not understand English are effectively foreclosed from any meaningful education. (Douglass, 1974)

As Lau ruled on a violation of the Civil Rights Act of 1964 and not the Fourteenth Amendment, the legal precedent on which *Guey Heung Lee et al. v. Johnson* (1971) was founded, his rationale shifted; not to pro-scribe bilingual education for unity, but to pro-scribe language access and thereby, language rights under the Civil Rights Act of 1964.

Meanwhile, Edward Steinman on his long commute from San Francisco to Santa Clara University, where he was now a Law Professor, heard the announcement on his local radio channel, KCBS. '*Lau v. Nichols* rules in favor of the Chinese plaintiffs'. Ed remembered his reaction as he held onto the steering wheel.

> Lead story 8:00 news. The US Supreme Court ruled unanimously. Court to avoid the constitutional issue. Oh, sh-t! Because of course, to legalize you one over the Constitution. Yeah. And that was the reason it was unanimous. It is not a constitutional decision. That means the decision could be changed by Congress. If you made a decision based on a statute or in law, it is actually federal regulations, those regulations could be changed.

Ed described that what prevailed with the Supreme Court was that *Lau v. Nichols* was a violation of the Civil Rights Act of 1964 and not the Fourteenth Amendment of the Constitution, unlike the Brown cases which were a violation of the equal protection clause within the Fourteenth Amendment. Ed's hope of them having parallel aims made the announcement a mixed celebration.

The *East West* Chinatown paper's Chinese version had a lengthy description of Lau's passage, entitled a 'Day of Victory'.

> 勝利的一天 On January 21st, in the case of Chinese-American children (CAC) in San Francisco accused the Department of Education of negligence in education responsibilities, the United States Supreme Court ruled in favor of CAC. CAC won the lawsuit. As a result, firstly, educational institutions in San Francisco and other areas of the US must no longer ignore the educational needs of CAC. Secondly, based on this Supreme Court's decision, the government can allocate funds to support the schools which CAC study in. The term 'government' includes federal, state, and local governments. Thirdly, the demand for Chinese-American educators in schools will increase, which is a great thing for Chinese-Americans working in the education industry. Remember, not long ago, regardless of their academic achievements, Chinese-Americans faced difficulties to become teachers. Fourthly, bilingual (Chinese & English) and bi-cultural education will receive funding. (East W*est*, 1974: 1)

Lau's passage did not detail the language provisions that should be furnished. The *East West* announcement draws from the collective belief that a substantive commitment to Cantonese-Chinese bilingual education was forthcoming.

The Lau Consent Decree Annual Reports

SFUSD had to swing into action quickly. Bilingual administrators, divisions of instruction and the personnel department, along with its school board had to respond to the remedy for Lau: The Lau Consent Decree for SFUSD. The Lau Consent decree of SFUSD, born just one year after Lau's passage in 1975 was overseen by the Ninth Circuit, the very courts that had regarded language deficiencies as the fault of the families in 1973, leading to Lawyer, Edward Steinman filing an appeal and its assent to the Supreme Court. The defendants would change in the Lau decree from Nichols *et al.* to Hopp *et al.*, to reflect the new school board president and its members of 1974 (*Kinney Kinmon Lau, et al. and the United States vs. Dr. Eugene Hopp, et al.*, 1974). None of the school board members that worked with Nichols remained on the board. This is due in part to the tumultuous nature of busing, but also that school board members were no longer appointed by the mayor but now elected by the voters.

On March 25, 1975, the SFUSD School board approved the Master Plan for Bilingual–Bicultural Education, which began to inform what they submitted to the court supervisors. The plan's development was facilitated by the Center for Applied Linguistics in collaboration with the Citizens' Taskforce on Bilingual Education. Its four-part series, set the Lau decree tenets from 1975 to 2005 (Center for Applied Linguistics and the Citizens' Taskforce on Bilingual Education, 1975a, 1975b, 1975c).

SFUSD had to produce large-scale reports for the courts annually. Its first report for the Lau Consent Decree was submitted to the United States District Court Northern District of California on November 15, 1976. The consent decree had four paragraphs that required their annual response, all aligned with the details in the four-part plan developed by the Center for Applied Linguistics and the Citizens' Taskforce on Bilingual Education:

- Paragraph #1: SFUSD shall implement a Master Plan for Bilingual–Bicultural Education.
- Paragraph #2: SFUSD will identify the number of Non English Speakers (NES) and Limited English Speakers (LES) not receiving ESL or bilingual education.
- Paragraph #3 and 4: SFUSD will create structures and processes for implementation of the Bilingual–Bicultural Education Master Plan.

(Bilingual Department of San Francisco Unified School District, 1976)

The first Lau decree report would begin with apologies, stating that schools did not meet the deadline to report their demographics and 'new BBE [Bilingual–bicultural] classes have started and new students have arrived not reflected in the survey' (Bilingual Department of San Francisco Unified School District, 1976: 5). The Bilingual Department was newly transforming and their system for collection was still developing.

Victor Low (Chapter 5) who was the Project Manager for Chinese Bilingual talked about the new bilingual department being in an old high school gym and 'growing like and amoeba', but not necessarily with a clear and consistent direction on accountability for the courts. Their focus was on implementation in the schools, so he did not participate directly in the preparation of the first decree report, even though the Bilingual Department was noted as the author of the 1976 Lau consent decree report (Bilingual Department of San Francisco Unified School District, 1976).

Identification of Eligible Students

To prepare the first Lau decree report, all SFUSD teachers received a memorandum from the district asking them to fill out a home language survey of their students. Item 1 and 2 required documentation of US born or not-US born, and items 3–6 solicited information about the type of language learner they had in their schools, using these naming conventions (Table 11.1).

As shown in Table 11.1, the descriptions were broad brush strokes, combining level of English proficiency with program type for students classified as a Bilingual-English speaker with no mention of program model for students in the lower levels of proficiency. Thus, NES and LES students were somewhat muted within this reporting request as to what program type they should be assigned. Lastly, on a report about language minoritized students or what we would reference today as identified-English learners, there is a designation of Dominant English Speaker (DES), denoting language majority students or what we may now reference as English-only (EO) students. Busing was now in its fifth year and DES children could opt into bilingual programming with parental consent. While the Lau consent decree was focused on the language minoritized students, SFUSD created a distinct category of DES for the court report, an intersectional dimension of student category and representative of the maturing seeds for what we now call two-way bilingual education or dual language bilingual education (DLBE).

The decree also required information related to ethnicity and preparers of the report used the same descriptors that were used for the racial desegregation decree, which were indicative of how race was counted during the 1970 Census (Humes & Hogan, 2009; Pratt *et al.*, 2022). The ethnicities included: OW: Other White [meaning: White]; N/B Negro/Black; C: Chinese; J: Japanese; K: Korean; SS: Spanish Speaker; F: Pilipino; A.I.: American Indian; ONW: Other Non-White. The Asian diaspora was disaggregated across east Asian, Southeast Asian and Pacific Islanders, whereas Hispanics were already clustered into a category of Spanish speakers to cover their vast diversity in national origin and language identity.

Language Program Type

Program types were described as English as a Second Language (ESL), Bilingual–Bicultural Education (BBE) with specifics on how many

Table 11.1 Identification of eligible students by teachers

Type of language learner	Description (1976)	Description (2024)	Construct of measure 1976
#3: Non-English Speaker (NES)	A student who communicates only in a home language that is not English. Such a student is unable to conduct basic conversation in English or to benefit from classroom instruction given only in English.	Newcomer Beginner-level of English	1. Recency of immigration 2. Low level of English proficiency
#4: Limited English Speaker (LES)	A student who has not sufficiently developed English language skills of comprehension, speaking, reading and writing to benefit from instruction only in English. (Such a student usually comes from a home where a language <u>other than English is spoken</u>).	Limited English Proficient (LEP)	3. Low level of English proficiency
#5: Bilingual-English speaker (Bil)	A bilingual student who can understand and participate at various levels of proficiency in two (2) languages. He has sufficient English skills to succeed in class taught only in English or in a bilingual class. He may current be in either type class	Intermediate level of English	4. Level of English proficiency 5. Eligibility for more language program options
#6: Dominant English Speaker (DES)	A student in a self-contained bilingual class whose home or first language is English	English majority student or English-only (EO) student	6. Bused students who are English majority and wish to participate in BBE models

Home language survey collection from SFUSD teachers as reported in the Lau Consent Decree Report (1976) (Bilingual Department of San Francisco Unified School District, 1976: 8)

NES, LES, Bil and DES students were at each school and/or newcomer center, followed by a description by ethnicity. Latter pages detailed how many different student types were in ESL or BBE models by language group. The 1976 report documents the number of NES and LES children *not* in ESL or BBE models (Bilingual Department of San Francisco Unified School District, 1976: 11). A total of 210 NES and 1245 LES students were not in any program. The breakout by language is circled with a pen if the numbers were high. Cantonese was among the starkest. A total of 47 NES and 364 LES Cantonese speakers were not in any ESL or BBE model (total = 411). They were in a sink or swim context like Kinney Lau was in his earliest years at Jean Parker Elementary.

Eight hundred and forty (840) DES students were documented as participants in the district's different BBE model by ethnicity in the report. Bilingual programs included Chinese, Spanish, Filipino and Japanese. A total of 304 of the 840 DES students were in the developing Chinese bilingual programs in large part due to busing versus the explicit recruitment that happens in present-day districts to promote dual language education (Delavan *et al.*, 2022). The mechanism for DES placement in bilingual programs was largely busing and a parent's willingness for their DES child to participate in the BBE strand, as we learned from Lucinda's students, designated as NES, LES or DES students at the time.

So, 411 eligible Cantonese emergent bilinguals received no help, and 304 DES (English majority students) received a Chinese BBE. Most of the BBE DES students were White (OW) and illuminates how busing created the conditions for racial and linguistic integration, but that the White students bused to their assigned school with a Chinese BBE program may have been the primary beneficiaries; a form of interest convergence (Palmer, 2009). Interest convergence within the context of DLBE posits that families from English dominant backgrounds are fine having native speakers (in this case, LES, or NES) students in the mix, provided their child is the primary benefactor. In short, if busing is a bummer for my child, at least they have a BBE model to enrich their experience. This stand is in stark relief to the many Chinese who had no programming, meaning their access to schooling was compromised, while many DES students were enjoying a BBE enrichment model. The logic drawn from this report, coupled with the narratives of our Chinese participants demonstrates early signs of DLBE gentrification, both discursive and material (Morita-Mullaney & Chesnut, 2022; Valdes, 1997; Valdez *et al.*, 2016).

This early gentrification move was also due in part to the reauthorizations of the Bilingual Education Act in 1974 and again in 1978, which permitted up to 40% English majority speakers to participate in a bilingual education (Public Law 93-380, 1074; Public Law 95-561, 1978). Within a desegregating SFUSD, the aims of racial integration formulas could be met by satisfying the interests of English majority families to a bilingual education, as was the case with Lucinda Lee's families who were bused into Commodore Stockton's Chinatown school. Importantly, English majority students was also inclusive of racially minoritized students. Thus in a racially integrated school, students of color experienced '…negative equality, which consists of removing morally untenable discriminatory practices to ensure equality via similar treatment' (Thompson, 2013: 1249) which was the ideological premise of Brown. Racially minoritized bilingual students could also benefit from 'positive equality, which consists of ensuring equality by customizing treatment depending on a group's particular needs' (Thompson, 2013: 1249). Yet, while combining White students, students of color, some of whom were bilinguals, the customization of treatment requires differentation. At the onset of Lau and its remedies, how this differentiation manifested was through a focus on the bicultural domain within the Cantonese program as evidenced by Lucinda's classroom (Chapter 5) and what you will later read with Laureen Chew (Chapter 13).

Trained Teachers

The last part of the report described how BBE models were staffed along with the language proficiency and content expertise of all SFUSD teachers, not just those in BBE programs. SFUSD's personnel division was charged with collecting this data, having teachers self-identify their 'foreign language abilities' as 'fluent, limited, and minimal' (Bilingual Department of San Francisco Unified School District, 1976: 16). The personnel department accounted for three of the main language groups including Chinese, Spanish and Pilipino.

The report went on to detail the proficiency levels of certificated teachers in BBE programs, using the terminology of fully bilingual, partially bilingual, or minimally bilingual. For Chinese BBE, 32 identified as fully bilingual; 11 as partially; and 15 as minimal. In comparison, 46 native speaking Chinese aides were working in Chinese bilingual programs.

Lucinda Lee affirmed that the aides that assisted in her bilingual classroom were native speakers from Hong Kong or Southern China, and instrumental to the implementation of the BBE program. During the day, the aides taught the NES and some of the LES Cantonese students during Chinese time, while Lucinda taught the bused-in DES students during Chinese time, referenced as Chinese as a Second Language (CSL). According to Lucinda, she rated herself as fully bilingual and Laureen, her student teacher rated herself as partially proficient, an early indication of the range of proficiencies of Chinese bilingual teachers.

The first Lau consent decree report's author was the Bilingual Department of SFUSD (Bilingual Department of San Francisco Unified School District, 1976). Yet in conversations with members of The Association of Chinese Teachers (TACT), the pen name of Yu Rat, John Lum reemerged. He was the origin author. John Lum shared,

> My role in the Lau Consent Decree was generally non-political. I was employed by the SFUSD which assigned me to write the Consent Decree. I would then periodically send drafts to City Attorney George Krueger,

who suggested a couple of places where I could better restate my words in a more legal way. I never met with federal court personnel; Mr. Krueger and Mr. Ray del Portillo did all of the meetings with the feds, and occasionally informed me that the feds never expressed any negative feeling. In fact, the only thing I heard in the years I was writing the Decree, was from the respected head of the Center for Applied Linguistics, Rudy Troike, who was checking in on 'how I was doing.'

John demonstrates the many roles and tasks happening behind the scenes; ones that were not publicly noted in the development of the decree and its subsequent reports. The Consent Decree portion of the Lau-Nichols Decision was a collective effort, but without retrospective inquiries, the complete social picture would be lost.

Victor Low, the Project Manager of the Chinese Bilingual program, who seemingly could be a contributor to the decree reports, was not called upon nor asked to furnish any expertise on how to assess teachers in Cantonese. The only instrument was self-identification, perhaps due to the swift nature of assembling the report. Further still, the lack of solicitation from the Chinese Bilingual Program leadership for advice is evidence of the developing program, but that historic systems were assigned to complete the report, in this first iteration, the personnel department to complete 'Paragraph 1-2'. As the Lau decree serves as a narrative source of bilingual education, understanding its oblique authors is important in understanding how particular actors, like Victor were in/excluded in its preparation and how John Lum was positioned as their ghost writer.

The Late 1970s: Building the Structure within the Structure

In the 1977–78 school year, the Bilingual Community Council was established, drawing from bilingual educators, community agencies and universities with teacher education programs bringing in multiple perspectives, contributing to the direction of bilingual education, and thus the shape of the report. The report, now bounded in a tidy yellow covered booklet held the authorship of the Office of the Superintendent, and not the Bilingual Department (Office of the Superintendent of San Francisco Unified School District, 1978).

For the 1977–78 report, counseling, licensure acquisition and professional development for BBE teachers and administrators was added. Counseling detailed the type of advising students would receive when they came to a variety of intake centers throughout the city to enroll their children. In the centers, students would be assessed and identified and then placed based in schools with language programs. Discussion of a battery of testing was furnished (Office of the Superintendent of San Francisco Unified School District, 1978: III-2) In this report, we see the term DES disappear from the report, the English majority students who were participating in BBE at places like Commodore Stockton with Lucinda. Instead we see the naming convention of LES, NES, Bil, Dom (for dominant), to articulate a continuum of proficiency levels from beginner to advanced and only in relationship to identified-English learners (Office of the Superintendent of San Francisco Unified School District, 1978). Professional development included sessions available to bilingual educators, including the provision of a bilingual workshop in the summer months and continued work with the Center for Applied Linguistics. Discussion of licensure was a big topic as many of the BBE educators were not licensed in this area and nearby universities were scrambling to develop such models.

California's adoption of Assembly Bill 1329, Chacon-Moscone Bilingual–Bicultural Act (1972) required that BBE teachers be assessed for their proficiency in the minority language they were teaching. The process for assessing them was internally developed and teachers were furnished with a 'Certificate of Competence' and 'waivers' were furnished should teachers not meet the minimum standard (Office of the Superintendent of San Francisco Unified School District, 1978: III-11).

The provision of waivers was a heavy weight to carry for Cantonese-Chinese bilingual educators. Even though they had a teaching license, they did not have the bilingual specialization. Chinese teachers also had to demonstrate bilingual proficiency in English and Cantonese. At that time, nearby universities were just beginning to develop models for bilingual licensure, and thus, it was incumbent upon the district to create the standard, which only relied on language proficiency for which Chinese educators had various levels of proficiency in relationship to a fluent standard. The construction of waiver made BBE teachers uneasy. Laureen and Darlene (teachers you will meet in subsequent chapters) both spoke of being on waivers, continually worrying about their contract from year to year. This was also a big concern within TACT, who persistently advocated for waiver teachers' retention, and that their benefits and years of service would go toward their final pensions. They were devoted to bilingual education, yet, they were precariously positioned, something that ESL teachers did not experience.

1979–1980

Proposition 13 passed by California voters in 1978 made its way into the 1979-1980 report. Proposition 13 meant that taxes were summarily frozen for property owners reducing funding to public schools.

Remarks about Proposition 13 articulated that the state context of California made the decree challenging to implement (Office of the Superintendent of San Francisco Unified School District, 1980: i). A district wide school boycott went on for six weeks due to financial cuts, including layoffs and the writers of the report were apologetic, testifying to the large lift given reduced staffing during the report's preparation. During this upheaval, written within the decree, SFUSD committed to retaining BBE teachers on waiver, a term to describe those not yet licensed in bilingual education.

California Assembly Law 1329, called the Chacon-Moscone Act (1976) required the proficiency in the minoritized language for those teaching in BBE programs, but also that BBE teachers must seek out a bilingual certification from a university's teacher education program. University of San Francisco and San Francisco State were mentioned explicitly. No funding was furnished for such licenses and BBE teachers had to invest their own personal resources into the additional licensure along with developing their language proficiency to the district's standard. In short, making one's way off the waiver roles required personal and financial resources, exponentially experienced by Chinese BBE educators.

Advances were made in the areas of counseling, curriculum, instruction and promotion based on the 1979–1980 report. Counseling at the high school had expanded to include a procedure of evaluating transcripts of students from within the district, transfers and/or those coming in from another country, so appropriate placements could be made. Funding from Emergency School Assistance Act was solicited, but mostly Hispanic programs were funded, so resources to support this procedure was scant for the Chinese (Office of the Superintendent of San Francisco Unified School District, 1980: 3).

Curriculum was being acquired commercially for Spanish BBE programs, but the Chinese BBE program was largely creating their own with Title VII staff, including Robert Sung's and Gordon Lew's (Chapter 4) materials. Other content areas were being developed, especially in social studies at the secondary level. BBE teachers were also creating their own units and TACT was actively involved in curriculum-making for the bilingual and bicultural aspects of the program. For instruction, there was an emerging understanding on the amount of time students should receive within their mother tongue in the BBE programs. This was a heavy focus in the high schools as students transitioned through multiple subjects and teachers throughout the day.

Promotion for BBE teachers was discussed, detailing how the district was in the process of developing criteria for who would evaluate BBE teachers; the principals or the Bilingual Department? Reference was made of other districts who had a career ladder program for BBE teachers and that SFUSD needed to duplicate such processes (Office of the Superintendent of San Francisco Unified School District, 1980: 25).

The late 1970s were indicative of SFUSD building a BBE model with the pillars of student identification, curriculum, instruction and adequate and qualified staff. Yet this happened during a time of huge financial strain across the state given the passage of Proposition 13. Laureen Chew (Chapter 13) discussed the consistent threat of layoff, and how it was demoralizing especially given her significant contributions with TACT and the development of bilingual resources and support for Chinese BBE. Ultimately, this strain would lead to a different direction in Laureen's professional trajectory (Chapter 16).

The 1980s: Positions, Promotions and Pupil Proportion

The 1980 decrees were indicative of bilingual education on the rise. California Assembly Bill 507 called the Bilingual Education Reform Act of California (1980) replaced the Chacon-Moscone Bilingual Bicultural Act as its original iterations lacked girth and specificity. Further, the revision also discussed bilingual education more explicitly and that every LEP child must be given a bilingual education. The sharper contours of the Bilingual Education Reform Act of California (1980) were evident in the decree reports of the 1980s.

Within management, the Bilingual program Department now had a Supervisor, a higher position within the administrative ranks creating new conditions and influences for oversight (Office of the Superintendent of San Francisco Unified School District, 1982: 2). The Bilingual Education Improvement Reform Act of California (1980) was passed, creating trigger numbers. If there were 10 or more students of a given language, then a bilingual education in that language was to be furnished (1980: 32). Further, there was now funding of BBE through competitive state funds, increasing the dollars available to SFUSD by writing grants to solicit the state funds (1980: 65). Given the exponential increase in the number of identified LEP students in SFUSD, alongside of the teacher to student ratio requirements, bilingual educators were needed. To meet the demand, waivers were still being furnished to BBE teachers.

In 1982, California Assembly Bill 507/80 stated that bilingual teachers on waivers could maintain their contracts, provided they had a bilingual paraprofessional whose proficiency in the minoritized language was supervising them at least three hours a day. Thus, we see the privileging of many immigrant Chinese speakers who take on a larger role in mentoring and modeling Cantonese to the mostly American born Chinese teachers. As Lucinda and Laureen continually shared, their aides were instrumental for the linguistic components of the program, but also that they could be primary interlocutors for the cultural histories of their student communities.

For the 1982–83 Lau consent decree report, a new area filtered into the mix. In addition to the historic requirement of testing BBE teachers in the minoritized language they were teaching, also reinforced by the Bilingual Education and Reform Act (1980), BBE teachers also had to take an exam for their English proficiency in listening, speaking, reading and writing. While this was not a requirement of the original Master Plan for Bilingual–Bicultural Education, it was a clear messaging coming from the Bilingual Department, now under new leadership; an administrator that was not in SFUSD when the Lau case was established. SFUSD's Department of Bilingual Education set up a process for its completion. In the end, nearly all BBE educators took the exam with only two refusing to participate. Clearly, the emphasis for English was leaning back into the fold. The content of English testing for BBE teachers was only evident in the 1982–83 Lau decrees; an agenda item of insertion and ideology of the 'new leadership' (Office of the Superintendent of San Francisco Unified School District, 1983).

Other additions in the decree included discussions about students who were both LEP and special education (Office of the Superintendent of San Francisco Unified School District, 1983: 8), opportunities for vocational education, and students who recently arrived with interrupted formal schooling (1983: 7). Dually classified students identified upon enrollment or at their schools were to be assessed by bilingual staff for the learning need of concern (1983: 8–9). Collaboration between BBE and special education teachers was articulated. If a bilingual psychologist was needed in a particular language, then a consultant would be brought in to evaluate.

Students with limited formal schooling were classified as 'preliterate' and special programming was developed that fell outside of the scope of the original Master Plan (1983: 9). Regarded as a survival program, 'it will stress orientations needed for survival in an urban society' (Office of the Superintendent of San Francisco Unified School District, 1983: 9).

The 1990s: English Heavy and Bilingual Light

In the early 1990s, diminishing affordances for bilingual education, policy procedures and systems, presented itself discursively in the 1990–91 Lau decree report. The theme of the 1990s was English heavy and bilingual light. Program re-descriptions, placement and redesignation were detailed.

English language development occupies a large section in the 1990–91 report with discussion of English language development (ELD) placement being done by English language proficiency level at the secondary level. The term 'clustering' is used stating, 'ESL Language Development and ESL Reading classes must be organized according to English language proficiency level; ESL classes are not grouped homogeneously by primary language; ESL classes should be scheduled during the same block of time to accommodate movement of students from one level to another' (Office of the Superintendent of San Francisco Unified School District, 1991: 20). As one of Lau's original premises was grounded in belief and scholarship that opposed tracking, we see its pernicious reemergence. First, students must be grouped by level of English proficiency, replicating a model of a high school foreign language program and ascribing to a premise that students can only learn from a teacher, dismissing the vital resources of their classmates. Further, it sets aside the importance and value of biculturalism which was central to bilingual education's beginnings. Heterogeneity is only valued when there is a mixture of language groups, discouraging the use of students' home and native languages in the classroom, making the medium of instruction only English and thereby, the language of power in the classroom. Programmatically, ESL classes were to be held at the same time, so if students moved to a higher level, they could easily do so without a significant disruption to the master schedule.

For the elementary program, there was admission that not every child was in a bilingual program and if they were not they could be taught by a language development teacher, regular teacher trained in ESL, ESL teacher, resource teacher, bilingual aides, tutors, volunteers (Office of the Superintendent of San Francisco Unified School District, 1983: 18). Such students required a Bilingual Individual Learning Plan, called a BLIP which could justify the district as attempting bilingual education, albeit light or unfurnished. In short, a commitment to a BLIP was a strategy of absolution.

Redesignation or reclassification of students as fluent English proficient occupied three pages in the decree report. The pattern of reclassification was documented, stating that in 1984-85, 6.6% of emergent bilinguals were exited, whereas 1989–90 reflected an exit rate of 11.1%. While the identified-EL student constituency is not monolithic, always progressing and changing, the fact that reclassification doubled in the short period of five years indicates that a timeline of exiting was being accelerated. Schools were responsible for redesignating and the Bilingual Education Department monitored and approved/denied the recommendation, but clearly, its emphasis was having a growing impact to reclassify students quickly.

Upon investigation of supporting appendices within the report, a letter from the Wade Brynelson, Assistant Superintendent of Compliance of the California Department of Education congratulated SFUSD on addressing concerns of non-compliance during the 1980s. Conditions of compliance included: (1) Daily ELD instruction offered by qualified staff; (2) group data on the achievement of LEP students; (3) adequate number of qualified teachers to teach ELD at the secondary schools; and (4) adequate number of qualified teachers to teach the primary language of its students (Brynelson, 1988: 1–2).

Clearly, the rudder was steering toward more English medium instruction. As there was a persistent emphasis on leveled tracking of students based on their LEP level while concurrently mixing them heterogeneously by linguistic group, we see the potential for the foregrounding of race to meet the aims of the desegregation decree within the schoolhouse, while simultaneously eroding the progress made in bilingual education.

The tensions between policies of race and language had long been a challenge with the overlapping forces of SFNCAACP and Lau. The 1990–91 Lau decree report included a lengthy report and memorandum from the Bilingual Community Council on this dispute.

> Under the present court order to integrate our schools and to provide a meaningful education for all children, we find there is a basic incompatibility and injustice that staff has not yet found a way to resolve. A case in point. A youngster arrives in mid-semester from China. He does not speak English. There is no room at the newcomer center. A Chinese bilingual program in another school may have space. Unfortunately, the school already has its quota of Chinese students. Too frequently, the expeditious solution is to send the student to yet another school where there may not be an appropriate program but where the ethnicity of the student will not impact the racial quota. The dilemma members of the Board, is faced on a daily basis at the intake center and the Student Assignment Office. (Tsukamoto, 1990: 2)

The constructs of race and language were measured and systemized by the Bilingual Department's Intake Center (for language) and the Student Assignment Center (for race). The intake center and the assignment center operated too autonomously and race was constructed with greater value, diminishing the possibilities of *negative* and *positive liberty* for racialized, bilingual students. This was argued by Chinese and Hispanic members of the BCC with a resolution to approach the SFNAACP in mitigating their respective decrees (1990: 3). By calling out this inconsistency, we are reminded that Brown was decisioned on the Equal Protection clause of the 14th amendment and the Civil Rights Act of 1964, whereas Lau was attached only to the Civil Rights Act. Thus, the policy force privileged Brown. But, the BCC actors on the ground did not oppose one decree over another, rather requested coordination and hopeful congruence across the intake centers, facilitating cross-racial and cross-linguistic discussions. The BCC illuminated the early challenges of engaging in solidarity across identities of race and language.

12 After Lau: California's Proposition 227 and English for the Children
Federal Decrees Combat State Language Policy

On June 2, 1998, Proposition 227's 'English for the Children' was passed in a voter-led ballot initiative with 61% of its voters supporting, significantly eroding the foundations and programming of bilingual education (California Congress, 1980). The English-only movement was taking hold.

'All children in California public schools shall be taught English by being taught in English' (California Education Code, Chapter 3, Article 1. Section 305). Led by conservative politician and businessman, Ron Unz, instructional provisions were to be done exclusively in English with a focus on quick exit into mainstream instruction within one year, claiming it would save California money. While a bilingual education could be furnished, the decision was decentralized to the school and district, leaving it incumbent upon them to mediate placement, many of whom prioritized English as a Second Language (ESL) placements over bilingual ones. The proposition, creatively named 'English for the Children' had five items on the ballot with specific language about the role of schools and parents; and state funding for English tutoring.

School Responsibilities:
- Requires all public school instruction be conducted in English.
- Provides initial short-term placement, not normally exceeding one year, in intensive sheltered English immersion programs for children not fluent in English.

Parent Roles
- Requirement may be waived if parents or guardian show that child already knows English, or has special needs, or would learn English faster through alternate instructional technique.
- Permits enforcement suits by parents and guardians.

Funding Outside of Schools
- Appropriates $50 million per year for ten years funding English instruction for individuals pledging to provide personal English tutoring to children in their community. (California State Congress, 1998)

Instead of outwardly naming bilingual education as unlawful, the Attorney General of California stated, '...or would learn English faster through alternate instructional technique', a loophole for bilingual education. This statement left the door open. Districts could solicit waivers from parents who signified the need or the emergency for their children to receive a bilingual education. One of the districts who actively pursued the waiver route was SFUSD. Under the leadership of Superintendent Waldemar 'Bill' Rojas, the district quickly restructured itself along with ironclad strategies to solicit waivers from parents. SFUSD became the district that 'ignored' Proposition 227 (Wagner, 1998: 1).

Waldemar 'Bill' Rojas was a force in SFUSD. At the onset of his seven-year leadership (1992–1999) he was entertaining a return to the New York City Public School system after just one year in the SFUSD seat. The SFUSD School Board, desperate to retain him, offered him a longer contract and increased his salary from $120,000 to $136,000, making him one of the highest paid Superintendents in the country. The Board's strategy worked, and Rojas stayed on to usher in his primary agenda: capital bonds to fund much-needed building projects.

A series of four voter approved bond and tax measures totaling $337 million began in 1988 in advance of Rojas' tenure, but he would come in just as the dollars began to flow. He ushered in two of the four bond and tax measures in 1994 and 1997, all approved by San Francisco voters who anticipated massive renovations to decaying school buildings, many further damaged by the 1989 Loma Prieto earthquake. Under his leadership, building projects were overbudget and delayed with students attending school in unsafe conditions. The expense of the projects was higher than anticipated as necessary retrofitting was needed to meet new California building codes for earthquakes.

Further, an investigation by the *San Francisco Chronicle* found that over $68 million of the $337 million was not used on capital projects, rather on non-teaching salaries, funding administrative priorities, which would later be the focus of a state investigation and the primary project of the new Superintendent, Arlene Ackerman when she came into the Superintendency in 1992 (Guthrie, 2001). SFUSD, Rojas and the school board became the center of negative press and demands from voters who questioned the financial ethics of SFUSD. In what is reported a massive financial cover-up, Rojas was creative at narrating a positive story about his leadership, dissuading the doubters. Rojas also ignored attempts from the press, the city, the courts and the community to investigate any wrong-doing. He was described as an astute autocrat where principals were expected to fall in line with his demands, including the edict of strictly ignoring requests for information, even those solicited by the courts during the implementation of Proposition 227 (Asimov, 1998).

Embroiled in the financial investigation, Rojas continued his resolve to 'ignore' any government oversight or interference with the implementation of Proposition 227. A *San Francisco Examiner* article criticized Rojas' leadership stating,

> 'We're disappointed by his vow to go to jail rather than implement the law, which was approved June 2 by 61 percent of California voters. It may be, as Rojas says, that the law is unconstitutional, but that is for others to determine' (San Francisco Examiner, 1998: A-16).

After all, Rojas claimed that SFUSD was under a federal court order as managed by the US District Courts of Northern California following the passage of *Lau v. Nichols* (1974). The subsequent 1975 Lau consent decree, and a state requirement for an English-only education was a violation of the federal law. In a report to the press in 1998 upon 227's passage, Rojas stated,

> What this is, is a sinking immersion ship. Everyone's going to learn English and that's it. But there is no program. What they're doing is denying access to science and social studies and other content areas that students now can learn in their native languages while they're learning English. You can't have a conversation if the kids don't understand it. You're saying to these kids that you're going to shut them out for one year, that you can shut them out for two years, however long it takes to learn English. (Wagner, 1998)

Much like the argument that Mrs Lau made when her son, Kinney was in Lucinda Lee's classroom about her son needing access to content in Cantonese, Rojas was asserting the same, but was doing so as the district Superintendent.

The Chinese for Affirmative (CAA) actively opposed Proposition 227 and rallied for its failure among California voters. When the proposition was first proposed, Christina Wong, their education specialist recalled,

> At that time, it was like, oh, wow, yet another anti-immigrant initiative. We were really fearful that the rhetoric out there was so anti-immigrant. (Smith, 2017)

Yet other advocacy groups came to the fore to resist the ban on bilingual education. On June 3, 1998, one day after Proposition 227's voter victory, Multicultural Education, Training and Advocacy (META), the American

Civil Liberties Union (ACLU), the Mexican American Legal Defense and Educational Fund (MALDEF), the Asian Pacific American Legal Center, the Asian Law Caucus, the Employment Law Center and Public Advocates filed suit against the California State Board of Education, Governor Pete Wilson, and the Superintendent of Public Instruction (ACLU of Southern California, 1998). Ted Wang, also of the CAA who had helped Ling-Chi Wang in the Lau case in 1973 stated,

> Proposition 227 sets back public education in California by 25 years… This proposition treats children who are not fluent in English as if they have a disease. They will be isolated from other children, placed in English immersion classes, and denied other academic programs. We just can't tolerate this. (ACLU of Southern California, 1998: 2)

While not explicitly stating Lau, Ted Wang referred to the premise of Lau, that access to learning would be restricted isolating Chinese children from academic content and their peers.

US District Judge of the Northern California, Charles A. Legge presided over the enforcement of California's Proposition 227. Legge served on the same court as Lloyd H. Burke who presided over the Lau case, even though Burke ruled against Lau on its initial hearing in 1971. Legge was appointed by President Reagan and like Burke was a Republican. Burke and Legge's time did not overlap as Burke passed away in 1988. Legge was adamant that there was no violation of any federal laws and that SFUSD should implement Proposition 227 with all due speed. Multiple lawsuits from civil rights and immigrant right groups, opposing the proposition claimed that they would have little access to the content of instruction. Other suits asserted that immigrants would receive an inferior education, and thereby, structuring a racially discriminatory practice. In response, Legge claimed that there was no basis for the discrimination claim and that SFUSD should implement the state law with greater urgency (Asimov, 1998).

In the wake of 227, the Language Academy was created under the leadership of Superintendent Rojas and Dr Rosita Apodaca served as its Assistant Superintendent. The programs under the Language Academy included such names as English Plus, Dual Language or English immersion. This discursive naming was also adopted by other districts throughout the state to elude investigators from the term and construct of bilingual. Yet, a Grand Jury investigation led by Judge Legge of the US District Judge of the Northern California investigated the Language Academy in 1998 given Rojas' absolute refusal to implement and the court's concerns over how dollars were being spent on language programming. A Grand Jury report from 1998 stated,

The Grand Jury was desirous of determining what effect Proposition 227 would have on the District's educational system and particularly the impact on the funding of the system. The Grand Jury was also interested in whether Proposition 227 would impact the District's right to use funds that it received from various state, federal, and local sources for bilingual education purposes and whether the District would have to change any of its numerous language programs to comply with the new law. The Grand Jury did note that the District's Superintendent, Waldemar Rojas, stated publicly that the SFUSD would not obey the mandates of Proposition 227. (San Francisco Civil Grand Jury, 1998: 1)

The primary focus on dollars spent on language programming was stonewalled at multiple intervals. The SFUSD administration referred the Grand Jury to the City Attorney office, as they had some involvement over the implementation of the Lau consent decrees. A list of schools with bilingual programming which were to be visited by the Grand Jury were to be furnished by Rojas by April 16, 1999, but such reports were never provided (San Francisco Civil Grand Jury, 1998: 3). In requests to speak with the auditor for 1997 and 1998, he excused himself due to his busy tax schedule (1998: 4). School visits where interviews were to be conducted with principals about the funding of their language programming were attended by the district lawyer, Ms Den, who often instructed principals not to answer the questions. Ms Den was consistently at these school visitations, even when Rojas had assured the Grand Jury that they could speak freely with administrators. According to the Grand Jury investigation, the SFUSD-furnished data on student achievement was regarded as falsified.

The Grand Jury investigation continued into the 1998–1999 school year, where similar barriers were erected by SFUSD, restricting the jury's access to personnel and information. The focus on the Grand Jury was on the finances related to implementation of language programming. They focused on what sources were funding language programming, specifically, bilingual programming and its cost effectiveness. Clearly, English for the Children had another aim of cost savings (San Francisco Civil Grand Jury, 1999). A bilingual education was framed as frivolous and costly.

Between 1998–1999, area school districts in Oakland, Berkeley and Hayward sued the state of California, requesting district wide waivers to continue the provision of bilingual education. Alameda County Superior Court Judge Henry Needham made this decision, but only a short month later, the state of California resisted this provision. Yet, the fervor of waivers alongside other lawsuits forged by immigrant right's groups were gaining traction.

By 1999, Superintendent Rojas was on his way out, having been recruited by Dallas Independent Schools for the Superintendency. Further, the attention over his mismanagement of funds was becoming even more heated, demonstrating the simultaneous push and pull of his departure

(Guthrie, 2001). By 1999, the California legislature was focused on implementing new academic standards, alongside of new testing and social retention of students, a grave stressor to California educators complicating energies placed upon 227's enforcement (Gándara et al., 2000).

Christina Wong, the educational specialist of Chinese for Affirmative Action (CAA) worked closely with the Language Academy of SFUSD to organize meetings with Chinatown parents, explaining the impact of Proposition 227 for their children. She shared that there was little interest in the Proposition itself as SFUSD had aggressive plans to acquire waivers from parents, keeping their bilingual education intact.

Christina explained that parents largely trusted their school's teachers and principals. In coordination with the newly named Language Academy, CAA worked with area schools to solicit 10,000 waivers from EL-identified families, enabling bilingual education to continue. Ronald Unz had originally conceived waivers to be a bureaucratic nightmare for districts, discouraging their use. Yet, SFUSD and other large districts throughout the state used the waivers to maintain bilingual provisions. Darlene Lim, a teacher, principal, and active in the The Association of Chinese Teachers (TACT), later became the director of the SFUSD Enrollment Placement Center (EPC) in 2007. All incoming students with home language surveys other than English would come to the EPC. She revisited the practices after 10 years of implementing the waiver,

> ….language programs were encouraged as it was the district's belief that students would be provided more access to content through the language programs. Additionally, the Consent Decree under the DOJ required that all parents of potential EL students be informed of the program options. (email, January 15, 2024)

The bilingual program was encouraged. Darlene continued, '…in order to enroll into a biliteracy or immersion program, the parents must sign the waiver. The waiver needed to be renewed annually'. Despite Ron Unz's hope of waivers being too big a headache for districts; SFUSD actively used them, and bilingual provisions continued. For the Chinese community, bilingual education was an allowable provision and signing a waiver became part of the EPC's annual protocol.

Proposition 227 reveals the power of proximity within educational and language policy. State and local laws can attempt to circumvent federal provisions, including the Lau consent decrees that in their local origins asserted a mainly bilingual approach (Bilingual Department of San Francisco Unified School District, 1976). Given that the Civil Rights movement was in the past and there was widespread bi-partisan support for Proposition 227 passage, many schools in California limited or dissolved their bilingual programs. Just a few short years later, the No Child

Left Behind Act (2001) and the elimination of the Bilingual Education Act (1968) within it would further turn the rudder toward English medium instruction. In SFUSD, this was observed in Lau consent decree reports that became more focused on English proficiency and exit. The sun was shifting on the landscape.

13 A Third World Rights Federation Activist in the Midst

Laureen Chew, EdD

Laureen Chew was born in San Francisco's Children's Hospital on the other side of the city. Her mom did not trust the two male Chinese doctors in Chinatown where they resided, so she traveled across the city to have Laureen and, later, her younger brother. She attended Washington Irving Elementary where Lucinda Lee went, but her mother wanted her to have a Catholic education, so when she entered Junior High, she began attending Saint Mary's Catholic Church, located on 838 Kearny Street in Chinatown. She walked to school with two other Chinese American girls from Chinatown, where they would learn among mostly White-European students from the greater San Francisco area. She would meet her Chinese classmates on the corner and take the short walk to Saint Mary's. Every day after school, Laureen and her Chinese classmates scurried home and then headed to Chinese school for several hours.

In reflecting upon her time growing up in Chinatown, she quickly came to understand the social deficit of speaking Chinese and a Chinatown variety of Chinese, which was also cast with lesser value among the greater diaspora of Chinese immigrants. She remembered the inferred and direct messages from her public elementary education and her seven years in a Chinese school, where she studied five days a week after school. She remembered how language hierarchies played out for her as a youngster at Washington Irving Elementary and explained her swift understanding once she started attending public school.

> And I think I remember like there were times we would play jacks on the floor on the concrete, and we played with some of the kids and speak to each other in Chinese. And then you had the teachers and… they used to have these bells, those huge loud things getting really, really loud. Ding-Ding-Ding! Right? …The teacher would go, 'Ding-Ding-Ding … You know, don't speak Chinese! You're in an American school now! Speak English'. And then we would go, 'What? Speak English?' [The teacher would respond] 'Because if you only speak Chinese, you'll never learn English'.

While Laureen's experience reflects an assumption that English immersion will render English mastery, we also see how language was drawn to her seeming lack of national identity, not aligning with the ideals of an American school, because she and her classmates were speaking Chinese on the playground. Laureen chuckled at the absurdity that she and her playmates would have such a sinister agenda as 8-year-olds. Laureen went on to describe how her parents also sent a message that polarized and supported the bell-dinging teachers' linguistic judgements.

> Now, what's interesting is that you couple that with parents that tell you when you go to school, you listen to a teacher. They know best. If you want to succeed in this country, you got to do what they tell you. In other words, defer to the teachers.

The deference to the authority of their parents along with deference to the bell-ringing teachers inscribed English as the language of substitution and power, yet this was coupled with her negative experiences at Chinese school which she attended five days a week after school. Laureen talked about hating Chinese school, where she would often check-out mentally, and cope with her disdain by copying assignments and daydreaming. Her Chinese instructors judged her lack of engagement and her proper use of Chinese as she had Americanized and butchered the Chinese language, consistent with Victor Low's (Chapter 5) description of his college attempting to eradicate his 'Chinatown accent'. Laureen was being evaluated for her Chinese as being imprecise and her bell-dinging teachers were nationalizing her away from Chinese toward English. Two distinctly different adult sources devalued all the languages she brought to her classrooms.

When Laureen arrived at San Francisco State, critiques of her Chinese would persist. As a Chinese-Mandarin major, she had frequent courses with instructors that regarded her Chinese as non-standard.

> I chose that major because I had a background in Chinese literacy. I spoke Cantonese and went to 'Chinese' school for seven years and wanted to recapture what I had learned and forgotten. But the professors were not kind to me, because the prof told me my Mandarin will never be 'good' because I spoke Mandarin with a 'Cantonese' accent, and they 'looked down' on me because of it.

Additionally, Laureen had become accustomed to varied teaching methodologies from her American schools and that asking for help was acceptable. She remembered advocating for herself in a Mandarin course, where many of her classmates were from Hong Kong and Taiwan and spoke Cantonese.

> Once, I raised my hand and asked the teacher to please slow down and speak slower so I can better understand….my classmates [most from Hong Kong and Taiwan] responded by saying, 'Well we aren't from here,

> and no one slows down for us when they speak English in the classes they took', essentially telling me 'tough sh-t'. The professor just went on like I didn't make a request. (Chew email, July 11, 2023)

Laureen's heuristic of asking for help drawn from her school experience in Chinatown, coupled with the linguistic foundation from Cantonese-Chinese school, her language and cultural constructions were still being called into question. This multifaceted sword of having the wrong Chinese combined with Westernized notions of teaching and learning were not represented for her in formal school spaces. San Francisco State did not have a Cantonese program, so Laureen had to find her syncretic identities outside of school (Asian American Political Alliance (AAPA), 1969).

Laureen was responsible for supporting her tuition at San Francisco State during her undergraduate years. Laureen took a job as a counselor for Chinese women in a home for runaway girls at the Salvation Army in a program called 花木, Mulan, symbolic of the 'multiplying of in the spirit of strong women' and mirroring the legend of a young girl who took the role of her brother in the army and became strong and independent. While at Mulan on the corner of Waverly and Stockton, Laureen began to see the utility of her Chinatown Cantonese and how it worked with the young girls she was mentoring.

> And the parents were having a hard time with them…I took my role seriously… we were the house mothers. So that was my job for a couple of days a week. And I had to stay overnight there because the girls stayed there. And our job was to feed them, to help them with their homework, make sure they had a schedule and then to make sure they went to school… I also had to negotiate conversations between the girl and the mom. So, I found another role that I found interesting… being like a counselor…

Laureen went on to describe how she mitigated challenges between young American born Chinese girls who struggled with their immigrant mothers, remembering a particularly difficult case when talking to Jeannie's mother (pseudonym). She said to Jeannie's mom:

> They just have freedom to do what they want to do. And, you know, this is not good for you, you know, but I know you are trying, so I appreciate that…and they exhale a bit.

Laureen who had her own struggles with her immigrant mother was able to connect with Jeannie and her mom as she empathized with the cross-cultural challenges among immigrant born parents and their US born children along with having the language facility. Laureen was beginning to recognize how her Chinatown language and how her culture intermingled across generations. At Mulan, her identities were becoming invited and affirmed.

While at San Francisco State, Laureen joined the Intercollegiate Chinese for Social Action (ICSA), an organization responsible to leading her to the Mulan program, where she was paid to work with runaway girls like Jeannie. ICSA was formed in 1967 and was principally focused on making localized change in their communities given poor housing conditions, employment discrepancies, educational in quality, and access to adequate healthcare. Chinese students, many commuting to San Francisco State, formed and volunteered or worked part-time at social service agencies in Chinatown, including tutoring programs and the War on Poverty office (Umemoto, 1989). Ultimately, ICSA would request monies from their student association to fund the maintenance and expansion of such programs in Chinatown (Hekymara, 1972).

Shortly after ICSA's formation, their Chinese student leadership voted and although the response was mixed, they joined forces with the Third World Liberation Front (TWLF). TWLF was an international movement of student solidarity focused on disrupting colonialism and capitalism, critiquing how higher education was concomitant in its reproduction. Locally at San Francisco State, the TWLF was multi-coalitional, drawing from different student groups, principally, the Black Student Union and then, Latino, Native-American and other Asian groups, like ICSA and the Philippine-American Collegiate Endeavor (PACE). TWLF student activists recognized the pernicious tracking system of the university and how they worked with area industries to satisfy their need for low-paid workers with the university summarily reducing its acceptance rates of Blacks from 11% in 1960 to a mere 3% in 1968. The naval base by Hunter's Point, home to a mostly Black community, was a case in point, as the military valued their labor to suit their aims. While TWLF efforts were indeed local, they were also done in solidarity with other student groups and coalitions throughout Latin America and Asia where oppressive conditions rendered the poor to subjugation (Okihiro, 2016).

TWLF conducted the longest standing student strike in US history lasting from November 6, 1968 to March 1969 where over 80% of students were not in class and with faculty joining them in the strike. During these five long months, college administration was given 15 non-negotiable demands including the admission of more Black students and other minoritized groups, and the provision of a Black studies program with full time faculty lines. Appointed San Francisco State President, Samuel Ichiye Hayakawa, a Canadian Japanese and California Governor, Ronald Reagan believed their demands were being solicited by means of anarchy and opposed the TWLF's militant approach, prolonging negotiations and engagement (Dong, 2002; Hekymara, 1972). As the TWLF movement was a more militant form of activism, focused on very specific demands, grounded in self-determination, Hayakawa saw this as a threat to the civility of the campus. He became infamous for pulling the cords out of a loud speaker posted on a truck to prevent students from protesting and to return to class. He had attempted to reopen the college multiple times since the strike's start (Champion, 1969). Hayakawa brought in a strong police presence to quell the energy of the strike.

In the Spring of 1969, the 20-year-old Laureen was leaving the library and she was drawn into the physical movement of a large crowd of students, but now there were police mounted on horses with clubs poised for striking.

> They [the police] basically rehearsed how they were going to not allow us to leave. They had these huge horses come in... the guys. The cops sat on the horses with their batons and started just hitting everybody that they saw. So, I saw, you know, so many people, especially the Black guys, you know, they were in the back, and they were just trying to get pushed in, pushed in. And then they started swinging and these guys got their heads busted open... blood everywhere ... because the crowd from that rally in the front were pushing out... So, they arrested 400 something people, and *I was one of them.*

Laureen was eventually tried and convicted for civil disobedience and spent 20 days in jail, whereas the charged men were incarcerated for 45 days.

> I get it why people think incarceration is inhumane because your world is just so petty and small. It comes down to cigarettes, candy bars, your little turf of a chair and it can blow up because there's nothing else for you to do.

As Laureen progressed through school and reflects now, she detailed the significant impact that the Black Student Union and the TWLF had on her language identity and her professional trajectory.

> I think the Black Student Union and TWLF student strike was absolutely instrumental for me to look in my first 19–20 years in terms of the whole thing of racism and discrimination. Yes, I was angry. Yes, I was lashing out. Yes, I probably was inappropriate in terms of a lot of things. How I try to communicate with people, especially in the community. Right. But the difference is, in terms of my own growth, as I had compared to maybe some people who just went on their merry way until they're like 40 or 50. You know, I feel like, okay, I need to change this trajectory and how ever ways that I can, you know, like. Being bilingual as much as you can.... is something that we need to do.

Although TWLF was not specifically focused on language rights, its premises were based on self-determination (Hekymara, 1972) and for Laureen, her language, her Chinatown Chinese was becoming a self-determinate for her.

Throughout college, Laureen remained involved in the TWLF and continued her work at the Mulan group home in Chinatown. ICSA, now a part of TWLF, took the theme of 'power to the people' and applied it to the working class of Chinatown (Umemoto, 1989: 13). Community agencies and churches, along with pastors Larry Jack Wong, Ed Sue and Harry Chuck and ICSA held a march in Chinatown advocating for better education, housing, immigrant resources and health services (East West, 1968a, 1968b) and improved treatment from police to Chinatown youth (San Francisco Examiner, 1968b). While Laureen attended San Francisco State, the connections between the university and Chinatown were steadfast, educating its students to become activists and supporters of their home communities: Develop the local to contribute back to the local. Such was the theme of the National Teacher Corp program, which Laureen would join upon her graduation from State in 1972.

After Laureen finished her bachelor's degree in Mandarin Chinese at San Francisco State, she enlisted in the National Teacher Corp program, just like Lucinda Lee had done two years earlier. Consistent with ICSA and the TWLF, Teacher Corp was localizing 'power to the people' (Hekymara, 1972). For Laureen's Teacher Corp cohort, the Chinatown cluster had expanded from Jean Parker Elementary to include Commodore Stockton, Washington Irving, Sarah B. Cooper (now Yick Wo Early Childhood) and John Hancock Elementary (now closed). Unlike Lucinda, her Teacher Corp time overlapped with the implementation of Chinese bilingual programming. In her first internship year, she was placed with Lucinda Lee in her second-grade Chinese-bilingual classroom in 1971–1972, just a year after busing had begun. Laureen was mesmerized by Lucinda's teaching methodology. She shared,

> I really admired her [Lucinda] as a teacher, I learned a lot from her, the whole part. The thing about centers, of having kids engage in activities because you had learning centers and stuff. I read about it when I was a teacher. You know, I had never seen it. I saw it in the suburbs, but I had never seen it in a Chinatown school. And every year that I taught there, I did it because I really believed in it. And it was messy and it was a lot more work, but I loved the energy that the kids like, I have second graders who are 50 something now.

Importantly, students were contributing in their home language both in the classroom and the playground and within the bilingual strand there was no bell-dinging teachers. Cantonese was welcome. Her historic judgmental teachers' attempts to eradicate her Chinese and her parents' advocation to respect the teacher were settling differently within a bilingual classroom. Chinese children were maintaining and developing their Cantonese while learning English. Laureen found bilingual education magical as it represented an experience that addressed the self-hatred she had constructed from the school messengers at Washington Irving

Elementary and her Chinese teachers demand for Cantonese precision. Her languages were always ascribed as imperfect. Her variety of English and Chinese were being honored vicariously through 8-year-olds in Lucinda's classroom. She recalled,

> I stepped into Lucinda's class where I heard the kids speaking Chinese, you know, to each other, and nobody stopping them. And they were like free flowing and happy... I was blown away. You know, like, wow, what a simple thing of having a language accepted that created verbal Chinese kids. Kids were not afraid to speak up. And you give them a platform where they can talk to each other, discuss something that they're learning... *But they're helping each other and no one's silencing them.*

Consistent with the theoretical groundings of Teacher Corp, which linked to the foundations of TWLF, bilingual education was informing the children's self-determination.

Following her two years in the Teacher Corp, Laureen got a job at Commodore Stockton due to a teacher leaving and not having the appropriate visa status to return in time for the new school year. She got a phone call from Victor Low (Chapter 5), now in an assistant role of bilingual education at the district offices just two days before the school year began in 1973. Excited to begin her career as a teacher, she embraced the open concept model she had learned from Lucinda. Her Teacher Corp co-teacher and mentor, Dr Roger Tom[1] diplomatically described her initial years in the classroom as 'organized chaos'.

Laureen described how Roger, her co-teacher, and she organized their time within their bilingual education model at Commodore Stockton which included (1) English as a Second language; (2) Chinese as a Second Language (CSL); and (3) Chinese literacy. These three blocks involved division of children into various groups throughout the day depending on their identification as a 'bused student' or a 'local Chinatown resident', essentially English majority speakers and Chinese speakers. The bused children were mostly English dominant students, so when it was Chinese time, they would come to Laureen for CSL time. The native speakers of Cantonese and local to Chinatown did Chinese literacy and went to Ms Betty, her paraprofessional, who was an immigrant teacher from Hong Kong. At the time, Betty's group had a high representation of newcomers and thus, it was like a continuation of their literacy skills from their schooling in Hong Kong and Southern China and, of course, Chinese school, which most attended after school. Laureen would then teach all the other content in English including math, science and art. English as a Second Language focused on all the other subject areas but was taught using the tenets of Krashen's theory on 'comprehensible input' (Krashen, 1977). While Krashen's language teaching theories on comprehensible input were not yet published, Laureen now has the repertoire to describe what they were doing in the early 1970s. For English as a Second Language (ESL) time, the students would go to Roger. Thus, Laureen taught math, science, and art in the morning to one set of students, and then the same to another set of students from Roger's classroom. She called it the 'flip-flop' to demonstrate how they organized their time, but also to recognize the messy experimental nature of their program as they were still 'figuring it out'.

The conditions of busing alongside the bilingual program enabled an examination of biculturalism and thus, the later naming of the program as the Chinese bilingual and bicultural program. Roger Tom, Laureen's mentor, and Teacher Corp supervisor worked with the district offices to bring in programming that she remembers as the Human Development Program (Palomares & Rubini, 1973).

The Emergency School Aid Program (ESAP) program was a federal provision, a law approved in 1970 for non-profits and school districts to support school desegregation and/or reduce residential minority isolation (Kimbrough & Hyman, 1978). Congress and President Nixon were debating over the larger Emergency School Assistance Act that would be later authorized into law in 1972. During this interim period, the ESAP was intended to support the primary objectives of desegregation by adding resources to communities and districts to support its implementation. Given mixed signals from the executive branch, President Nixon and the majority Democratic Senate and House of Representatives, ESAP was an interim measure to fund any contract, personnel or material resources to meet desegregation's aims (Kimbrough & Hyman, 1978: 4). Most of the applicants were large school districts, like SFUSD. Roger Tom worked with district administrators applying for ESAP funds and the human development activities in which Laureen would embark was supported by the acquisition of the materials and the training.

As bilingual education was a more newly allowed provision within California code, and the SFUSD Chinese Bilingual federal Title VII program was identified as experimental, and the need for resources that addressed sociocultural aims, ESAP was an important form of support. Federal, state and district dollars for bilingual education were specified for language programming in personnel and material resources. The Human Development Program was non-linguistic and not necessarily tailored for addressing racial nor linguistic integration within a community, but Roger and Laureen saw it as a needed resource and approach to create an inclusive approach to the racial project within bilingual education. Roger demonstrates the creativity of bringing together multiple policies, grants, and resources to holistically develop a bilingual–bicultural program. Laureen recollected,

...the busing piece and the language piece was really, really moving for me to be involved for five years or six years… and because of Roger, who

> really cared about a building community in a classroom. I mean, he had a real heart and he put us through programs called the Human Development Program, which was basically how to run class meetings.

Laureen recognizes the opportunity to consider racial integration and bilingual language programming as an endeavor of curiosity and disruption. Recognizing that busing had brought racially segregated communities into contact with each other, the class meeting was the platform for children sharing their feelings and asking questions of one another. While the human development curriculum focused on feelings, guided by simple prompts and questions, Laureen recognized the complexity that such invitations brought to a classroom of young students who did not reside in the same communities. She described how the Chinese girls had negative stereotypes about their Black classmates who came from Hunter's Point, a community largely employed by the military industry close to a naval yard. While such stereotypes were never stated explicitly, Laureen could see the separation on the playground, where White and Chinese girls would play Chinese jump rope together (jump rope made with linked rubber bands), and a Black classmate, Wanda (pseudonym) would just observe. Although the aims of busing were to have no more than 40% of one racial/ethnic group in one building, such was not the case at Commodore Stockton at the time, where most of the children were local and Chinese. Thus, what happened on the playground was largely guided by Chinese children's interests, including who could play with one another. Laureen took the class meetings as a time to interrogate this division.

Laureen described the necessity of these types of conversations within classrooms to disrupt students' constructions of one another that were reproduced when communities were segregated. She did not stick to the script of the Human Language Development Curriculum but was committed to explicit story telling.

> You know what I'm saying is like young kids, when we don't teach them about difference in a way that would resonate with them at a very young age, you can't wait. You know, I mean, you can't wait for just osmosis… that is some things have to be deliberate. Like stories are deliberate.

Laureen illuminates the early sociocultural aims of bilingual education and she saw this manifest on the playground. Due in part to these explicit conversations 'Wanda eventually was invited to play [Chinese] jumprope'.

Laureen demonstrates that a project focused on racial and linguistic perspectives is one that must start when children are young. It is an explicit and intentional act meant to disrupt historic and cumulative attributions of negativity and subjugation. Importantly, she describes how the history of segregation and isolation created by the conditions of White property owners dictate contact and community, oftentimes constructing negative attributions among different groups of color among one another. Yet, such understandings detour us from understanding that racial integration, and language rights operate in relationship to those with power. Laureen saw the wedges that were being arbitrated on the playground and in the classroom, and disrupted this construction with the young children, devoting time to class discussions drawn from the children's behaviors amongst each other.

As I think about the 'wait time' that is a reliable tenet applied within bilingual teaching, whether it is waiting for others to process or waiting for someone to fill in the ambiguity of a term or an idea, I am struck by Laureen embracing this idea of storytelling fully. It was not just wait time for linguistic processing, but wait time for children to consider how they were racializing one another, particularly how they were racializing Wanda, a Black child. Given Laureen's history in the TWLF and her work with the Black Student Union at San Francisco State, she was an early navigator of addressing anti-Blackness within bilingual education. Such stories from Laureen's Commodore Stockton Elementary bilingual classroom demonstrate the multifaceted criticality in the early years of bilingual education. The younger the better mantra often invoked for introducing other languages early on extends beyond the mere linguistic to a commitment of extrapolating raciolinguistic ideologies to unsettle perspectives among young children. Shifting and troubling perspectives as the sun rises.

Note

(1) Roger Tom was one of the founders of the Association for Chinese Teachers (TACT) and eventually served in district leadership, including the role of Associate Superintendent. He passed away unexpectedly at age 62 in 2003 and TACT honors his memory by having an annual walk-a-thon to raise dollars for Chinese youth in Chinatown.

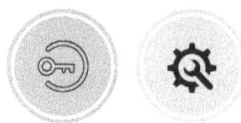

14 Remedies and Remediation in Higher Education

Interpreting Language Rights at the University

Following the passage of Lau, Ed Steinman, Ling-Chi Wang and Laureen Chew entered higher education in the Bay Area of California. Each higher educator had a continued contribution to language rights and did so in their various capacities at their universities as lawyers, professors and activists.

Edward Steinman, Santa Clara University

Edward Steinman began his post at Santa Clara University as a young 26-year-old after his few years as a Reggie in Chinatown. He was the youngest among his faculty colleagues, but regarded as a rock star as he had four large cases that were moving through the US District Court of the Northern District of California and the Ninth Circuit Court of Appeals, where two would eventually land for oral arguments at the Supreme Court (Table 14.1). While at Santa Clara, he continued to shepherd the various cases through the courts, holding fast to never taking a penny for a case. 'I don't work for money. But in law, you know, all my clients have been what's called in forma pauperis', people of poverty.

All the cases were filed while he was at the Chinatown office or the Youth Law Center, his post after the Chinatown office. Ed remembered,

> As for the 1970 Census case, *Quon v. Stans*, I filed that case in October 1969, less than two months after becoming a practicing attorney, alleging that impoverished, Chinese non-English speaking persons in the Chinatown district in San Francisco would not be counted in the taking of the 1970 United States Census. The contention was that the basic method of enumeration proposed to be used by the US Commerce Department …Stans was Nixon's Secretary of Commerce – census questionnaires mailed out to known dwelling places and then mailed back by

Table 14.1 Edward Steinman's argued cases for language rights and affirmative action

Case	Quon v. Stans (1970)	Lau v. Nichols (1974)	National Labor Relations Board v. Western Addition Community Organization (1975)	Hampton v. Mow Sung Wong (1976)
Construct	Affirmative Action & Voting Rights	Language Rights	Affirmative Action	Affirmative Action
Court	Northern District of California	US Supreme Court	US Supreme Court	US Supreme Court
Attestation	Violation of US Constitution and federal statutes	Violation of the Fourteenth Amendment and the Civil Rights Act of 1964	Violation of the Title VII Civil Rights Act of 1964	Violation of the Constitution's Fifth Amendment
Status	Dissented	Prevailed on premise of Civil Rights Acts of 1964	Dissented	Prevailed

the occupants thereof – would fail to include all or even most of the poor, Chinese non-English speaking plaintiffs in the class action. Such failure was arguably a violation of the US Constitution and federal statutes.

The US District Judge Gerald Levin in San Francisco attested that no constitutional or statutory rights would be violated and thus, Ed's hope for relief ended in denial. Ed continued,

> Given the 1970 United States Census was set to begin two months later, I decided there was no chance of winning an appeal in the US Court of Appeals for the Ninth Circuit and did not pursue any further legal action in the case.

Despite the case stopping short of the US District Court level, the Census did change its practices and returned to collecting the Census in person versus through the mail that would significantly undercount communities like Chinatown. So even without the case prevailing, an impact was made on future collection procedures for the Census. Distinctly, the continued advocacy of Ling-Chi Wang and the Chinese for Affirmative Action (CAA) pressured the Census to change its ways. The courts and the community galvanized collective pressure for changed practices and protocols that include the provision of translation and interpretation and conducted by trustworthy members of given ethnolinguistic communities.

In *National Labor Relations Board v. Western Addition Community Organization* (1975), racially minoritized employees of the Emporium Capwell, a department store argued that there was racial discrimination as evidenced by Whites occupying the highest earning roles in the store. Discriminated employees, mostly workers of color, argued that the union should bargain individually with its employees and not just collectively. Ed was busy preparing his oral arguments for the Supreme Court and good friend, colleague and co-counsel, Ken Hect, argued the case. While it did not prevail, Ken was able to solicit a $1 million dollar settlement from the company for the chronic underemployment and maltreatment of its minoritized workers.

Hampton v. Mow Su Wong (1976) involved a challenge to a United States Civil Service Commission regulation that excluded resident aliens from applying for or holding jobs in the federal civil service. This case was brought to the fore by fellow activist, Ling-Chi Wang (Chapter 7), then at the CAA when the case first was launched in 1970. Ed reminds us that in the case at the level of the Ninth Circuit Court of Appeals, if it fails at the Supreme Court level, the Ninth Circuit ruling prevails. In the original decisioning the Supreme Court was deadlocked at 4–4, with Justice William Douglas not represented as he had died. The new appointee, John Paul Stevens, a Republican appointee, would be the tiebreaker, ruling in favor the plaintiffs in a 5–4 vote. Ed demonstrates that the Supreme Court albeit leaning conservative in a post-Lau period still could prevail in areas of affirmative action.

And of course, there was Lau. Ed continued to brood over the 'bad law' arguing that Lau should have been called the *United States v. SFUSD*, compelling the US government to interpret the constitution more robustly for national origin students as a protected class, and that the case would 'show purpose' as it did for Brown. In short, Lau should have demonstrated that race was an arbitrating factor in the purposeful exclusion of language learners from an accessible education (Steinman, 1974). Lau was looking inside classrooms to see if students like Kinney had access to instruction. In Brown, the view was looking numerically from outside of the schoolhouse to see if a building was sufficiently integrated based on race. If the United States could demonstrate such purposes of exclusion based on national origin/language within the classroom, then a new kernel within the Fourteenth Amendment could be arbitrated legally.

Ling-Chi Wang, University of California, Berkeley

Ling-Chi Wang went on to serve as Professor of Ethnic Studies and Asian American studies at UC Berkeley in 1972, regarded as the founder of Asian American studies at the campus. Ling-Chi still maintained his advocacy for language rights within Chinatown, continuing to support the plaintiffs and the various committees for the Lau case. Ling-Chi maintained his post at the CAA, being engaged in local San Francisco politics in addition to his full-time professorship. At Berkeley, Ling-Chi began to see how inequities played out in admissions of Asian and Asian American students. While Ling-Chi had been principally focused on the Chinese constituency of San Francisco, he had now broadened his view to include the larger Asian diaspora who were now his colleagues and students.

In 1984, Ling-Chi observed that his campus' admissions policies were elusive and not in explicit policy, and it was having a direct impact on Asian American applicants. Ling-Chi intended to uncover what his campus was trying to shield. Working through the local and campus press, and through the California legislature, he shared what undergraduate applicants needed to submit on their admission applications.

> ... It was several things that are so blatant. Number one, Berkeley admission policies require every applicant to submit two achievement tests plus three achievement tests of your choice, like history, math or what have you. So, SAT verbal and SAT math and three achievement tests. The way the admissions office calculates the use of those tests, the five test scores is to average them out. And that was the thing... that gets a total of five is what counts. But Berkeley found out that SAT verbal test for Asians, for typical Asians is 100 points behind Whites. That's where the mistake was. You only single out in the verbal test. And then if you take a look at the SAT math as the Asian typically outscore, the Whites, and they do not make that minimum requirement. So, when I found that that was the most secretive decision that they made internally and ... in violation of university policy. That's why they're protecting. Oh, they knew that they were doing something illegal.

I presumed that Ling-Chi had launched an internal probe, and litigation, so I asked, 'What's the name of the case?' He responded, 'No, there was no case. I decided early on when this issue came up in 1984. I decided that I am no longer going to go by litigation, because litigation takes too long'.

As *Lau v. Nichols* had taken over five years from conception, to filing at the US district court, then to the Ninth Circuit Court of Appeals, and finally, to the Supreme Court alongside of all the other cases on the 1970 Census and citizenship requirements for civil service, he had collaborated with Ed Steinman on, he was trying a different approach. Over several years he pressured his university chancellor and the other nine chancellors of the University of California system to open the locked door on their admission practices with a keen focus on his own campus. Ultimately, Ling-Chi and other gathered advocates began to push for a report to study the elusive phenomena of Asian admissions. The Asian American Task Force for the Admissions on University Admissions brought light to what Ling-Chi had long noted issuing a report in January 1987 after several years of study. Through Ling-Chi's advocacy and that of the Student Coalition for Fair Admissions, a group of young Asian American students and activists at UC Berkeley lobbied Asian American Assemblyman, Phillip Ting, insisting on meetings with Chancellors and politicians who would hear their call. In 1987, the Office of the Auditor General of California commissioned a report studying the specific admission criterion for Asian and Caucasian students (Hayes, 1987). The audit found that between 1981 and 1987, the overall admission rate for Asians had decreased, yet increased for White students. The conclusion: test score bars were intended to benefit Whites and not Asians or other groups of color. The commissioned study by the California auditor led to an apology by the University system and the UC Berkeley Chancellor and ultimately led to the Chancellor's resignation (New York Times, 1989).

While at Berkeley, Ling-Chi also critiqued the larger system of testing and their means of excluding Asian students and Asian languages. The College Board did not have any advanced exams for Asian languages, diminishing students who had participated in bilingual Chinese, Japanese or Korean as early as elementary school or after school or weekend language programs. The College Board's touchpoint was only at the high school level, where French, Spanish and German were standard. Ling-Chi strategized and invited the College Board president to a meeting.

> I organized a conference in California for all the universities, and I invited College Board President, Don Stewart. At that time, he came and asked him, you know, I told him …I mean, out in the open, I said the reason why I'm inviting you here is to talk about foreign language education and whether the College Board can do something about it. So, he agreed. He came. He gave a talk, but he got criticized because I prepped the people already in the audience. I asked him, 'What about Chinese, what about Japanese, what about Korean?'

College Board President Stewart was candid, sharing that such exams took years to field test and were not profitable for the College Board. Ling-Chi persisted, gathering the next year and inviting Stewart again. Armed with data from California's community language schools, along with bilingual education schools teaching Asian languages throughout the state, he furnished evidence for the demand. When such efforts continued to be delayed, Ling-Chi moved to the California legislature.

> Assemblyman Floyd from Gardenia and Senator Carr from Santa Barbara, both agreed to introduce parallel legislation, because I found out… I also told a politician that the College Board made about $40 million a year from SAT tests!

Collaborating with the legislators Floyd and Carr, both proponents of bilingual education described their shared strategy.

> We're going to give College Board two years. And by the way, UCs [Universities of California] provides 10% of their income. They call it a sport because of large number. So, they introduced a bill requiring the

College Board to come out with Asian language tests in two years. Failing that, you see, will be prohibited from using the College Board tests [in the state]... as soon as that bill hit.... they have Don Stewart calling me!

As a result of Ling-Chi's local and political advocacy and College Board's access-oriented agenda under Stewart's leadership (College Board Communications, 2019), Chinese and Japanese became field tested in 2003 and later administered officially in 2007, directly benefitting future Asian undergraduate applicants of East Asian languages. The implementation of a College Board Chinese exam also coincided with deepening interest of China to spread Mandarin throughout the globe through their Ministry of Education, namely, the Confucius Institute (Morita-Mullaney, 2024; Peterson, 2020).

As an academic, we see how Ling-Chi's work in setting up the Lau case, was the start of a long-term commitment to language rights. Ling-Chi aptly intersected language rights with fair admissions practices and affirmative action, principally focused on the underrepresentation of Asian students at the time.

Laureen Chew, San Francisco State University

After Lau's passage, Laureen continued to work as a bilingual educator at Commodore Stockton Elementary, while continuing her master's degree in education at San Francisco State funded by the Teacher Corp program. She was an active member of The Association of Chinese Teachers (TACT) from the start of her intern years and eventually was elected as TACT president in 1975 when teacher layoffs were announced. TACT was full of social advocates advancing their education even further and in the late 1970s, she moved into a doctoral program at the University of the Pacific as a Title VII Teacher Fellow Program.

In 1974, the federal Bilingual Education Act was reauthorized to provide more girth to its altruistic beginnings. Requirements for teacher preparation were articulated along with committing to training more bilingual education specialists with Master's degrees, EdDs and PhDs in bilingual education through its Title VII fellows program (Stewner-Manzanares, 1988). Educators from area schools were recruited to universities to obtain advanced degrees focused on bilingual education to more adequately structure the burgeoning profession. Graduates at the Master's level were targeted for district leadership, whereas PhD and EdD candidates were prepared for teacher education faculty roles, state education agencies, and local school districts in senior leadership roles (Coballas-Vega *et al.*, 1979).

Between 1975–1978, 49 universities applied for and hosted advanced degrees in bilingual education. In many cases, existing faculty had rudimentary to no foundations in the bilingual education, and they had to develop and recruit faculty to meet the demand of the newly implemented discipline. During the 1975–78 period, the Office of Bilingual Education (OBE) regarded bilingual education as 'interdisciplinary approach to special educational needs' and not a legitimate subject area nor field (Coballas-Vega *et al.*, 1979: 12).

The OBE worked under the Health Education and Welfare (HEW) (contemporary US Department of Education) and HEW had a structure of 10 regions throughout the US. Northern California was nested in Region IX and was the second most populous participant in the Title VII fellows program. From 1975–1978, the first three years of its implementation, 176 doctoral students were enrolled with the Title VII financial support and another 41 with other types of support, including self-funded. Importantly, this big difference between Master's and the doctorate level illustrated how bilingual education doctoral studies would not have been possible without the support of BEA's Title VII fellows program (Coballas-Vega *et al.*, 1979; Katz, 2004).

Laureen chose the University of the Pacific in Stockton, a 90-minute drive from San Francisco, where she and Roger Tom, her co-teacher and Teacher Corp mentor, would attend school on Friday evenings and all-day Saturday. Laureen and Roger were identified as full-time students, but they continued their full-time work in SFUSD along with all their activist activities within the city including their work with TACT. When Laureen reached the stage 'all but dissertation (ABD)' stage, San Francisco State's School of Education recruited her to begin the Cantonese teacher education bilingual program. The Bilingual Education Act of 1974 and California Senate Bill 1355, brought in the licensure area of Bilingual/Crosscultural Specialist Credential. Ironically the California bill passed in 1973 before Lau prevailed (Mitchell, 2019). The Bilingual Cross-Cultural Language and Academic Development (BCLAD) license was to be a combination of bilingual pedagogy as well as proficiency in a language other than English. She began as a lecturer in the School of Education charged with developing the Cantonese BCLAD, yet she was told that she was not eligible for a tenure track role in education given her ABD status.

Yet, Laureen found a tenure home in the very young Ethnic Studies program, a program she had fought for as an undergraduate in the Third World Liberation Front. The Dean in Ethnic Studies saw her as a practitioner-scholar and saw how her experiences could shape their developing Asian American studies program. Laureen would ultimately serve across both colleges as her Ethnic Studies dean believed this collaborative relationship was essential, so the distinct identities of different groups were represented in voice and content in education. Her dean also saw how Laureen could broker decisions. Laureen shared, 'I really respected our dean. He goes, "you know, you get in there and you become part of the faculty. Then you be part of the decision making"'. Laureen contributed to future faculty hires in the School of Education, increasing the proportion of multilingual faculty of color.

As Laureen built the BCLAD teacher credential in Cantonese, supported by Title VII grants for pre- and in-service teachers, she initially worked with teachers who were on waivers at SFUSD and needed to add on a BCLAD credential. She described the Chinese constituency of the BCLAD program.

> The American born or American educated Chinese, the rest of you, even if you came here young, you know, their Chinese literacy level was not very high. It was very difficult for them to pass the language piece of our, you know, to get, you know, to get certified. So, we had to offer classes to bump that up, which was never optimal.

In addition to bilingual pedagogy, Laureen had to identify resources for teacher candidates to prepare for the Chinese proficiency tests they would ultimately have to take to get the BCLAD, and also to meet the Cantonese proficiency required of SFUSD's Lau consent decree.

Other Cantonese bilingual teachers who would eventually serve in SFUSD were more recent arrivals from Hong Kong, different than the initial influx following the Immigration and Naturalization Act of 1965. Laureen described the complexity of wanting teachers to have strong Chinese literacy, but also to have the syncretic and distinctly cross-cultural context.

> …we need the Hong Kong types who are the people that basically came here as adults. And many of them, a lot of them were already teachers somewhere else [in Hong Kong]. The piece that I found most difficult to work with, with many of them is the cross-cultural piece.

Laureen continued to describe their stand and deliver instructional style and how it reminded her of her Chinese School as a youngster. She saw the disengagement of the children and saw how Black youth were often mistreated or regarded as poor language learners. She began to identify the conservative turn in teaching stating,

> At that time, by the late 80s and stuff, because of Reaganomics, the whole country was turning conservative. It was like it was nothing like how I taught in the 70s… But the teaching is becoming much more monotonous. And not very critical thinking oriented.

She also recalled that when she taught her Chinese American history course in the Ethnic Studies program, she polled her students in her class to see who planned to vote for Reagan in the 1982 presidential election and 75% of the hands went up, including Chinese Americans. Laureen remembered, 'You see their faces out there and they're raising your hand and you're like, who are you?'.

Recognizing the political landscape shifting while preparing Chinese teachers to work in SFUSD, she realized that the Chinese and Chinese American diaspora was also changing. Laureen saw the expansive diversity within the international Chinese community coming to San Francisco State, who were more focused on standard language proficiency and less so on the bicultural element of a bilingual education and were less likely to come from Chinatown proper. Laureen realized that her roots in Chinatown had distinctly framed how language rights were localized to the Cantonese-Chinese community and not always shared by the greater Chinese diaspora; contributing to the dynamics of a conservative turn. Importantly, Laureen struggled with historicizing and localizing the Chinatown language landscape to her international Chinese students, recognizing that while important, it is challenging when it has not been experienced first-hand (Cervantes-Soon *et al.*, 2017).

Ed, Ling-Chi, and Laureen used both legal and local strategies to advocate for language rights and affirmative action for their clients and university students. But, by the time they were serving in their higher education roles in the 1980s onward, the courts were becoming more conservative, and the federal courts became less active. Ling-Chi and Laureen had to rely on their state and local networks to continually strategize on recentering the rights of Chinese and Chinese American students. The conjoined efforts of the Lau period of the courts and community were diminishing.

Section 3
Beyond Lau: The Sun Setting

15 Post Lau: The Association of Chinese Teachers

TACT Advances its Advocacy in Bicultural Identity

The Association of Chinese Teachers (TACT) continued its advocacy across multiple intersecting strands. TACT committed to community and school district education about the merits of bilingual education within the context of racial integration. They also continued the development of curriculum materials for the Chinese bilingual program, ushering it out of its pilot stage. One of its largest advocacy activities was fighting against teacher layoffs that disproportionally impacted teachers and administrators of color, including Chinese bilingual teachers. In this chapter, we become reacquainted with some historic agents of Lau along with administrators and teachers in Chinese bilingual, Irene Dea Collier, Sophie Lee, Darlene Lim, Laureen Chew, Helen Joe Lew, Anna Wong, Sophie Lim and Lonnie Chin.

Teacher Layoffs

With the racial integration plan in full implementation, the district's transportation budget was stretched alongside the start of declining enrollment. Cuts had to be made to sustain court-ordered busing requirements and address the $8 million shortfall. In 1975, Superintendent Morena and the school board voted to layoff administrators, teachers, instructional assistants, or cut any programs that were too small in scale to justify (Dooley, 1975). This was a possible hint that small bilingual programs were at risk, especially given the small scale of Chinese bilingual relative to Spanish bilingual. But TACT's advocacy done in collaboration with the Ethnic Minority Educators (EME) led to a softening of Morena's original proposal. Morena and the Board rejected a suggestion from Board member, Cannon to send layoff letters to 'probationary teachers' in 'mandatory programs' (San Francisco Examiner, 1975: 18).

Lau had created the conditions for mandatory bilingual, but Lau always stood in contention with the teacher's union heuristic of seniority, teachers being certified in areas of instruction, the continued construction of bilingual education as experimental and the small scale of their program relative to other models of language education, like English as a Second Language (ESL). ESL had a longer precedent and was navigable capital for the mostly monolingual English-speaking principals. TACT formulated their strategies to critique such constructions and attempt to dismantle them.

To address the teacher union's 'last hire, first fire' construct, TACT collaborated with the EME group, which consisted of mostly Black educators, who were also young and more newly hired like the Chinese; a direct impact of the Teacher Corp program's earlier inculcation of teachers of color to serve their local communities. Collectively, teachers of color within EME and TACT had to push back on the construct of seniority among their mostly unionized White colleagues.

EME, and the Latino and Black community had a long history of organizing and these were coalitions that TACT's 1975 president, Laureen Chew, had developed while a student at San Francisco State within the Third World Liberation Front (TWLF) movement. Laureen had learned in solidarity about community organizing. She described their quiet working together across teacher groups of color sharing,

> We need to do a boycott, a school boycott for one day. And then someone asked, 'Why? Because it's going to cost them money. Because it's about your ADA [average daily attendance], right?' Everyday your kid goes to school, you get money. I said, 'Can you imagine if our kids out for that one day? You know, what it would do to the school district? And we go, oh, good idea, right?' I mean, we all agree that was a great idea. That shows you how. How do you say?.... Audacious!

TACT arranged a boycott for teachers and students in early 1976. Laureen continued,

> We have to organize our people in our communities to take the kids for the day. So we went to churches, we went to community agencies. We got it organized, or they didn't go to school, but they would go to places or our parents who can keep their kids home for that one day. Great. But if you can't, we're going to have these sites where we're going to have our teachers there because we're not going to do it. We're not going to go teach that day. We're going to all be sick. So, we organized the places and we planned it all out.

The anticipated scale of the strike was so large that the new Superintendent Alioto cancelled all the layoffs for the 1976–1977 school year. Yet TACT knew that this victory was temporary, and that continued pressure was necessary, as the layoff proposal would reemerge. TACT continued to write letters to the school board and Superintendent's Cabinet articulating the specific impact to all students of color and students in bilingual programs.

In 1978, California voters passed Proposition 13, instituting a cap on property taxes, rationalized by inflation, and thus rising property taxes and at the time, a state surplus. California propositions are initiatives that amend the state constitution, and Prop 13 capped property taxes at 1% at the time of purchase. For example, a home bought at $100,000 in 1978 with a 1% tax rate of $1000 would remain steadfast with no more than a 2% increase per year based on the $1000 rate, not the current value of the property. Only when renovations or changes in ownership would the 1% tax cap be altered. The 1% cap was in force and had a deleterious impact on schools creating the conditions for major budget shortfalls and thus, the proposed reduction in staffing.

In 1979, TACT addressed layoffs head-on with the SFUSD administration and School Board in writing (Figure 15.1).

TACT addressed the measurable impact to Chinese teachers, minoritized teachers, bilingual teachers and children needing language services. Using the Lau consent decrees, now in force with the US District Court of

> We do not want program or staff cuts in the San Francisco Unified school District. The school district is presently operating on a bare bone budget due to Proposition 13. To further cut the school budget by $23 million would be a detriment to equal and quality education in San Francisco.
>
> Teachers of Chinese descent have been hired in large numbers beginning in 1970. And it is these teachers who were hired since 1970 to the present who are going to be laid off. Presently in the school district, 24% of the teachers are minorities while minorities compose about 79% of the student population. Employment of minorities in recent years have been increasing due to affirmative action. But since the state education code states that seniority should be the first consideration in laying off teachers, not only are minority teachers going to take the brunt of the budget cuts but minority students as well. The state education code does not protect children's rights as its first priority in education.
>
> If the school district reduces staff soley on the criteria of seniority, 60% of the teachers in the bilingual department would be cut. This would mean further limiting, if not eliminating bilingual services to those children who desperately need it.
>
> The Lau vs. Nichols Consent Decree of 1975 states that it is unconstitutional to deny children on an equal education. Children who receive instruction in a language which they cannot comprehend are not getting an equal education. These children should therefore be provided with bilingual education whereby they would continue learning in the cognitive areas as they are learning English. Our children deserve an equal education, their academic growth should not be hampered because of their lack of English language skills.

Figure 15.1 TACT's Letter to SFUSD Administration and School Board on Teacher Layoffs (The Association of Chinese Teachers (TACT), 1979)

the Ninth Circuit to administer and supervise, TACT makes a strong stance in coalition with other teachers of color. Notable within this letter is the simultaneous amplification of race and language identities. Herein, we see how TACT is arguing that a reduction in the teacher force among bilingual teachers is both a racial and linguistic project (Morita-Mullaney, 2018; Rosa & Flores, 2017). Additionally, any cuts to other teachers of color means the 'brunt' is experienced by the students of color, disrupting equitable aims of schooling for all students of color. Importantly, we see how language rights and affirmative action policies are happening in tandem, representing a distinctive policy moment.

Waivers: Not Yet Highly Qualified

Many of the Chinese bilingual teachers were not fully credentialed in bilingual education and were regarded as teachers on 'waiver', meaning they were permitted to teach in bilingual education, but had no guarantee of a continued contract given their non-specified teaching credentials. Although the district and TACT was providing professional development and Cantonese language development training for Chinese bilingual teachers, the licensure area of bilingual education was really needed, even though area universities were still in the developmental phases of establishing the bilingual license.

Darlene Lim, TACT member and a new Chinese American teacher certified in elementary education, shared her experience as a teacher on a bilingual waiver.

> I started getting really involved because I was in the bilingual program at that time, but I was a teacher on waiver, which meant that I wasn't fully certified to be a bilingual teacher... And so, the district had set up some training programs for teachers on waiver at that time. Language programs kind of get your reading and writing shored up.

Darlene identified as a Cantonese speaker, but she did not regard her level of reading and writing as meeting a high level of proficiency, so the district had set up language training for teachers like Darlene. She continued,

> ... there was a rush to kind of get everybody certified. But the training was very poor that the district provided. I mean, they tried a lot of iterations of training that didn't work. So that was when TACT started getting involved and advocating for a better quality of training. And that was at the time there were some layoffs happening ... even though bilingual programs were a priority, a high need area, we were still laid off... we were still on the layoff list. So, TACT got involved in advocacy in terms of trying to get these teachers who are on waiver skipped over in the layoff process.

As the Chinese bilingual program began to scale with increasing numbers of Chinese throughout the city, the need for Chinese language teachers was constant. Nearby San Francisco State was the only higher education program in the area to have a BCLAD Cantonese program, which Laureen Chew, former TACT president had started (Chapters 13 and 14). TACT worked with the district and eventually, the California Department of Education to protect bilingual teachers on waiver, shielding them from any future layoffs. The Chinese bilingual teachers became a protected class, again at the intersection of language rights and affirmative action.

When the history of seniority is the strongest marker of teacher retention and bilingual and minoritized groups disrupt this formula, they are refuting the dominant narrative of the system by saying that their specialty and identities trumps longevity. For Chinese bilingual teachers, this made things very awkward among their White colleagues as shared by Darlene Lim and Laureen Chew of TACT. Importantly, Chinese, and Latino bilingual teachers were able to claim race and language as rationale for retention, nested within the legal requirement of Lau and Brown. Black educators could claim race and align with *SFNAACP v. SFUSD* (Brown) case (racial integration) for their retention. All educators of color could claim affirmative action and prevent layoff. Herein we see the construct of negative liberty and positive liberty operating in parallel (Berlin, 1958; Thompson, 2013). Black, Latino and Asian educators could claim their retention because it satisfied elements of the racial consent decrees, affording students with an integrated and thus equal education (negative liberty), galvanized by the earlier federal policies with the Teacher Corp program (National Teacher Corps Task Force, 1965). Drawing from Berlin's (1958) work, this constitutes freedom from a sense of inferiority, and thus the rationale for racial integration. SFUSD racial decrees were unique in that they included multiple groups of color, including the Chinese, whereas most of the US operated on a Black/not-Black binary (Quinn, 2020). In addition to negative liberty for an equal education (or freedom from), language educators, Latino and Asian could claim positive liberty which posits a freedom toward or to, with an aim of increasing autonomy and self-determination (Thompson, 2013), consistent with the TWLF movement of which Laureen Chew was a participant. Lau, protected bilingual teachers of color on the grounds of positive and negative liberty, language rights and affirmative action, creating opportunity and access to a system that historically excluded them.

The call for the preservation of jobs among Chinese teachers was also coupled with the same advocacy for Chinese administrators, many of whom were acquiring their administrative licenses, yet could not secure such senior-level positions. TACT pushed for Chinese representation. While

TACT had a regular protocol of speaking to the board, when it came to personnel matters, such could not be discussed in a board venue, so TACT actively used letter writing for personnel concerns. During Helen Joe Lew's TACT presidency in 1985, she wrote to Superintendent Alioto,

> In the most recent administrative appointments, only one of the twelve new administrators was a Chinese American. We believe that this constitutes only a token effort in affirmative action for Chinese Americans; the gap will continue to widen unless a more assertive posture is taken by you and your staff to resolve this problem. Moreover, we are deeply concerned not only with an under representation of Chinese American administrators in our schools, but we are as concerned that there is also the lack of Chinese American counselors, deans, and department heads. (Lew, 1985: 1)

Helen furnished a list of qualified Chinese educators with administrative credentials, invoking Alioto to take action. Instead of a response or a meeting, Helen was called into the central office.

> A senior official grilled me about my authority and TACT's authority to question the Superintendent. After my encounter, I must have called a former TACT president who called other past presidents who met with me to calm me down. They presented me with a 'Trial by Fire' certificate.

Helen articulates how TACT remained steadfastly involved in promoting not just language rights, but affirmative action ones that reflected the growing Chinese community throughout the city. Further, TACT served as an important coalition of support for each other.

Community Education

After the passage of Lau at the Supreme Court, remedies were rendered back to the US Ninth Circuit for oversight. The Ninth Circuit represented the very courts who had previously denied the Lau case stating the reasons as the 'deficiency of the parent'. Ironically, they would now be the courts to oversee Lau's implementation. SFUSD had to furnish an annual comprehensive report to the Ninth Circuit on how the language needs of identified English learners' were being met, inclusive of identification, provision of services, staffing, training and community engagement. As TACT operated as an autonomous unit, they were not directed to address the demands of the decree, but they became deeply involved in the Bilingual Community Council which shaped the policy moves of SFUSD and community engagement for the Chinese.

In January 1975, TACT held a community event on the merits of bilingual education for Chinese parents. While sentiments about bilingual education were mixed among TACT members at its introduction in

1969, TACT was now largely on board by 1975 shared Irene Dea Collier, a Chinese bilingual pre-school and elementary teacher. The event was hosted in the Chinese Cultural Center's auditorium located on the third floor of the Holiday Inn, the hotel that cast a shadow over Chinatown's Portsmouth Square. TACT had created a play, reenacting the lifelike conditions for their children in schools. *East West,* Gordon Lew's (Chapter 4) Chinese-American weekly covered the story.

> The capacity crowd in the Chinese Culture Center auditorium roared with an understanding kind of laugh when the mean-talking teacher with a blond wig chewed out her simulated class of Chinese Students, 'You are Americans now. You speak English – English!' Many among the 400 present in the auditorium last Sunday have heard that before. Or their children have. They were to laugh and applaud many more times before the well-attended community meeting on bilingual education came to an end. (Hui, 1975: 1)

A second skit illuminated the conflicts that could emerge between children and parents if schools dismissed or belittled their ethnic languages. Another skit humored the ignorance of the American teachers in how they treated minority students poorly. Time was offered for educators and parents to give testimony and many Chinese bilingual teachers spoke of the affirming conditions of a bilingual education. Slide shows demonstrated real-time Chinese bilingual classrooms in SFUSD and the greater Bay Area, heralding its benefits (Figure 15.2).

Figure 15.2 Bilingual Education Parent Summit hosted at the Chinese Culture Center at the Holiday Inn (Hui, 1975)

Curriculum Creation and Professional Development

Gordon Lew (Chapter 4) and Robert Sung were hired as curriculum writers for SFUSD's Chinese bilingual program. Gordon Lew was on contract and created resources addressing the bicultural aims of the bilingual program and the simple stroke moves for numbers and simple vocabulary. Robert Sung worked full time for SFUSD, writing literacy curriculum that was accessible to the diverse constituency of language learners: newcomer Chinese students from Hong Kong and Southern China, American born Chinese (ABC) students who attended community Chinese language schools, Chinese as a Second Language students and ABC teachers who were committed to developing their biliteracy proficiency. For teachers on the bilingual waiver, it was a necessary skill to meet the language proficiency standard for the bilingual license. While the Title VII dollars continued to support Gordon and Robert's curriculum development, TACT found that strong augmentation was needed to support classrooms at different grade levels, including the secondary level. Darlene Lim, Irene Dea Collier and Sophie Lee, leaders within TACT and bilingual educators, found such resources needed to be supplemented.

TACT actively pursued funding for the Emergency School Assistance Act (ESAA), authorized as federal policy in 1972 (Kimbrough & Hyman, 1978). As TACT was regarded as an autonomous entity, they qualified to apply for this grant as a non-profit organization (NPO), apart from SFUSD. Intended to augment the desegregation efforts of the school system, multicultural activities to promote any type of inclusivity, racial or linguistic were permissible. On June 23, 1975, TACT issued a press release soliciting educators to apply for the ESAA funded 'Project for Cross Cultural Understanding: The Chinese Americans'.

> The Association of Chinese Teachers (TACT) announced a forthcoming grant from the Office of Education, Department of Health, Education and Welfare (HEW) under the Emergency School Aid Act (ESAA). The goal of the TACT Project will be to support the San Francisco Unified School District's desegregation program by complementing its efforts to increase multicultural understanding within the school community. Major activities of the Project include:
>
> - Inservice training of teachers on the instructional materials developed by the project.
> - Community conferences on Chinese American lifestyles and their implications for education.
> - Bulletins on curriculum resources on Chinese Americans.
>
> (The Association of Chinese Teachers (TACT), 1975)

Within this project were affordances for additional salary and work that could be done on 'evenings and weekends' (The Association of Chinese Teachers (TACT), 1975: 2). Other qualifications included proficiency in spoken and written English, awareness and understanding of the Chinese American subcultures in San Francisco, and residence in the community preferred. While the application could not explicitly state that only Chinese-American from San Francisco would be considered, the call definitely leaned toward privileging local ABC candidates (The Association of Chinese Teachers (TACT), 1975: 7).

The imprint of the ESAA project made its way into its monthly newsletters. Instead of a TACT Newsletter, it now stated TACT/ESAA newsletter as they used this venue to promote its professional development sessions for SFUSD educators (The Association of Chinese Teachers (TACT), 1977b).

Filmstrips were one of the main productions of the Chinese-American ESAA project, and much of the effort led by Anna Wong of TACT. The filmstrips were accompanied by narration furnished on tape cassettes along with background music. Cantonese translations were also being developed. The filmstrips were regarded as the first of their kind to exhibit Chinese Americanness and were solicited from others across the country for use in their burgeoning Cantonese bilingual programs (Moy, 1975).

The TACT/ESAA newsletters also contained journal articles on how to assess the cultural appropriateness of curriculum resources being used in bilingual programs and/or resources being used in general education classrooms. In an article entitled, 'Criteria for analyzing books on Asian Americans', teachers were directed to critically analyze all their resources with such guidance about transcending stereotypes including the resistance of the model minority stereotype. Artistic images should reflect the diversity of the Asian diaspora and not portray all Asians as cloned 'China dolls' (Council on Interracial Books for Children, 1976; The Association of Chinese Teachers (TACT), 1977a: 2).

The ESAA funds provided seed funding and the momentum for representation in the curriculum. This focus endured even beyond the initial ESAA funding provisions. For Irene Dea Collier, the continual creation and implementation of Chinese focused curriculum was a means to localize the history of Chinese America and to invoke the bicultural aims of a bilingual education. She shared,

> I worked really hard and a lot of the TACT curriculum that would sort of bring me back to the community... because bilingual didn't only encompass the language. It was also the history, the culture, the contributions, the biographies. It was more. It should have been bilingual, bicultural, or bilingual, multicultural. And for me... I did the bicultural, the history things. But I also always had other links to other groups who were experiencing the same thing. Like, I have one of Mamie Tape. And not only was there Mamie Tape ... then links to *Brown v. the Board of Education* and Linda Brown...

Irene discussed the need for localizing the Chinese experience to San Francisco proper and inviting all educators to commit to at least one lesson on the Chinese community. Bicultural should be integrated beyond the bilingual program and used within general education classrooms as SFUSD had high proportions of Chinese and Asian students. No longer were the Chinese living in Chinatown alone, but throughout the city.

Bean Sprouts and Island of Secret Memories

The largest component of the TACT ESAA project were its television productions and its curriculum resources. One of the TV programs, *Bean Sprouts* (1978) would go on to win two Emmy awards. TACT collaborated with the Chinese for Affirmative Action to produce a student-designed series of life in San Francisco with a focus on Chinese Americans. Linda Chu, a student of Lucinda Lee remembered being recruited to support the project with scenes filmed at Commodore Stockton Elementary, site of the first Chinese Bilingual program. Students even received a stipend for their contributions.

Bean Sprouts was a five-part narrative series focused on Chinese American children in their school, family and community contexts addressing themes of 'personal identity, intercultural contacts, and generational relations' (Center for Educational Telecommunications (CEL), 2022: e1). Loni Ding, Chinese American, and an independent filmmaker, television producer and university instructor worked with the children of SFUSD to produce the Emmy-Award-winning series, completed in 1978 and aired through 1980 on KQED; the Bay Area's public television station. Each episode had music with a visual introduction of mostly Chinese children throughout San Francisco, on playgrounds, their yellow buses or walking the streets of Chinatown, or the Mission with their friends. The series even had a theme song with lyrics about the complexity of being Chinese American and being stretched like a rubber band, and how sometimes 'it's not super to be super Chinese' given the pull they felt between their Chinese community and their newly integrated schools.

Bean Sprouts tackled complex topics of linguistic racism, cultural relativism, and beauty during the beginnings of racial integration. In Episode 1, we see a yellow school bus heading down the hill from North Beach, adjacent to Chinatown with a driver hurrying the students onboard because there are many more stops to make to get to their assigned Chinatown school (Ding, 1978c). On the bus are three boys; Chinese, White and Black. While on the bus, the Black and Chinese student converse in Cantonese, both students in the Chinese bilingual program at Commodore Stockton. As they converse, the White student makes fun of them, but ultimately the bilingual students of color take the upper hand and assert their linguistic skills. Scenes in classrooms depict the racial integration, the Chinese instruction and highlighting the challenges of the more newly arrived Chinese immigrant student whose parent does not want him to attend a school camping trip. Episode 3 takes us to the campaign headquarters of Lillian Sing, Chinese American running for the Community College Board and she shares why it is important to be politically active despite the Chinese construct of not bringing attention to oneself (Ding, 1978d). Other vignettes take us into the sewing factories, and students' Chinese schools that meet after school. On the playground, Black, White and Chinese students discuss how parents' language backgrounds shape the ways in which they speak; a playground discussion of translanguaging (Ding, 1978a). While there is a lilting humor as each child shares about their parent(s), there is no ridicule, rather engagement and curiosity (Ding 1978a, 1978b, 1978c, 1978d, 1978e).

Island of Secret Memories also produced by Loni Ding followed Joe, a young elementary Chinese student on a field trip to Angel Island (Ding, 1988). Angel Island, located in the San Francisco bay, was an immigration station where immigrants from around the globe would be processed between 1910 to 1940. Met by immigration officers, the Chinese were subjected to multiple rounds of interrogation which delayed their entry to San Francisco and in some cases, prevented it. In contrast, other immigrant groups were processed within days, particularly White Europeans.

The Chinese Exclusion Act was still in force and only eligible merchants could legally have passage, yet every Chinese person was regarded as a suspect class. The Chinese endured questioning from immigration officers that asked them minute details such as the number of chickens their neighbor owned. The focus on such detail was to ensure the credibility and the honesty of the Chinese with the aim of detaining them until their authenticity could be proven. Loni produced this film in collaboration with students from Spring Valley Elementary, where Mamie Tape tried to enroll and where Lonnie Chin was principal. Anna Wong, member and leader within TACT assisted with the curation of the film alongside Loni Ding. Anna also developed multiple film strip units that focused on the Chinese American experience that were designed not just for Chinese bilingual classrooms, but also classrooms throughout SFUSD.

The continual pushback for representation that was authentically voiced within curriculum was a consistent mission among its members. Helen Joe Lew, who served as TACT's president between 1983–1985 and again in 1990–1991, reviewed the state approved social studies curriculum for 1990 which was laden with omissions and inaccuracies of the

Chinese. Helen and TACT members testified at the State Curriculum Commission and State Board of Education hearings against the adoption. The slogan was, 'We cannot and will not accept being sidebars in textbooks!'. The scale of TACT's advocacy was not just localized but expanding on behalf of the greater diaspora of Chinese America in California.

For the initial years following the passage of Lau, TACT actively combined efforts of desegregation, language rights, alongside of affirmative action for its bilingual Cantonese-Chinese teachers and community. They did so through civic engagement within and outside the Chinese community creating curriculum for schools which increased understanding among all SFUSD teachers about the history of Chinese America. TACT's co-production of *Bean Sprouts* and their involvement in *Island of Secret Memories* built awareness across the greater San Francisco Bay Area about what it meant to be Chinese American. But TACT's most systemic contribution was the retention of Chinese educators systemwide who were the younger and newer employees of the district. Without TACT's insistence on affirmative action nested within language rights, Cantonese bilingual education may have faded, privileging more ESL models, and changing the teacher constituency of the district.

16 Post Lau: The Chinese Principals
Interpreting and Implementing Lau

With a three-person Chinese teacher quota lifted in or around 1960, along with increased immigration to SFUSD following the passage of the Immigration Act of 1965 legally ending nearly 80 years of Chinese exclusion, Chinese teachers were now among the teaching faces of SFUSD. Some of teachers would obtain their administrator licenses and go onto to be building principals. In this chapter, you will be reacquainted with Victor Low, who became a principal outside of Chinatown. You will meet for the first time, Lonnie Chin, who served as principal at Spring Valley Elementary, where Mamie Tape once tried to enroll. Irene Dea Collier served as the Director of Wah Mei Preschool in the Sunset district right after Lau was passed. Darlene Lim from Chapter 15 also reemerges as she shares her experiences as a principal just outside of Chinatown. As principals (with the exception of Irene's preschool), they had to oversee the 'Lau plan' in their buildings, alongside of the continuing provisions of desegregation and busing.

Far Away

Victor Low's wish of having his student teaching outside of Chinatown materialized pre-Lau in Hunter's Point, where most of his students were African American. His years after student teaching drew him back into Chinatown and the promising time of growth and creation of the Chinese bilingual program. Victor served in the assistant leadership role for Chinese bilingual for several years with what he described as 'all of the work and none of the pay' as his position was administrative in title only and he was salaried as a teacher on special assignment. During his time in this quasi-leadership role at the dilapidated gymnasium at Commerce High School, he was recruited alongside of other Chinese teachers to pursue his EdD as a Title VII fellow; a provision under the revised Bilingual Education Act (BEA) that Laureen began at the same time (Chapters 13 and 14).

The University of San Francisco (USF), a private Jesuit University, was one of the schools that participated in the Title VII fellows program beginning in 1979. From 1979 to 2002, they conferred EdDs to 121 educators in International and Multicultural Education, representing one third of their total graduates within the program. Thirteen graduates went on to serve in the California State University system as bilingual teacher educators: nine served in high-level administrative roles in their districts, two served at the California Department of Education and another two at California Community Colleges (Katz, 2004: 149). Many continued in their roles as bilingual teachers in their districts. Importantly, at USF, nearly all fellows identified as racially minoritized bilingual speakers.

Victor was among several bilingual and/or ESL teachers in SFUSD who was interested in the opportunity, where tuition would be paid, and class schedules would be accommodated for the working educator. He applied and enrolled in the Fall of 1976 at the University of San Francisco (USF). There was neither a teaching nor bilingual program to speak of at USF and the campus focused on recruiting Asian scholars to begin an EdD program in international and multicultural education. As USF was the applicant for the Title VII program, they had to commit to enhancing and/or building a program focused on linguistic and cultural diversity. Victor remembered, 'All I knew is that they hired some Asian scholars to help the program of multicultural education'.

The Asian scholars came from China and Taiwan and had no background in bilingual education nor in Cantonese language instruction. They were also privileged scholars, one living in nearby Marin, a wealthy suburb across the bridge from the city. Victor described his coursework and time at USF as one that was cobbled together, and that his dissertation work was done in relative autonomy. Victor was most interested in studying the history of his community in Chinatown with a specific focus on Chinese bilingual education. His advisors agreed after Victor did some convincing.

> I went to the doctoral committee, and I said, Look, I'm only interested in this study. If you allow me to do it, if you want me to do this kind of a study, a historical study, I'll go for my doctorate... So, I told them my plan and I said, why not give you a trial chapter just to see ... you know?

From there, his dissertation study was affirmed, and he proceeded with logging hours at the district's Teacher Professional Development Library, where old board meeting documents dating back to the days of the Chinese

Exclusion era and the segregated Chinese Primary School. Victor searched with three key words: Chinese, Oriental or Mongolian. Therein, he found a plethora of board notes, handwritten notes from Superintendents trying to ameliorate the Chinese, heathen problem by excluding them from White schools (Low, 1982). His study culminated in the early 1980s focused on the implementation of Chinese bilingual programming and its challenges.

Victor defended his dissertation in 1981 and he shared in celebration with Superintendent Alioto and senior leaders of the bilingual program. For SFUSD to have so many newly graduated Masters, EdDs and PhDs among them, the celebration was collective. At last, there was substantive representation of Chinese bilingual educators, leaders, activists, authors, and doctors of philosophy within SFUSD.

His dissertation did not end at its deposit at USF but also as a published book entitled, *The Unimpressible Race: A Century of Educational Struggle by the Chinese in San Francisco* (Low, 1982). The description of the Chinese as 'unimpressible' was drawn from the words of San Francisco School Superintendent, George Tait in 1864 who contested the continuation of the Oriental School based on low attendance and what he described as lack of interest and engagement in education among the Chinese. Superintendent Tait argued that the failure to adequately evangelize and convert the Chinese, ascribed them as unimpressible or impermeable to Christian ideals (1864: 23). Tait wrote in the San Francisco School's Annual Report.

> If missionaries after a life-long devotion to the spiritual regeneration of this unprogressive and unimpressible race, show but little fruit of their exhaustive labor, surely no sudden or extensive progress of American ideas can distinguish the only Chinese public school-house outside of the Celestial Kingdom. (San Francisco Annual Report, 1864: 45)

Only 20 years later, however, would the on again/off again Oriental School be reopened to educate Mamie and Frank Tape who were 'impressible', converted Christians (Independent Calistogan, 1885) (Chapter 1).

Victor's book publisher was *East West*, Gordon Lew's publishing company who also issued the weekly *East West* bilingual newspaper in Chinatown. Victor wanted his work circulating and applied within his SFUSD home and had 3,000 copies run, anticipating the impact it would have on the district. Victor reached out to various teacher and administrator groups, and local Chinese organizations, but his request to share his books went unanswered. Ultimately, his book would be taken up by universities throughout the US, but locally, the interest in historicizing the educational struggle of the Chinese sat on quieter ground, demonstrating a long-standing blindspot within the field of bilingual education. We do not adequately nor appropriately historicize our racially and linguistically minoritized student communities. Schools are concerned with pragmatic and immediately implementable practices and recollecting history is regarded as a poor use of time. Yet, more recent scholarship within dual language bilingual education suggests that 'historicizing', is a critical tenet in creating equity grounded spaces for minoritized youth, families and teachers (Cervantes-Soon *et al.*, 2017; Palmer *et al.*, 2019). Historicizing deconstructs the mainstream or majoritan ideals of the past, and recenters the voices and identities of minoritized youth, families, and teachers. Through such narratives, greater understandings are built, which then inform the shaping of curriculum. Victor recognized this bilingual blindspot when the book was taken up nationally, but not as much locally. One could claim that 'you cannot be an expert in your own land'.

Frustrated with the lack of progress and energy within his leadership role at the district level, he began to seek out other opportunities, eventually moving into a teaching role and assistant principalship outside of Chinatown. At the age of 50, he moved to Cleveland Elementary in the Excelsior district to become principal. His elementary was mostly Hispanic with no Chinese students. His desire to become a principal in a school with a mostly Chinese population never materialized. The Redesign plan for desegregation was privileging more family choice, summarily rendering his school to one of proximity versus the 'opportunity' that the racial integration plan and the bilingual program had once so boldly established.

An Angel in Nearby Chinatown

Lonnie was a bilingual teacher at Commodore Stockton Elementary and joined The Association of Chinese Teachers (TACT) immediately following its founding in 1969 and served in various leadership roles including as Treasurer, and later as President in 1973–1974. Early in TACT's formation, Lonnie organized a trip to China among SFUSD educators. The timing of the trip was further enhanced by President Nixon's visit to China, increasing curiosity about a country that had historically been closed. Further, Lonnie and TACT leadership advocated for there to be representation of Chinese Americans in Nixon's entourage to China (The Association of Chinese Teachers (TACT), 1999: 15). Under the support of TACT, Lonnie led a trip to China with SFUSD educators, many of whom were TACT members.

> I organized a trip to China in the summer of 1973 to learn something about the land of our forefathers. As educators we did not find any materials in China that would be useful in the bilingual programs the SFUSD were trying to organize…. (email, January 26, 2024)

Distinctly, we learn from Lonnie that merely bringing in materials used in a Chinese national setting to a US context may not represent the linguistic and cultural experiences of the Chinese landscape of San Francisco, particularly American born Chinese. Further, the review of materials demonstrated Lonnie's and TACT's early efforts of curriculum inclusion and appropriate interpretive representation.

When *Lau v. Nichols* passed in 1974, Lonnie was TACT's president, and she prepared an amicus curia for the Department of Justice. She supplied testimony on the rights of immigrant families and their need for a bilingual education. Lonnie advocated that this direction was a necessary move in framing language rights as an enduring principle of social justice and equity.

Lonnie Chin demonstrated early qualities of leadership and was encouraged by her White male principal at Commodore Stockton to pursue her administrative license because she was willing to engage in debate and be 'feisty for change'. In SFUSD at the time, you must be assistant principal before moving into the principalship, but her entry differed as she swiftly moved from teacher to principal. The principal at Spring Valley Elementary had died of a stroke during yard duty, and they needed someone immediately. Given her proximity to Spring Valley on the border of Chinatown and her experience in bilingual education, she was quickly appointed. Her first day at Spring Valley was October 31, 1977: Halloween.

> So, the first day was… I had to come in costume. So, I came as an angel. I had an old Chinese robe that was kind of like, you know, a cream color. And then I bought wings and a halo. So, that's how I came. That's how I was introduced to the school.

Her introduction to the school as an angel is a historical metaphor, as Lonnie, a Chinese-American was the principal of Spring Valley, where Chinese-American, Mamie Tape had attempted to enroll in 1885 (Chapter 1). During her principalship at Spring Valley, Lonnie ensured that her students knew about Mamie Tape. Since Mamie was eight, the age of a third grader when she tried to enroll, she wanted all third graders to learn about Mamie and her family.

Lonnie: And my feeling is every third grader in San Francisco, because she was 8 years old, should know…
Trish: So, what does it mean for you to retell Mamie's story?
Lonnie: So that the kids understand that they have rights, and that other people have rights, and that this thing we call freedom and all that is not necessarily free. You have to do stuff. You have to lead. Anyway, I think because I see this… that's the reason why I stayed at Spring Valley for 30 years.

The district attempted to move Lonnie to other buildings, but she remained devoted to Spring Valley, building a creative resistance that emulated a freedom that must always be aggressively maintained. Lonnie took nothing for granted, and consistently advocated for her students, and learned how to work around her large, bureaucratic district to bring in needed resources for her racially integrated school, which was also home to a Spanish and Cantonese-Chinese bilingual program. Lonnie discussed the intersection between racial integration and Chinese bilingual programming and how they worked together.

> And so, thank goodness for bilingual ed, because that was the beginning of the bilingual program. So, we had Spanish bilingual and Chinese bilingual. And so, I used those teachers to introduce new ideas.

In 1977, racial integration was in full swing, and the Lau consent decrees were also in force. Lonnie thought deeply about her grounding in cognitive research to support her racially and soon to be linguistically integrated school. She adopted 17 principles of 'Habits of Mind to Improve Thinking', which included such qualities as 'seeks to be informed' and 'strives for clarity' and 'admits mistakes and recognizes what they don't know' (Chin & Costa, 1977). More simply, intelligence was not something that was fixed, but one that could be developed through deep inquiry in the content area of science, but also through building an integrated community. To facilitate such an ecology, she had students serve as conflict mediators. Donned with red jackets and carrying clipboards, student mediators facilitated disagreements among their peers. With groundings in such principles, Lonnie worked with the two bilingual strands (Spanish and Chinese) to integrate children whose home languages were other than the target/partner language, including Hispanic and Black children in bilingual education classrooms.

Lonnie created the conditions for a two-way bilingual program, by integrating Black and Hispanic children outside the immediate Chinese and Hispanic neighborhoods into the bilingual classrooms. I asked Lonnie what experiences around racial and linguistic rights informed such decisions, aside from cognitive science principles. Lonnie reflected on her formative years at the Cameron House and the YWCA and how these experiences helped her imagine a different possibility of integration for Spring Valley.

Before Lonnie began college, she met Dorothy Height, an African American activist through her work at the YWCA in Chinatown. When Lonnie entered college, she was a youth delegate to the Presbyterian Church's national convention where she served on the Church and Society Committee. Lonnie then met Jesse Jackson, and a Black writer from Life

Magazine. These interactions shaped Lonnie's perspective as an emerging school leader and activist.

> So, these very prominent, smart African African-American people actually spoke to me. I was impressed with how they dealt with what was happening in history. And that they had a handle on making change and the necessity for people to be involved in making change and that it was not just the African-American to bear the mantle of social justice, but that everybody could be involved and would be involved.

These formative experiences alongside her deep understanding of Mamie Tape's exclusion from school in 1885, impressed upon her the need to integrate Spring Valley racially and linguistically. Language rights and racial equity were conceived as incongruous in other buildings within SFUSD, and thus, the bilingual strands and the non-bilingual strands were sometimes racially stratified (Chesnut & Morita-Mullaney, 2023; Morita-Mullaney & Chesnut, 2022). From the outside of the schoolhouse, the numbers say 'integrated' but inside, resegregation takes hold, dismantling the construct of integration and equity. Lonnie helps us see how she resisted the framing of only Chinese and Hispanic kids having access to the bilingual program, drawing in students of all language and racial backgrounds into the fold, satisfying the bicultural aims of the program and racial integration at the classroom level. Even before a two-way dual language had a formal naming convention, Lonnie was already integrating across multiple identity categories, coupling racial and linguistic integration, the hopeful outcome of the model and practicing negative and positive liberty concurrently (Berlin, 1958; Gándara & Orfield, 2012).

> Lonnie continued to describe the primary aim of the Chinese bilingual program as bicultural. She had previously taught at Commodore Stockton, and she knew as an American born Chinese (ABC), that even with her Chinese after-school program, and growing up in a Chinese home and community, that her reading and writing proficiency in Chinese was no better than a fifth-grade level, where she could read the local newspaper and converse within her home and greater community. She found that the SFUSD bilingual office was very focused on language proficiency and expected a particular model with explicit goals of language development. Yet, the district had appreciably less resources in Chinese both in personnel and curriculum. She shared her ongoing debate with the central office.

> …the Chinese bilingual program is about culture and identity. You see, language is… it's a tool. Just as computers are a tool. Learning… using the computer is not a skill, it's a tool. And you better use the tool to create something inside.

Lonnie continued to reinforce that bilingual education was a method for teaching, not a model based on language proficiency alone. Lonnie lamented, '...they [the district] never considered us as a model'. When visitors would come from Washington, DC, they would go to Cesar Chavez Elementary, site of a large Spanish bilingual program. But Spring Valley Elementary was named in the *SFNAACP v. SFUSD* racial consent decree. Court-appointed experts in racial desegregation would come to the building to ensure that they were sufficiently integrated, in part due to their large Chinese constituency.

> We were part of the [racial] consent decree. I don't know why! Because Commodore Stockton actually was worse. But they chose us, you know. Orfield from Harvard? Yeah. He used to come all the time. Yeah. What are you doing here? They will come and check that we have no more than 40% Chinese. That's how they looked at us anyway. They never named Jean Parker or Commodore Stockton... [they] had 1,000 kids in those days. They were huge!

Lonnie draws attention to where the court was assigning its energy for Spring Valley: racial integration. But the courts and the district were not paying as much attention to her Chinese or Spanish bilingual programs as she consistently articulated their lack of support for resources and professional development. Despite this lack of support, Lonnie created her own framing and practices for linguistic and racial integration. Decentralization was starting to take hold.

Irene and the Wah Mei Preschool

Irene attended San Francisco State where she got her degree in anthropology and participated in the San Francisco State Student Strike. Following college, her spouse's number came up for the draft. Her husband, Malcolm Collier, was a conscientious objector, and they spent a year together on a Navajo reservation doing Malcolm's alternative service. When they returned to San Francisco in 1973, layoffs in schools were beginning to grow and Irene found herself serving as an instructional assistant within SFUSD and actively working with TACT on curriculum development.

In 1978 she became the Director of the Wah Mei School, located in the Inner Richmond district and later relocated to the Sunset district. Its site outside of Chinatown reflected the growing Chinese diaspora throughout the city as detailed by Alan Nichols during his attempt to establish a racial integration plan in a small portion of the city. Wah Mei was founded by well-regarded Chinese residents like Ling-Chi Wang (Chapters 7 and 13) and Judge Lillian Sing originally featured in *Bean Sprouts*, who had a vision for a bilingual education within early childhood. Wah Mei fulfilled a growing need among young families needing high-quality bilingual preschool. Irene expressed the fervor of showing SFUSD that preschool could be done well and done mostly on public funds. Importantly, Irene wanted the program to be economically accessible to the growing Chinese community outside of Chinatown, both domestic and immigrant. In an interview on Wah Mei's 50th anniversary, she remembered,

> Wah Mei provided quality education to various income levels. At the time I became director, there was consideration of eliminating the state preschool program because of its cumbersome reporting requirements. It would have been much more profitable to grow in the direction of having more private slots which at the time was in great demand. Thankfully, the board decided to keep the program. (Dea Collier, 2024)

Irene also described her talented and 'dynamo' staff, making reference to how preschool was done in Hong Kong.

> Chinese speakers who were good teachers in Hong Kong and other places, didn't have jobs in the city. In no other community can you see this push for preschool education and part of it is because in Hong Kong, there are, school stores ... They open up store fronts to provide preschool, not always free, but accessible. They don't have to pay very much, but there is a tradition of it in Hong Kong.

Irene described the unique context for bilingual education among its youngest learners and how it provided the opportunity for area Chinese educators from Hong Kong to make a livable wage within their profession alongside of their Chinese American colleagues. She shared, 'It was an interchange that created a dynamic program that reflected our bicultural heritage in America, and not just a transposition of Hong Kong preschools'.

In the 1970s and 1980s when Irene led Wah Mei, hiring and wage discrimination was rampant and SFUSD was going through its first rounds of teacher cuts and layoffs. Wah Mei became a school that welcomed and honored the professional expertise of its Hong Kong and Chinese American educators.

Irene's leadership at Wah Mei demonstrates how the preschool became a social location for newly immigrated educators and American born Chinese teachers that was not as possible within SFUSD given their layoffs due in large part to California Proposition 13's freeze on property taxes. Further, the grassroots developed preschool demonstrated that quality bilingual education was possible and could be sustained on public dollars without 'Lau' enforcing its implementation.

Darlene Near Chinatown

Like Lonnie and Victor, Darlene Lim was born and raised in Chinatown, but came to the district as an SFUSD teacher, administrator, and enrollment manager, serving the district administratively from 2001 to 2016, as racial desegregation was eroding, and Lau was deep into its implementation. Darlene became a principal through an apprenticeship program instituted by Superintendent Arlene Ackerman that allowed her to intern as an assistant principal for an entire year with the increased hope of an administrative placement. After her internship, Darlene did not actively seek out a role but was recruited and became the principal of Yick Wo Elementary, near Chinatown and adjacent to Russian Hill and the Coit Tower in 2002.

Yick Wo and Wo Lee were Chinese laundrymen in the Chinese Quarter who were arrested by San Francisco Sheriff, Peter Hopkins because they refused to pay $10 for operating a wooden laundry. At the time, the city ordinance required that any laundries that were wooden would be subject to a fine. In its enforcement, all those being fined were Chinese merchants, demonstrating that when any policy or law is enforced and the outcome has a disproportionate impact on a given group, then it violates the equal protection clause of the Fourteenth Amendment (*Yick Wo v. Hopkins*, 1886). Yick Wo and Wo Lee prevailed. To recognize this important contribution, SFUSD officially changed the school's Sarah B. Cooper name to Yick Wo School on February 23, 1982 (Lang, 1982).

When Darlene began at Yick Wo in 2002, racial desegregation was still in force through the *SFNAACP v. SFUSD* but was beginning to erode with the construct of choice beginning to take a stronger hold. Yick Wo was in a mostly White neighborhood who had brought the arts to the school where students learned to play the xylophone among other creative endeavors. Yick Wo formerly had a Cantonese-bilingual program, but it had phased out right before Darlene began. Darlene described the phase-out as shared with her by others.

> They would only have two kindergarten classes a bilingual and the general ed. At that time, I think there was an opening in the bilingual program and for some reason they placed a monolingual teacher in there... and I think that kind of had a domino effect on the program...

Darlene illuminates how a seeming tinker that is meant to be temporary, can be the one pebble that initiates erosion. Gradually, over time, as less children matriculated from kindergarten into the upper grades, the program slowly declined in enrollment and evaporated. Because SFUSD was transitioning to yet another school assignment system centered on parental choice, the language as a right orientation of the 1970s (Ruíz, 1984) was becoming a distant construction for the Cantonese-Chinese community. While provisions for bilingual education were still available to families as managed by the educational placement center (EPC), families had to mitigate among a range of content choices (e.g. STEM, arts), while still attending to the language rights of their children.

Despite the loss of the bilingual program, many Cantonese-Chinese staff still worked at Yick Wo and were committed to having Chinese families at the school. Darlene and her team actively recruited students from nearby Chinatown, even though there was not a bilingual–bicultural program available.

> So, I would get our Chinese speaking teachers to go to functions that we would hold in Chinatown. We would go to the Newcomer Center and talk to the parents there. What we had in common was they wanted to continue to serve those students. So, I remember that. I don't remember really having a conversation about the demise of the program. I still felt like there was a commitment on their part to serve those families… They never leave the neighborhood. So, I felt that that was an important focus of the school that we could broaden our reach in terms of opportunities for disadvantaged or bilingual students.

Darlene and her Chinese staff demonstrate the historical value of being and coming from Chinatown and how their shared experiences could be a part of shaping a new education for Chinatown students with Chinese teachers; an experience that Darlene and her colleagues did not have as young children in Chinatown. When Darlene left as principal, the Chinese constitution in the building began to decline; another pebble in the erosion of racial diversity within the school.

With choice as mechanism for schools, it became incumbent on SFUSD principals to recruit their student body versus the system placing students. In 1971 when mandatory busing had begun, the option of 'choice' was arbitrated outside the system for many of the Chinese in Chinatown in the formation of Freedom Schools (Chapter 10). For White students, many chose a private system rather than be integrated. Their choice was vocally arbitrated by their ideologies of anti-busing and integration. But in 2002, the new system directs the principals to be the arbiters of their student community, a decentralized focus within the public system (Gobby, 2013). In Darlene's portrait, she drew from the shared identities of her fellow Chinese faculty to diversify her school and furnish opportunities for the Chinese of Chinatown.

In 2008, Darlene was recruited into a supervisory role with the educational placement center (EPC), where she oversaw the counseling and placement of identified-ELs (English learners) throughout the city. She explained the complicated process that was based on the Lau consent decree. When she joined the team, she worked diligently to tighten the descriptions of language programs, so families could be appropriately informed about their language rights. For Latino and Asian student who were also language learners, their array of choices was larger.

> But, you know, I think in terms of the Latino and Asian student of Chinese students, they had more options in terms of what they could apply for.

Working within the construct of content choices and language rights, instrumentally, it appeared as if Latino and Asian families had a greater representation of options, but what Darlene illuminates is the combination of language rights (required) with content choices (options). She continued,

> And so, part of the work that we did when we would bring them in for language assessment and part of what the Lau consent decree required of us was that the parents would know immediately. The counselor would meet with the parent and say, 'Okay, according to the test, your child is proficient in Chinese or Spanish. And the here are the programs that we offer'. So, you could apply for immersion. You can apply for biliteracy. You can also apply for general ed, which would be English only. But parents have to sign off that they've been informed. And they can choose whatever it is they wanted to choose.

Darlene identifies that families become eligible for particular language models: ESL, biliteracy (self-contained of same language group) or bilingual immersion (two-way model) for their language rights. Thereafter, they can then add on the layer of choice (selection) for a building with a particular focus. For Yick Wo, identified students could be *placed* in an ESL model and then *choose* the school because of its art's focus. But, if a student is eligible for an immersion program and it does not have an art's focus, then parents must arbitrate this matrix of decisions, potentially foreclosing on the possibility of a bilingual education or their language right being satisfied, but their content choice not possible as a school does not have both.

Lonnie served in principal role during the height of busing and racial integration. Victor served in a principalship when busing was beginning to fade and the proximity of the neighborhood was more likely to reflect the constituency in the school. Darlene, who served as a principal later than Lonnie, Victor, and Irene was at the tail end of *SFNAACP v. SFUSD* (1985) racial consent decree and eroding. The construct of parent choice was scaling quickly. Collectively, their portraits demonstrate the shift from external and centralized construction of student constituency to an internal and decentralized method of student recruitment. Things were beginning to turn, and the language policy landscape was beginning to shift.

Other Chinese Americans became principals and central office administrators throughout SFUSD. Many served in communities with large Chinese populations, but others served far from such sites, including Victor Low. Sophie Lee served on the Presidio's active military base, with very few Chinese. Helen Chin[1] served as a principal at several schools outside of Chinatown, but returned to Commodore Stockton Elementary in 1990, when it would be later named Gordon J. Lau, in honor of San Francisco's first Chinese American supervisor (no relation to Kinney Lau). Roger Tom[2] who served with Victor Low on the Title VII bilingual pilot would go onto serve as an Associate Superintendent. This powerful cadre of Chinese American administrators would eventually develop their own association of administrators called the Asian American Administrator's Association. Today they remain an active force drawing from their racial, linguistic and teacher identities to inform their leadership.

Notes

(1) Helen Chin served as a Cantonese bilingual teacher in Chinatown and later a princcipial throughout SFUSD. She would later return to SFUSD Commodore Stockton's Elementary as principal. She is regarded as a young activist for language rights.
(2) Roger served as an Associate Superintendent of SUFSD. He was an active mentor to many Chinese bilingual educators within SFUSD.

17 The Modified Lau Consent Decree to the Sunset

Sunsets. Metaphorically, sunsets represent the passing of time. If we take time to notice a sunset, we recognize what and how we have changed over the day, or over the years. Sunsets symbolize how time has shaped the growth of humans, their ideas, beliefs, practices and social relations. Sunsets are retrospective. For those that are historic characters in the sunrising of Lau, the sunset represents their contributions to a rich history of language rights for Chinese Americans for which they can remember and retell: a narrative policy portraiture.

The legal naming convention of *sunset* describes the closure of a decree and release from court oversight or that the old decree needs to be replaced with a different one. More simply, a sunset suggests that a decree is no longer necessary because an emergency has been resolved or the decree was intended to fulfill a temporary need that is now satisfied, no longer necessitating court oversight.

SFUSD has encountered two large-scale legal sunsets. First, *SFNAACP v. SFUSD* consent decree and secondly, the *Lau v. Nichols* consent decree. The racial desegregation case of *SFNAACP v. SFUSD* sunsetted in 2005, following 35 years of court oversight. The original *SFNAACP v. SFUSD* plan contrasted deeply with where the decree ended in 2005. The Horseshoe Plan (1971–1978), an outcome of the *Johnson v. SFUSD* (1971) preceding *SFNAACP v. SFUSD* perniciously reduced minority isolation and its impacts manifested in the 1980s with few schools having 45% or more of one race (Quinn, 2020). But, by 1999, race-based admissions were eliminated in SFUSD due in part to the Chinese American Democratic Club who rallied for its demise and voter-led California proposition 209, which made race a non-factor in school assignments (San Francisco Unified Schools, 2020). This set stage for the demise of Brown and the *SFNAACP v. SFUSD*. US District Courts throughout the country would follow suit with race no longer counting as a selection criterion for magnet schools and school assignment, polarized by many districts reaching unitary status (sufficient racial integration), and closing any future integration and eroding plans for affirmative action in K-12 and later, public universities. Further, the US Courts are far less active than they were in the 1960s and early 1970s (Edward Steinman, pers. interview, May 1, 2023).

With California Proposition 209 (approved in 1996) prohibiting use of race in admissions in K-12 education, a new metric was used for integrating schools. The SFUSD Diversity index allowed for families to choose up to seven schools, which may or may not be within their given neighborhood. Herein, we see the final stages of court oversight ending with choice, race-neutrality and the likelihood of proximity contrasting with the originally equity grounded pursuits of racial integration of assignment, racial proportions, and less likelihood of attending a school in one's neighborhood. *SFNAACP v. SFUSD*'s consent decree ended with a complex formula that attempted to integrate the court decree, and ideologies about choice instead of race as a simple and direct formula, a significant erosion to the spirit and the aims of Brown and to the Johnson family of SFUSD. On December 31, 2005, the *SFNAACP v. SFUSD* consent decree concluded, lifting the district from court oversight for racial desegregation.

The second sunset was the *Lau v. Nichols* and its consent decree. From 1974 to 2019, Lau became the longest standing civil class action suit in SFUSD under court supervision, superseding the length of the *SFNAACP v. SFUSD* case monitored for 33 years. Lau was under court supervision for 45 years.

Indications of SFUSD wanting to sunset the Lau decree emerged in the 1981–82 annual decree reports, just five years after the decree's implementation. The original Master Plan for Bilingual–Bicultural Education had a timeline of 1975 to 1980, and the report detailed either completion or the adequate progress with given tasks and structures. The 1981–82 Lau report stated, 'With success completion of the timeline activities, this Department now seeks the court's favor for closure of the Consent Decree Reports' (Office of the Superintendent of San Francisco Unified School District, 1982: 1). Yet no action was taken, perhaps in part to the assigned judge from the US District Court of Northern California, Lloyd H. Burke.

Lloyd H. Burke (LHB) was appointed by President Dwight Eisenhower to the US District Court for the Northern District of California in 1958. Beginning in 1976, LHB would preside over the Lau consent decree, receiving annual reports from SFUSD and ensuring the Department of Justice visited the district to oversee the implementation of their Master Plan for Bilingual–Bicultural Education. But in 1979, shortly after the Lau decree's implementation, LHB was declared disabled by President Jimmy Carter, and he continued in a reduced role until his death in 1988. Following his death, his seat was abolished with no judge immediately reassigned to the decree. In short, the extent to which a US District court judge was involved in the Lau consent decree remains an area of debate and concern.

In 2005, SFUSD became even more earnest in its quest to be released and relieved from the Lau decree, making a formal request to the courts. Given that LHB was no longer living, his seat had been abolished and presently available documents do not indicate if a judge had been reassigned to the oversight of the decree. Yet in 2006, the Chief Judge of the US District Court for the Northern District of California, Vaughn R. Walker sent an order invoking SFUSD, the defendants to further justify why release from the decree would be necessary. Vaughn wrote,

> It has come to the attention of the undersigned chief judge that the San Francisco Unified School District (SFUSD) has continued to file with the court annual reports pursuant to the consent decree in this matter long after the retirement of the judicial officer to which this matter was assigned, Judge Lloyd H. Burke... The status quo may satisfy the requirements of form, but it is empty of substance. SFUSD is dutifully filling reports, but no judicial officer is attending to the consent decree compliance issues that the reports are intended in part to address. The fact that the parties have been content with this status quo suggests that the court may no longer be serving any useful role. (U.S. District Court for the Northern District of California, 2006: 1–2)

Vaughn describes SFUSD's dissatisfaction that the Lau decree is still in force when measurable and substantive changes have been made since the decree's inception in 1976. After 30 years of oversight, sunsetting required additional time and work to merit the request.

Yet not everyone supported SFUSD's request to sunset Lau. According to the Bilingual Community Council (BCC), a partner that was explicitly written into the 1976 Master Bilingual–Bicultural Plan (then called the Community Council) and formed in 1977 was opposed to the release from the courts in 2005. The BCC had communicated this with SFUSD and the Department of Justice directly. BCC's advisory role had been minimal with SFUSD, despite their advocation about the grave inconsistencies in program provisions throughout the district. BCC's complaints showed up when SFUSD, the defendant was denied relief from court oversight. Emily H McCarthy, Attorney for the US Department of Justice wrote the denial to SFUSD, detailing BCC's complaints.

> In the spring and fall of 2005, the BCC visited approximately 50 schools in the SFUSD. During these visits, the BCC found many problems, including but limited to the following: (1) some schools were not providing all EL students with the daily minimum of 30 minutes of ELD instruction; (2) staff responsible for teaching ELD classes were not adequately trained; (3) the articulation of the ELD standards across grade levels was insufficient; (4) bilingual programs had inadequate instruction in the native language; and (5) parents were not sufficiently informed of the services available for EL students. (United States Department of Justice, 2007: 4)

McCarthy also described findings from an external ESL consultant, Julie Maxwell Jolly who joined the US Department of Justice, visiting eight SFUSD schools with four of the six language programs available to identified-ELs. In her nine-page report, Maxwell Jolly found that curriculum materials for the Chinese were inaccessible, which was the founding for relief in the case. At this juncture, Gordon Lew's (Chapter 4) curriculum resources were no longer in circulation.

Maxwell Jolly takes us back to the origin of Lau and the spirit of the consent decree: the Chinese and a bilingual–bicultural education for them. Thirty years later, such provisions were still elusive. Emily McCarthy, the attorney for the US Department of Justice concluded the response to SFUSD stating, 'judicial oversight remains necessary' requiring SFUSD to create a new Master Plan for Bilingual–Bicultural Education (United States Department of Justice, 2007: 6).

In 2007–08, SFUSD's Department of Multilingual Education began its work developing a new Master Plan, called the 'Master Plan for Multilingual Education' (San Francisco Unified Schools, 2008). In 2008, the sunsetting of the decree was the focus of Superintendent Carlos Garcia's administration and the SFUSD school board. Garcia hired a Special Assistant to the Superintendent, Lawyer Christina Wong given her historic work as the Education Director for the Chinese for Affirmative Action to assist in working with the Multilingual Pathways Department (formerly the Bilingual Department). Christina collaborated with multiple stakeholders to bring their program into compliance for relief from the decree.

The Assistant Superintendent of Instruction of SFUSD, Dr. Francisca Sanchez, who was overseeing the Multilingual Pathways Department presented the new Master Plan to the SFUSD School Board on May 27, 2008 in anticipation of a June 10, 2008 court date at the US District Courts of Northern California to move toward a request for a Modified Consent Decree (MDC). Dr Sanchez shared the impetus for the remaking of the plan based on feedback from parents and the BCC. Concerns expressed included identification; lack of accurate information communicated to parents about the variety of language program choices; district furnished programs 'aren't always as strong as they could be'; and educators needing more professional development (Sanchez, 2008: Slide 3). The new Master Plan for Multilingual Education compared to the original 1976 Master Plan for Bilingual–Bicultural Education reflects nearly all the same concerns, but with the newer permutation of parent 'choice'.

In 1976, busing was in force, and students were attending their assigned school, with the hope of language programming being available. The Association of Chinese Teachers (TACT) consistently communicated the need for coordination with the Bilingual Department and the student assignment center to ensure students had access to a bilingual education versus nothing, or only English as a Second Language (ESL) models (The Association of Chinese Teachers (TACT), 1971).

Fast forward to 2008: language programming is available, but not just ESL or bilingual models, but (1) dual language immersion; (2) biliteracy; (3) English Plus; (4) newcomer; (5) underschooled; or (6) long-term English language learner and students must elect a 'language pathway' where the aspiration of support will be contiguous and coherent (Sanchez, 2008: Slide 12). Yet, choice is mediated by forces other than the family's decision. When new families enroll, they go to the Enrollment Placement Center (EPC), where they receive counseling about the best placement for their child, following a battery of assessments in English and their native language, then revealing their choices. For a child who has just immigrated from mainland China and has been consecutively schooled, their array includes four possibilities stated above. In contrast, a newcomer student who has had interrupted schooling, is likely assessed with one to two choices: the newcomer or underschooled program. Disparagingly, the latter three naming conventions of newcomer, underschooled or long-term English language learner are ascribed and labeled upon the child and do not refer to a language program, rather the deficient characteristics of the child, yet consistent with the naming conventions within No Child Left Behind Policy (2001). Thus, the construct of choice is mediated by the values of the system, tracking students, one of the original critiques in the *Lau v. Nichols* case: lack of access to the content will invariably lead to tracking.

The new Master Plan for Multilingual Education was approved on September 11, 2008 by the US District Court for the Northern District of California with Judge Claudia Wilkins now presiding, an appointee of Democratic President, Bill Clinton (U.S. District Court for the Northern District of California, 2008). The approved plan also included a new section – Section J that had more explicit content about the role of the BCC. The court ordered SFUSD to submit an annual report beginning in November 2008 and that the BCC would file a minority report (2008: 2).

Between 2008 to 2015, SFUSD continued to submit annual reports on the decree in hopes of arriving at a Modified Consent Decree (MCD) with the eventual aim of sunsetting. The BCC also submitted minority reports, which continued to express concerns about the implementation of the new Master Plan for Multilingual Education.

In 2015, after eight years under the new Master plan, a MCD was approved by the US District Court for the Northern District of California, essentially creating a new 54-page roadmap for language policy implementation within SFUSD (U.S. District Court of Northern District of California, 2015), compared to the relative brevity of the initial 1976 Lau Consent Decree report of a mere six pages (Bilingual Department of San Francisco Unified School District, 1976). Instead of the six areas that were to be followed and reported between 1976 to 2008, there was now eight areas with 109 points. The 2015 MCD paralleled much of the content found in the Master Plan for Multilingual Education (2008) (Table 17.1).

Comparing the original (1976) with the Modified Consent Decree for Lau (2015), there is a more explicit emphasis on English in the 2015 version. English is the required language for assessment, and 'The District will use a Primary Language Assessment to assess the student's

Table 17.1 Comparison of Lau Consent Decrees (1976 and 2015)

Lau Consent Decree (October 22, 1976) 6 pages	Modified Consent Decree (June 24, 2015) 54 pages
1. Implement Master Plan for Bilingual–Bicultural Education (1975) for Chinese, Filipino and Spanish students of SFUSD (Created in collaboration with the Center for Applied Linguistics)	1. Implement Master Plan for Multilingual Education (2008) for all identified-ELs
2. Establish timetables for plan implementation and placement of students in bilingual education	2. Identify, assess and place identified-ELs in one of six language program models; reclassify, and monitor reclassified students
3. Report progress of plan semi-annually (May and November), # of students by language, ethnicity, language program type (ESL, bilingual or other), placement, teacher's bilingual proficiency; and determine major and minor languages, identify model school sites	3. Furnish six different language programs to students and provide daily ESL instruction regardless of program model and ELD instruction within content instruction. Ensure access to specialized programs including special and gifted education.
4. Establish a Community Council to advise and participate in preparation of annual reports	4. Staff programs with highly qualified and certified staff in CLAD* or BCLAD** and ensure ongoing professional development for all educators
5. Report objections about content and/or progress of plan and/or decree objectives	5. Furnish translation and interpretation for families about all aspects of schooling; engage families in ELACs and DELACs at school and district levels
6. Courts have jurisdiction of all activities in execution of Master Plan	6. Court and county schools will not receive services in the same way and MOUs will establish types of service provision
	7. Monitor and coordinate effectiveness of programs with families, schools ELACs and DELACs, and the BCC
	8. Courts have jurisdiction of all activities in execution of Master Plan

*CLAD: Cross-cultural Language and Academic Development; **BCLAD: Bilingual Cross-Cultural Language and Academic Development.

proficiency in his or her home language, when the District determines that such testing is helpful to the effective implementation of the District's language pathways (e.g., dual language pathways)' (U.S. District Court of Northern District of California, 2015: 15). Thus, the nomenclature of school or program choice may elude bilingual students (Bernstein *et al.*, 2021). Only some bilingual students will be selected for dual language immersion or biliteracy, and for those that are not, they will be placed in a non-bilingual language pathway, a newly emerging concern about bilingual students being *placed* versus *selected* for a bilingual education (Delavan *et al.*, 2022; Morita-Mullaney & Chesnut, 2022).

The Lau MCD was in place for a short four years as SFUSD, the defendant requested release from oversight as they claimed sufficient systems, procedures and engagements were in place to address the historic harms originally experienced by Cantonese families like Kinney Lau. SFUSD's intent was to sunset the decree in 2018, but an extension was given and, ultimately, the sunset of the decree was approved on June 30, 2019 by the US District Court for the Northern District of California. *The Sunset*. The Lau sunsetting was eerily quiet. SFUSD issued a press release:

> After over 45 years of compliance with a federal mandate that the San Francisco Unified School District (SFUSD) provide services for English Language Learners, the District has been released from its Court-supervised obligations, and remains deeply invested in its comprehensive system of support for English Language Learners. (Dudnick, 2019: e1)

The district tweeted, 'Lau Consent Decree Sunsets for SFUSD #WeAreSFUSD' with only one like from the SFUSD handle and one retweet from the issuing press officer. Two other online venues put out a press release, one local to San Francisco (Bay City News, 2019) and another in Washington, DC (Targeted News Service, 2019). Yet, there was little buzz about its sunset, unlike the public radio announcement that proclaimed Lau's passage as Edward Steinman commuted to Santa Clara University in 1974 nor the celebrations expressed by members of The Association for Chinese Teachers (The Association of Chinese Teachers (TACT), 2004) and in the *East West* weekly (East West, 1974). The sunrise once celebrated had fallen to the other side of the landscape, and bilingual education experienced its second silent decline, a sunset.

The sunset was much like the 'silent obituary' originally asserted when the federal Bilingual Education Act of 1968 was replaced by the federal English Language Acquisition Act of 2002 (Crawford, 2008: 124). The English Language Acquisition Act had bipartisan support and little clamor was expressed by the Hispanic Caucus that rallied for the Bilingual Education's Act's original passage in 1968. After 45 years, the imprint of bilingual education had morphed into an English-centric agenda for bilingual students, later taking hold in SFUSD, the birthplace of *Lau v. Nichols*.

SFUSD's press release about the Lau sunset decree continued, describing its instructional provisions as abbreviated in Table 17.2.

Table 17.2 Lau Consent Decree Sunsetting and Continued Commitment to Language Provisions

Service	Description
Language instructional provisions	Provision of English language development (ELD) instruction until reclassified. Administrators and teachers have adequate resources to furnish ELD
Choice of language program model	Content in home language is available as students develop English skills. Provision of Seal of Biliteracy available if conditions of advanced proficiency are met.
Translation and interpretation	Families have timely access to translation of documents in major languages and interpretation is furnished at school and district convenings. Communication protocols in place for Individual Education Plans (IEP) for dually classified special ed/EL students.
District and site-based structures and protocols for programming and budgeting with family input	Site-based and district-based structures in place for families to understand current language programs and related protocols. Program and budget recommendations available in Local Control and Accountability program (LCAP).

Source: Lau Consent Decree Sunsets for SFUSD. Press Release by SFUSD (Dudnick, 2018).

Thereafter, a commitment is made in a press release to continue improving its programming with a plan for a new ESL master plan in the next two years, which has not yet been developed, due in part to the impact of COVID-19 pandemic.

The sunsetting does not absolve SFUSD from the requirements of *Lau v. Nichols* (1974) as premised on the violation of the Civil Rights Act of 1964, but it does mean the pressure is internal. SFUSD now has 51,000 students with 27% of those identified as English learners, inclusive of the Cantonese, now 3,361 students, but now represented in different parts of the SFUSD within and outside of Chinatown (California Department of Education, 2023). More simply, the district remains the primary force to hold themselves internally accountable for assurances of language rights.

18 Sunset and Beyond: Language as Problem, Right, Resource or Choice?

With the decree closure in SFUSD, the hope is that systems, beliefs, and values originally conceptualized in *Lau v. Nichols* are now embodied among the agents in the schools and community. As Edward Steinman asserted: 'Lau, unlike Brown was the first to go beyond the schoolhouse doors' and see what was going on inside in practice. To capture what this looks like after the sunset of the Lau decrees in SFUSD, interviews with educators demonstrate how Lau is now living in their multilingual schoolhouses and classrooms and how Cantonese is positioned as a language problem, right, a resource or a 'choice' (Ruiz, 1984). Capturing the experiences of educators during this post-Lau decree, time illuminates how they are mediating multilingualism for the Asian and Pacific Islander community, which presently represents 35% of the SFUSD student community (San Francisco Unified School District, 2023).

Interviews with present-day educators took place during the 2022–2023 school year, just a year after the closure of schools for nearly 18 months due to the COVID-19 pandemic. Anti-Asian hate was on the rise with many Chinese and Asian families being constructed as virus importers and carriers of the disease, a perniciously enduring and historic construction, leading to verbal and physical assaults. SFUSD educators regularly fielded the safety concerns of their Chinese families during school closures and upon their return to schools in the Fall of 2021. The Chinese for Affirmative Action and San Francisco State University worked to found the organization and the movement of #StopAAPIHate in an effort to stop public health scapegoating upon Asian communities (Stop AAPI Hate, 2023).

The current SFUSD educators are represented in their many voices as one as a collective autobiography. This collective strategy is not just to anonymize and protect participants, but as a means to affirm their shared ideas, stances and identities: a cumulative representation (Richardson, 1988). When educators' narratives intersected, I represent them in one unitary voice, drawing from their shared statements and inquiries. We now meet the multilingual educator collective, sharing about the present and future state of Chinese-Cantonese bilingual education in SFUSD.

Boutiquing and Gentrifying Dual Language Immersion while Eroding Bilingual Education

The collective: Bilingual education is the stepchild to immersion… the immersion program are as popular as ever. But biliteracy program are not so popular.
Trish: How does that sit with you?
The collective: It doesn't.

Each educator shared their concerns about dual language immersion where a small percentage of SFUSD's Chinese-Cantonese students were actually enrolled. Even though there was a desired formula of a half to a third of the classroom as native speakers as stated in the Modified Consent Decree (MCD) for Lau (2015) within dual immersion programs, in practice, it impacted a small proportion of the Chinese-Cantonese community with most being served by English as a Second Language (ESL) models, followed by Chinese-Cantonese biliteracy, and then Chinese immersion.

Biliteracy as a Strand is Segregation

Within the popularity of dual immersion schools, educators discussed the complexity of running biliteracy (bilingual education) in schools, where it operated only as a strand; a long-standing practice that biliteracy could not be school wide because it would systematize linguistic segregation. While the MCD and the Master Plan for Multilingual Education detailed that 'linguistic isolation' should be prevented (San Francisco Unified School District, 2008; U.S. District Court of Northern District of California, 2015: 20), in practice, the manifestation was linguistic and racial resegregation at the grade and classroom level.

Those classrooms rarely engaged with each other outside of being in the same space for recess and that had been going on for years. So, you look at class pictures and there's one… there's a class that's 100% Chinese kids and another class that's everybody else. And they didn't even know each other's names in the same grade level.

This set up created racial and linguistic student isolation except for recess and lunch, but also divided the faculty. Administrators struggled with the unevenness of the Chinese biliteracy programs as they had additional curriculum demands, but also had the benefit of what they described as a 'well-behaved Chinese classroom', whereas non-biliteracy classrooms struggled with the behavior challenges with Black and White children. The classroom differences in student constitution created envy toward their biliteracy colleagues, and racializing biliteracy as a form of faculty privilege, a dynamic that administrators wanted to equalize. During the pandemic when physical schools were closed for 18 months, all faculties began to collaborate online by a grade-level team, instead of by program strands. A new collegiality emerged that was energizing for all teachers and administrators and addressed that uneasiness of the separate programs.

> ...all of the teams worked together, so it wasn't separated into biliteracy and not biliteracy, except for if they found the capacity to have some Chinese time. The Chinese teachers would have like a little bit of time just spent there biliteracy kids, but it was easier on Zoom to have all the grade level together.

The emergency nature of moving into a fully online learning medium created a confessional among Chinese biliteracy teachers. They shared with their administrators about how little Cantonese instructional time they employed before and during school closures and what they believed was their 'lack' of standard Cantonese.

Cantonese Proficiency as Mediator of Biliteracy Decline

Educators expressed the language shift that was happening in Chinatown and throughout San Francisco. While the city has the highest proportion of Cantonese speakers in the US, most of its biliteracy teachers are American born Chinese (ABC) who learned Cantonese through their families and by attending after-school Cantonese schools. Educators described their ABC teachers in the Cantonese biliteracy strand. 'They could speak Cantonese just fine. They can read some. And their comprehension is pretty good. Writing—they feel like, minus school related words, they will have issues with writing Chinese'.

Educators recognized that in practice, the amount of instructional Cantonese time within the biliteracy program was declining as the linguistic complexity grew in the upper grade levels. Biliteracy teachers admitted that their own Cantonese proficiency did not align with the standards they were to teach within the model, so they began to spend appreciably less time in Cantonese. Without the expectation of their principal or district supervising language allocation during the designated Cantonese portion of the day, Cantonese teachers decreased their emphasis on the linguistic dimension of their biliteracy strand. Administrators shared it was a small opportunity for 'affinity time' or an emphasis on the bicultural elements.

Cantonese biliteracy teachers also made an additional stipend for their language skill, teaching craft, and Cantonese BCLAD license; a practice put in place in 1980 as reported in the annual Lau consent decree (Office of the Superintendent of San Francisco Unified School District, 1980). Yet, this stipend was not a sufficient incentive for current biliteracy teachers. 'I think the teachers are like, oh, ok. So, you end the program and the only thing they lament is not getting the stipend anymore'. Administrators continued that Cantonese biliteracy teachers were devoted to the school and the community and did not want to serve as biliteracy teachers in another part of the district. Administrators stated, 'They're devoted to the school and the community'.

Educators also critiqued the acquisition of a BCLAD-Cantonese license, a requirement among their biliteracy teachers, instituted in the earliest of the Lau consent decrees (Office of the Superintendent of San Francisco Unified School District, 1980). The local San Francisco State University where the first BCLAD program in the US was built by Dr Laureen Chew (Chapters 13 and 14) was no longer a program offering the primary licensure location for local Chinese teachers. Administrators shared, 'You actually have to take that test as the only way to get a BCLAD'. Acquiring a BCLAD in Cantonese was a test requiring language proficiency, methodology of bilingual education and bilingual and cultural knowledge, a subtest that was the same for Cantonese or Mandarin (Commission on Teacher Credentializing, 2023: e2). Cultural knowledge for Chinese is clustered together with Mandarin, assuming that both languages emerge from the same or similar cultural history. Without specific training in Cantonese teaching pedagogy, coupled with lack of historicizing the Cantonese immigration to the US and San Francisco, newer Cantonese teachers mostly constructed their capacity to be BCLAD teachers as contingent on their language proficiency alone.

Historic work with The Association of Chinese Teachers, Title VII and community-based funding supported racial and linguistic projects like Cantonese language support and development. Coupled with the fervor and the novelty of a bilingual education, a space of reclamation for teachers like Lucinda, Laureen, Irene, Darlene, Victor and Lonnie, they experienced an infrastructure of support for their continued language learning and affirming their capacities to serve as bilingual educators. SFUSD, TACT and San Francisco State furnished Cantonese language learning courses and opportunities funded by a variety of sources during the scaling of Cantonese bilingual. With declining funding, alongside the proliferation of school choice and charter schools, and limited training for teachers, such structures, dollars and community alliances are now more limited.

School Choice: Selection or Placement?

The educational placement center (EPC), a site of counseling and placement instituted in the earliest stages of the Lau decree furnished guidance to bilingual families about what language programs were rightfully available to them (ESL, biliteracy or immersion), mediating their assignment in coordination with racial desegregation efforts. Language rights and racial integration happened in tandem (albeit sloppily in the earliest stages of busing and Lau), yielding to the promissory aims of a racially integrated bilingual community as shared by Lucinda Lee and Laureen Chew's students.

The 1996 deletion of the use of race in school assignments per California law and the later sunsetting in 2005 of *SFNAACP v. SFUSD* in 2005 led to a colorblind system of placements, opening a market economy of school choice that had to simultaneously include language rights. Bilingual families have both rights and choices, an oddly concocted matrix. For example, a bilingual family may choose a STEM-focused school, but it does not have a biliteracy strand, delimiting them to an ESL model for language programming. Thus, their right is minimally met for language provisions (placement), and their choice is met (selection) or their selection is deleted because their language placement is more necessitated. These concurrent constructs of placement and selection emerge from different social foundations (Morita-Mullaney & Chesnut, 2022). Placement for language services denotes a right with origins in civil rights movements, inclusive of voting rights and affirmative action (Hsu Chen, 2012, 2014). Selection comes from neoliberal ideals of a market economy, reinforcing competition and meritocracy (Bernstein *et al.*, 2021; Morita-Mullaney & Chesnut, 2022). Thus, as we consider the Lau plaintiffs, the Chinese students in the classrooms before, during and after Lau, we now observe a retrofitted matrix of competing and incongruous ideologies, yielding to the continued tinkering of bilingual programming. *Language as choice erodes language as a right.*

Choice as the dominant and attractive construct within US schools has created a hierarchy when it comes to language programming. As administrators shared, 'the immersion programs are as popular as ever (selection), but biliteracy program are not so popular' (placement). As choice, the sunsetting of the decree and the Chinese teachers' confessional about their own Cantonese proficiency, biliteracy strands for Cantonese are being reconfigured.

> They've [the district] decided to collapse some of the biliteracy program that many of the schools have here. And so, we were asked if my community will be ok in phasing this out. My community actually thought it

was ok... and so that that struggle and also even the idea of having to pack everything that's six and a half hour a day, that's including recess time and lunch time and all that stuff, music, PE. Right? Yeah. How much time do I have to cover everything I perceive I need to cover? You know, it is a lot.

Educators reveal that biliteracy is seen an additional content area to cover instead of using the language as a medium for students to access the content. The Lau class action suit filed in 1970 stated that access was the moniker of creating equality for bilingual students and families, not adding time to the day, rather creating it as a medium of acceptable instruction so children would 'not fall behind' as expressed by Mrs Lau, Kinney's mom.

Mandarin is the New English

Not all Chinese is positioned equally, and Mandarin is becoming the new language of power, even in a city like San Francisco that has a lengthy history of families from Southern China and Hong Kong who speak Cantonese as their native or heritage language.

And when it comes to Chinese, you know, the fact that there's some people who are who want or wanting Cantonese, some folks want Mandarin. And for the Confucius Institute, the institute does try to, or they try very hard to support the schools.

The Confucius Institute of China has historically infused dollars into the instruction of Mandarin and such programs are represented in dual immersion schools throughout the city. Non-bilingual families enjoy the choice and the economic cache that a Mandarin education brings to their child as it makes them more marketable (Delavan *et al.*, 2022). Yet this making of the 'marketable' child is also impacting the Cantonese community. Educators shared how Cantonese families were constructing Mandarin stating, 'the kids are learning... that they will become more marketable' if Mandarin is part of their repertoire. In addition to the market of Mandarin, there is also interest in learning Mandarin as it is the official language of China. Having access to this additional language enables a deeper look into mainland China, helping to historicize the origins and conditions of their family's migrations to the US. Knowing Mandarin also is a window into understanding the contested history of US/China relations.

The narratives of the educator collective demonstrate a commitment to having teachers look like their school community, unlike the experiences of Lucinda and Laureen who never had a Chinese teacher in their public schools. Racial and ethnolinguistic affinity with their students is important to the Cantonese biliteracy teachers and families, but not necessarily within the formality of a bilingual education model furnished by schools.

Language as Choice Erodes Language as a Right

The original language in the Lau case described the Chinese-Cantonese as being handicapped and the schools serving as central mediators of addressing such limitations (Office of the Superintendent of San Francisco Unified School District, 1978). Thus, in its origins, Lau was framed as a language as problem and one to be remediated, which could be inclusive of a bilingual education (Ruíz, 1984). Yet, different stakeholders within SFUSD addressed this from different perspectives, including the Association for Chinese Teacher (TACT) who originally debated over ESL or bilingual models with the latter ultimately being framed as language as a right (The Association of Chinese Teachers (TACT), 2004).

Now, school choice based in competition has turned dual immersion programs into language as a resource for speakers other than the target language. In essence, this practice may delimit the possibilities for language as a right for its native and heritage speakers, yielding to a different type of exclusion in the post-Brown and post-Lau era. Often framed as the gentrification of dual language where the demands of the majority group outweigh that of minoritized students (Valdez *et al.*, 2016), affirmative gains in language rights for the Cantonese-Chinese are shifting within its schools.

19 Sunsetting and Choice: Co-Articulating Language Rights, Affirmative Action and Voting Rights

In the 1970s, the federal courts were extremely active, and funding was abundant for social programs that had a national civil rights agenda, like the Reggie program with Lawyer, Edward Steinman (Consortium for the National Equal Justice Library, 2018; Georgetown University Law School, 2009). Upon the implementation of mandatory busing throughout the US, the Health, Education and Welfare system's Emergency School Assistance Program (ESAP) had funds to support the multicultural aims of racial integration, which was inclusive of language rights (U.S. Congress, 1970). Schools and community agencies could apply for said funds, and in places like Chinatown, they distinctly created content for teachers of Chinese children and Chinese families: a localized and historicized approach. Through film, Loni Ding demonstrated how racial integration and its busing could create the conditions for racial and linguistic equity to operate in parallel (Ding, 1978c). The force of the court and the generativity of the community created a bright sunrise.

Affirmative action cases were being fought through the Chinese for Affirmative Action for representation of Chinese and Chinese American plaintiffs to be admitted as journeymen to the construction industry. Court cases were filed, fought, and prevailed for the inclusion of Chinese resident aliens to be represented in the civil services (*Mow Song Wong v. Hampton*, 1976). The US Census was sued for their overt omission of Chinese residents living in Single Renter Occupancy units (*Quon v. Stans*, 1970) and although it did not violate federal statutes, the fight in the press changed the Census protocols for collection, including the provision of bilingual collectors – a procedure that is still in force today. The Association for Chinese Teachers (TACT) fought for their retention as bilingual teachers of color during SFUSD's economic downturn and rallied the California legislature for their jobs as they satisfied the decrees of *SFNAACP v. SFSUD*

(1978) and *Lau v. Nichols* (1974). Chinese teachers did so in solidarity with Black and Latino teachers, albeit contentious, to realize a substantive impact on retaining their jobs. Without this advocacy, the racial and linguistic teacher portrait of SFUSD would likely be more homogenous today.

With the affordances of language rights within the schools, and increasingly in the civil sector, and the enforcement of affirmative action, an opportunity opens up for the Chinese American populace to become a significant voting segment. American born Chinese in this portraiture are politically active, mitigating changes within the greater SFUSD system and the city at large. Commodore Stockton, where most Chinese educators served at some point, is now renamed Gordon J. Lau Elementary. Gordon was the first Chinese San Francisco Supervisor elected to the city in 1977. Fred Lau, standing at 5 feet 6.5 inches tall, contested the height requirement of the police force, and went onto to serve as one of the first Chinese Americans in the San Francisco Police force and later as the Chief of Police. The portraits of the historic Lau architects for language rights, affirmative action and voting rights created a conducive legal and local movement for the implementation and development of bilingual education within San Francisco and throughout the US.

The Voting Rights Act of 1975 eliminated English literacy tests as a criterion for voting. Ballots were created in languages other than English, along with related election materials (Voting Rights Act, 1965, 1975). This significant amendment was largely due to the Chicano movement in Texas for Spanish speakers (Hunter, 1976) with lesser attention placed on the Cantonese-Chinese community of San Francisco and *Lau v. Nichols* (1974) (Hsu Chen, 2012, 2018). The lack of national attention on the intersection between Lau and the Voting Rights Act was in part due to the smaller scale of the Chinese populace who was eligible to vote at the time. The boon of language rights, affirmative action, and voting rights happening concurrently created a distinct trifecta for the interpretation of the Civil Rights Act of 1964 on which language rights and affirmative action were founded and voting rights and racial integration, as premised on the Fourteenth Amendment.

The architects of Lau identified the methods and resources they used within and outside their school system to develop a bilingual program that was adequately resourced and supported. The Civil Rights Act of 1964 addressed language rights mostly within the school system. Affirmative action addressed the employment of SFUSD teachers, but also included employment practices within the civil sector of San Francisco. The Fourteenth Amendment of the US Constitution addressed voting rights and racially integrated schooling. As Edward Steinman shared, for the US Constitution 'cases must show purpose'. In cases under the Civil Rights Act of 1964, the burden is on remedy and regulations, but because it is not decisioned under the umbrella of the Constitution, such cases are precariously situated.

While the courts have enforced and mediated language rights, affirmative action, voting rights and racial integration, the architects within Lau demonstrated their agency and advocacy through various organizations and strategies as detailed below (Table 19.1). The Lau architects are listed in relative time order.

The strategies used by the Lau architects for language rights show how much educators', community activists' and university professors' activities were focused upon the Civil Rights Act of 1964 with their incumbent remedies. Each player created or collaborated on such strategies within and

Table 19.1 The Lau architects for language rights

	Civil Rights Act of 1964		Fourteenth Amendment of U.S Constitution	
Architect	Language Rights	Affirmative Action	Voting Rights	Integrated schooling
Mamie Tape				Calif. Supreme Court *Tape v. Hurley (1885)* Daily Alta Newspaper
Alan Nichols	SFUSD School Board, Mainline Newspapers	Poetry by pen name, *San Francisco Commuter Poems (1965)*		SFUSD School Board, Mainline Newspapers
Edward Steinman	Courts *Lau v. Nichols (1974)*	Courts *Quon v. Stans (1970), Hampton v. Mow Sung Wong (1976)*		
Ling-Chi Wang	Courts, US Census, TV, radio, newspapers, school board, local legislature, College Board	Courts, TV, radio, newspapers, university systems, local legislature	TV, radio, newspapers, US Census, local legislature	TV, radio, & newspapers
Lucinda Wong Lee Katz	Mrs Lau, Teacher Corp, Cameron House	Teacher Corp, Cameron House		Counseling Chinese families to integrate
Victor Low	Teacher Corp, TACT Title VII fellow, *Unimpressible Race* (Low, 1982), First Chinese Baptist Church	Teacher Corp, TACT Title VII fellow, *Unimpressible Race* (Low, 1982), First Chinese Baptist Church	TACT	Principalship in the Mission

(Continued)

Table 19.1 (*Continued*)

Architect	Civil Rights Act of 1964		Fourteenth Amendment of U.S Constitution	
	Language Rights	Affirmative Action	Voting Rights	Integrated schooling
Lonnie Chin	TACT, protecting teachers on bilingual waivers, Cameron House, American Association of Asian American Educators, YWCA, Presbyterian Church	TACT, protecting teachers on bilingual waivers, Cameron House, American Association of Asian American Educators, YWCA, Presbyterian Church	TACT, American Association of Asian American Educators, Presbyterian Church	Racial integration at classroom level
Gordon Lew	Chinese pilot Title VII program *East West Bilingual* weekly	San Francisco Community College	*East West Bilingual* weekly	*East West Bilingual* weekly
Laureen Chew	Mulan of Salvation Army, Teacher Corp, TACT Title VII fellow, *Dim Sum*, American Association of Asian American Educators	TWLF strike, ICSA, Teacher Corp, TACT, SFUSD Teacher strike, American Association of Asian American Educators	TACT, *Bean Sprouts*	TWLF, TACT, ICSA
Irene Dea Collier	Wah Mei Preschool, TACT, American Association of Asian American Educators	SFUSD Teacher strike, American Association of Asian American Educators	TACT	TACT
Darlene Lim	TACT, protecting teachers on bilingual waivers, educational placement center, American Association of Asian American Educators	TACT, protecting teachers on waivers, American Association of Asian American Educators	TACT	Educational placement center

outside of their schools, yielding to language rights for students and families and affirmative action for bilingual teachers of color at risk of layoff. For the Chinese community, affirmative action meant access to jobs that once eluded them, allowing them to seek employment within and outside of Chinatown at a fair and living wage. For voting rights, we observe how

TACT and the Chinese for Affirmative Action through its public service announcements on radio and TV galvanized understanding around voting, drawing in a Chinese populace (Ding, 1978d).

The Chinese stakeholders in this story demonstrate that the courts are one method for invoking language rights. Social rights of access are best mitigated in multiple social locations and when left solely in the hands of schools (as was the case with *SFNAACP v. SFUSD* (1985)), then the reproduction of social inequalities seen throughout a given community is probable (Berlak & Berlak, 1981). Language rights for the Cantonese-Chinese of San Francisco demonstrate the intricate mapping of its players upon various social platforms, demonstrating that social equity is engineered across access to fair and affordable housing, access to health care, opportunities for employment, accessible and quality schooling, and voting rights (Anyon, 2005). If in the hands of schools alone, transformation for linguistic and racial equity is unlikely.

Legal scholarship in voting rights, which falls under the relative permanence of the Fourteenth Amendment, intersects with language rights and affirmative action (Hsu Chen, 2012, 2014). For language rights, there has been significant regress in bilingual education due in large part to English-only laws and movements throughout the US and the increase in testing in English for school accountability. Affirmative action in college admissions, and the reduction in what collective bargaining can arbitrate, also represents erosion (Poon *et al.*, 2019). But a focus on voting rights, which is constitutional, is the way forward to preserving and heightening language rights and affirmative action. Bilingual educators and activists must see their role of spreading their reach to this intersectional space, reconstructing, and reconstituting the trifecta of the 1970s. To expand the *positive liberty* experienced by the plaintiffs of Lau, the hope for the next 50 years is to consider how *positive and negative liberty* cannot just coexist separately but operate in tandem. Linguistic and racial justice must be a constitutive process as experienced and created by all groups of color to arrive at language as right and resource orientation (Ruíz, 1984).

As SFUSD moves into its Lau decree sunset, now five years behind us, how will the varied social platforms and its actors manifest over the next 50 years? What will we say about *Lau v. Nichols* in 2074? I invite scholars, practitioners and multilingual families from varied fields, social locations and identities to examine newer policy portraits of the characters of *Lau v. Nichols* in your specific schools and communities and challenge you to consider how linguistic and racial equity can be conjoined. Importantly, we must continually revisit how such intersections are made as our landscapes change over time. We learn from the Chinese community that language rights were not solely inscribed in the *Lau v. Nichols*' laws, policies and decrees, but were enacted from various social locations of activism and resistance. With the sunset of the Lau consent decree in SFUSD, how the sun will come across the horizon is incumbent on the next generation to unsettle.

References

ACLU of Southern California (1998) *Civil Rights Groups File Class Action Lawsuit to Block Proposition 227*.
Affadavit of Denise Lee, 38–39 (1970a).
Affadavit in Opposition to Motion for Preliminary Injunction and In Support of Motion to Dismiss (1970a).
An Act to establish a Political Code relating to public schools, Statutes of California 100 § 117 (1885).
Alcoff, L.M. (2003) Latino/as, Asian Americans and the Black-White Binary. *Journal of Ethics* 7, 5–27.
Anonymous. (6 March 1969) The Language. *San Francisco Examiner*, 30.
Anyon, J. (2005) *Radical Possibilities: Public Policy, Urban Education, and A New Social Movement*. Routledge. See http://www.loc.gov/catdir/toc/ecip051/2004023037.html
Appeal from the United States District Court for the Northern District of California (1973).
Art, Research and Curriculum Associates (1994) Revisiting the Lau Decision: 20 years after. *Proceedings of a National Commemorative Symposium, San Francisco, CA, USA*.
Asian American Political Alliance (AAPA) (1969) San Francisco State College Strike 1968.
AsianWeek (1988, August 19) 'Yee Decries SF School Plan'. *AsianWeek*.
Asimov, N. (1998, July 16) Prop. 227 Upheld by U.S. Judge. *San Francisco Chronicle*, A1.
Baecher, L., Knoll, M. and Patti, J. (2013) Addressing english language learners in the school leadership curriculum. *Journal of Research on Leadership Education* 8 (3), 280–303. https://doi.org/10.1177/1942775113498377
Bay City News (2019) *English Language Learners Retain Support After Lau Consent Decree Sunsets*. https://sfbayca.com/2019/07/01/english-language-learners-retain-support-after-lau-consent-decree-sunsets/
Before Hon. Lloyd H. Burke, Judge in Kinney Kinmon Lau, etc., et al., Plaintiffs v. Alan H. Nichols, etc., et al., Defendants, Oral Arguments (1970).
Berlak, A. and Berlak, H. (1981) *Dilemmas of Schooling: Teaching and Social Change*. Methuen.
Berlin, I. (1958) *Two Concepts of Liberty*. University of Oxford, Oxford, UK.
Bernstein, K.A., Alvarez, A., Chaparro, S. and Henderson, K.I. (2021) 'We live in the age of choice': School administrators, school choice policies, and the shaping of dual language bilingual education. *Language Policy* 20 (3), 383–412. https://doi.org/10.1007/s10993-021-09578-0
Bilingual Department of San Francisco Unified School District (1976) *Lau Consent Decree Annual Report*.
Bilingual Education Act, Pub. L. No. (90-247), 81 Stat. 816 (1968).
Bilingual Education Act, Pub. L. No. (93-380), 88 Stat. 503 (1974).
Bilingual Education and Reform Act of California, Chapter 1339 (California Congress, 1980).
Boyer, R.K. (1970) Repeal the Dentention Act of 1950. In A. Lai (ed.). Washington, DC: Congress of the United States: House of Representatives.

Brooks, K., Adams, S. and Morita-Mullaney, T. (2010) Creating inclusive communities for ELL students: Transforming school principals' perspectives. *Theory into Practice* 49 (2), 145–151. https://doi.org/10.1080/00405841003641501

Brown v. Board of Education II, 349 (1955).

Brown v. Board of Education of Topeka, 347 (1954).

Brynelson, W. (1988) Resolution of non-compliant findings. In L. Avenida (ed.). Sacramento, CA: California Department of Education and Form CTS 4A.

Burks, J. (1971, July 27) Chinatown's Bridge of a 1000 Controversies. *San Francisco Examiner*, 6.

California Civil Rights Initiative: Proposition 209 (2009).

California Department of Education (2023) *English Learner Students by Language by Grade for 2022–2023*. Author, https://dq.cde.ca.gov/dataquest/SpringData/StudentsByLanguage.aspx?Level=County&TheYear=2022-23&SubGroup=All&ShortYear=2223&GenderGroup=B&CDSCode=38000000000000&RecordType=EL

Center for Applied Linguistics and the Citizens' Taskforce on Bilingual Education (1975a) *A Master Plan for Bilingual-Bicultural Education in the San Francisco Unified School District: In Response to the Supreme Court Decision in the Case of Lau v. Nichols, Part 3B.*

Center for Applied Linguistics and the Citizens' Taskforce on Bilingual Education (1975b) *A Master Plan for Bilingual-Bicultural Education in the San Francisco Unified School District: In Response to the Supreme Court Decision in the Case of Lau v. Nichols, Part 4.*

Center for Applied Linguistics and the Citizens' Taskforce on Bilingual Education (1975c) *A Master Plan for Bilingual-Bicultural Education in the San Francisco Unified School District: In Response to the Supreme Court Decision in the Case of Lau v. Nichols, Parts I and II.*

Center for Educational Telecommunications (CEL) (2022) *about Loni Ding (1931–2010)*. http://www.cetel.org/ding.html

Cervantes-Soon, C.G., Dorner, L., Palmer, D., Heiman, D., Schwerdtfeger, R. and Choi, J. (2017) Combating inequalities in two-way language immersion programs: Toward critical consciousness in bilingual education spaces. *Review of Research in Education* 41, 403–427. https://doi.org/10.3102/0091732X17690120

Chacon-Moscone Bicultural Education Act (1972).

Champion, D. (1969) Hayakawa is firm: S.F. State Set to Open on Monday – Same Problems. *San Francisco Chronicle*, 1.

Chan, S. (2007) The making of a quintessential scholar-activist. *Amerasia Journal* 33 (1), 120–138. https://doi.org/10.17953/amer.33.1.21168r6302835138

Chesnut, C. and Morita-Mullaney, T. (2023) Dueling roles in dual language education: Exploring leader identity development in dual language strands. *Educational Administration Quarterly* 60 (1), 3–36. https://doi.org/10.1177/0013161X2312118

Chin, L. and Costa, A.L. (1977) Habits of mind to improve thinking. In S.V. Elementary (ed.) San Francisco, CA.

Chinese for Affirmative Action (CAA) (1972) Bilingual teachers needed in the marina. *Chinese for Affirmative Action (CAA) Newsletter* 1 (6), 1–9.

Chuck, H. and Chuck, J. (2019) *Chinatown Rising* J. Q. Chan.

Chuck, J. (1971) First Chinese Baptist Church. In T. Wong (ed.) San Francisco, CA: First Chinese Baptist Chruch.

Citizen's Advisory Committee Community Information Sub-Committee (1971). San Francisco School Desegregation Background Information.

Cloud, R.W. (1952) *Education in California: Leaders, Organizations, and Accomplishments of the First Hundred Years*. Stanford University Press.

Coballas-Vega, C., Espino-Paris, C. and Marra, A.F. (1979) *The Title VII Fellow Program: A Prelminary Report* (Bilingual Education Paper Series, Issue. L. A. California State University.

College Board Communications (2019) Remembering Donald Stewart. PhD, College Board. See https://allaccess.collegeboard.org/remembering-donald-stewart-phd

Commission on Teacher Credentializing (2023) *Bilingual Authorizations (CL-628b)* Commission on Teacher Credentializing. See https://www.ctc.ca.gov/credentials/leaflets/bilingual-authorizations-(cl-628b)

Cone, R. (1971, September 6) *San Francisco Examiner*, 1.

Consolidated Chinese Benevolant Association (1971) *Consolidated Chinese Benevolant Association Meeting Minutes*.

Consortium for the National Equal Justice Library (2018) *Persons: Reginald Heber Smith Fellows (Reggies)*. Consortium for the National Equal Justice Library. Retrieved June 28 from https://legalaidhistory.org/persons/reggies/

Coons, A.G., Browne, A.D., Campion, H.A., Dumpke, R.J., Holy, T.C., McHenry, D.E., Tyler, H.T., Wert, J. and Sexton, K. (1960) *A Master Plan for Higher Education in California, 1960–1975*.

Council on Interracial Books for Children (1976) Criteria for analyzing books on Asian Americans. *Bulletin* 4 (2 & 3), 4.

Crawford, J. (2002) *The Bilingual Education Act, 1968–2002: An Obituary* (Advocating for English language learners: Selected essays from James Crawford, Issue.

Crawford, J. (2008) *Advocating for English Learners: Selected Essays*. Multilingual Matters.

Crump, A. (2014) Introducing LangCrit: Critical language and race theory. *Critical Inquiry in Language Studies* 11 (3), 207–224. https://doi.org/10.1080/15427587.2014.936243

Daily Alta California (1885, April 16) Chinese Mother's Letter. *Daily Alta California*, Daily Alta California.

Daniels, L. (1971, February 20) The 'New' Peace Corps. *The San Francisco Examiner*, 4.

Dea Collier, I. (2024) *Wah Mei History* [Interview]. Wah Mei School.

Delavan, M.G., Freire, J.A. and Morita-Mullaney, T. (2022) Conscripted into thinking of scarce, selective, privatized, and precarious seats in dual language bilingual education: The choice discourse of mercenary exclusivity. *Current Issues in Language Planning* 24 (3), 245–271. https://doi.org/10.1080/14664208.2022.2077032

Ding, L. (1978a) Movin' Around, Movin' Out (Season 1, Episode 4). In L. Ding (ed.) *Bean Sprouts*. The Association for Chinese Teachers and Chinese for Affirmative Action.

Ding, L. (1978b) Growing Up From Here (Season 1, Episode 5). In L. Ding (ed.) *Bean Sprouts*. The Association for Chinese Teachers and Chinese for Affirmative Action.

Ding, L. (1978c) Try It, You'll Like It (Season 1, Episode 1). In L. Ding (ed.) *Bean Sprouts*. The Association for Chinese Teachers and Chinese for Affirmative Action.

Ding, L. (1978d) What Can You Show Me? (Season 1, Episode 3). In L. Ding (ed.) *Bean Sprouts*. The Association for Chinese Teachers and Chinese for Affirmative Action.

Ding, L. (1978e) Boys and Girls, Girls and Boys (Season 1, Episode 2). In L. Ding (ed.) *Bean Sprouts*. The Association for Chinese Teachers and Chinese for Affirmative Action.

Ding, L. (1988) *Island of Secret Memories*. California Historical Society.

Dong, H.C. (2002) *The Origins and Trajectory of Asian American Political Activism in the San Francisco Bay Area, 1968–1978* University of California Berkeley]. Berkeley, CA.

Dooley, N. (1975, February 26) School aides hint fight on pink slips. *San Francisco Examiner*, 1.

Douglass, W.O. (1974) *Certiorari to the United States Court of Appeals for the Ninth Circuit*.

Drewes, C. (1969, May 9) Dedicated to the Youth of the Ghetto. *The San Francisco Examiner*, 7.

Dudnick, L. (2019) *Lau Consent Decree Sunsets for SFUSD*. See https://www.sfusd.edu/about-sfusd/sfusd-news/press-releases/2019-07-01-lau-consent-decree-sunsets-sfusd

East West (1968a, August 28) *East West*, 4.
East West (1968b, September 4) *East West*, 12.
East West (1969) Chinese public school teachers to organize. *East-West* 3 (11), 1.
East West (1971a, October 6) Boycott or Busing: The Children Speak. *East West*, 1.
East West (1971b, June 2) Chinese Parents Firm on Anti-Busing Stance. *East West*, 1.
East West (1971c, September 27) Freedom schools rolls on with fund drive. *East West*, 1.
East West (1974, January 23) A day of victory. *East West*.
Ellsworth Jones, W. (1971, September 14) Chinatown's buses still nearly empty. *San Francisco Examiner*, 9.
Emergency Detention Act (1950).
Emergency School Assistance Program (1970).
English for the Children: Proposition 227 (1998).
Escamilla, K. (2018) Growing up with the Bilingual Education Act: One educator's journey. *Bilingual Research Journal* 41 (4), 369–387. https://doi.org/10.1080/15235882.2018.1529641
Evening Bulletin (1885, March 4) *Evening Bulletin*, 2.
Exclusion of Chinese, U.S.C. § 126, 22 (1882).
Executive Order 9066, Pub. L. No. 77-503, 56 (1942).
Flores, N. and Rosa, J. (2015) Undoing appropriateness: Raciolinguistic ideologies and language diversity in education. *Harvard Educational Review* 85 (2), 149–171. https://doi.org/10.17763/0017-8055.85.2.149
Gándara, P. and Orfield, G. (2012) Segregating Arizona's English Learners: A return to the 'Mexican Room'? *Teacher's College Record* 9 (114), 1–27. https://doi.org/10.1177/016146811211400905
Gándara, P., Maxwell-Jolly, J., García, E., Asato, J., Gutiérrez, K., Stritikus, T. and Curry, J. (2000) *The Initial Impact of Proposition 227 on the Instruction of English Learners*. UC Berkeley: University of California Linguistic Minority Research Institute. Retrieved from https://escholarship.org/uc/item/491925b7
García, O. (2009) *Bilingual Education in the 21st Century: A Global Perspective*. Basil/Blackwell.
Georgetown University Law School (2009) *Reginald Heber Smith Community Lawyer Fellowship Program*. Georgetown University Law School. Retrieved June 28 from https://aspace.ll.georgetown.edu/public/agents/corporate_entities/36
Gilmore, L. (1968, June 25) 'Forced busing' clarification to be asked tonight. *San Francisco Examiner*, 16.
Gobby, B. (2013) Principal self-government and subjectification: The exercise of principal autonomy in the Western Australian Independent Public Schools programme. *Critical Studies in Education* 54 (3), 273–285. https://doi.org/10.1080/17508487.2013.832338
Guerin, G. and Mohler, J. (1971) Chinese student need at Marina Junior High. In D.T. Shaheen (ed.). San Francisco, CA.
Guey Heung *Lee et al. v. Johnson* (1971).
Guthrie, J. (2001) 'A grave injustice against the children' / S.F. school officials squandered millions of bond, tax funds, concealed deficits from voters while seeking millions more. *SF Gate*. https://www.sfgate.com/education/article/A-grave-injustice-against-the-children-S-F-2858428.php
Hammond, A. (1965) *San Francisco Commuter Poems*. Pendragon Press.
Hattam, V.C. (2007) *In the Shadow of Race: Jews, Latinos, and Immigrant Politics in the United States*. University of Chicago Press. http://www.loc.gov/catdir/toc/ecip0713/2007011060.html
Hayes, T.W. (1987) *Report by the Auditor General of California: A Review of First-Year Admissions of Asians and Caucasians at the Univeristy of California at Berkeley*.
Hekymara, K. (1972) *The Third World Movement and Its History in the San Francisco State College Strike of 1968–69* University of California Berkeley]. Berkeley, CA.

Heritage on the Marina (2020) *History*. Author. https://heritageonthemarina.org/about-heritage-on-the-marina

Higher Education Act of 1965, Pub. L. No. 89-329, § 1001 (1965).

Houseman, A.W. and Perle, L.E. (2007) *Securing Equal Justice for All: A Brief History of Civil Legal Assistance in the United States*. Washington, DC: Center for Law and Social Policy (CLASP).

Howard, E.R., Lindholm-Leary, K.J., Rogers, D., Olague, N., Medina, J., Kennedy, B., Sugarman, J. and Christian, D. (2018) *Guiding Principles for Dual Language Education*. Center for Applied Linguistics.

Hsu Chen, M. (2012) *Regulatory Rights: Civil Rights Agencies Translating – National Origin Discrimination|| into Language Rights, 1965–1979* (Publication Number 3469237) University of California at Berkeley]. Berkeley, CA.

Hsu Chen, M. (2014) Language Rights as a Legacy of the Civil Rights Act of 1964. *SMU Law Review* 67 (2), 247–256.

Hsu Chen, M. (2018) Regulatory Rights: Civil Rights Agencies, Courts, and the Entrenchment of Language Rights. In L.G. Dodd (ed.) *The Rights Revolution Revisited: Institutional Perspectives on the Private Enforcement of Civil Rights in the U.S.* (pp. 100–122). Cambridge University Press.

Hsu, M. (2015) *The Good Immigrants: How the Yellow Peril Became the Model Minority*. Princeton University Press.

Hui, P.K. (1975, January 22) Bilingualism as a Right, Chinese Parents Told. *East-West*.

Humes, K. and Hogan, H. (2009) Measurement of race and ethnicity in a changing, Multicultural America. *Race and Social Problems* 1, 111–131. https://doi.org/10.1007/s12552-009-9011-5

Hunter, D.H. (1976) The 1975 voting rights act and language minorities. *Catholic University Law Review* 25 (2), 250–270.

Immigration and Naturalization Act, Pub. L. No. 89-236, U.S. Congress (1965).

Independent Calistogan (1885, September 16) Americanized Chinese. *Independent Calistogan*, 1.

Irizarry, R.A. (1978) *Bilingual Education: State And Federal Legislative Mandates: Implications for Program Design and Evaluation*. National Dissemination and Assessment Center, California State University.

Izumi, M. (2005) Prohibiting 'American Concentration camps': Repeal of the Emergency Detention Act and the Public historical memory of the Japanese American internment. *Pacific Historical Review* 74 (2), 165–193. https://doi.org/10.1525/phr.2005.74.2.165

Jenkins, R. (1967) *Bilingual Education in the San Francisco Unified School District*.

Johnson, L.B. (1964, May 7) *President Johnson's Speech at Ohio University*.

Johnson v. San Francisco Unified Schools (1971).

Johnson v. San Francisco Unified School District (1971).

Katz, S.R. (2004) Does NCLB leave the U.S. behind in bilingual teacher education? *English Education* 36 (2), 141–152.

Kim, C.J. (1999) The racial triangulation of Asian Americans. *Politics and Society* 27 (1), 105–138. https://doi.org/10.1177/0032329299027001005

Kim, C.J. (2000) *Bitter Fruit: The Politics of Black-Korean conflict in New York City*. Yale University Press.

Kim, C.J. (2018) Are Asians the new Blacks? Affirmative action, anti-Blackness, and the 'Sociometry' of Race. *Du Bois Review* 15 (2), 217–244. https://doi.org/10.1017/S1742058X18000243

Kim, C.J. (2023) *Asian Americans in an Anti-Black World*. Cambridge University Press. https://doi.org/10.1017/9781009222280

Kimbrough, J. and Hyman, J.B. (1978) *An Evaluation of the Emergency School Aid Act Nonprofit Organization Program: An Analysis of Federal Program Implementation and Funding Procedures*. https://www.rand.org/pubs/reports/R2312z1.html

Kinney Kinmon Lau *et al.* v. Alan H. Nichols *et al.*, 51 F.Supp 2d 1 (N.D. Cal. 1974).
Kinney Kinmon Lau *et al.* v. Alan H. Nichols, 51 F.Supp 2d 33, Affidavit of Denise Lee (N.D. Cal. 1970).
Kinney Kinmon Lau *et al.* v. Alan H. Nichols, 51 F.Supp 2d 1, Complaint for injunction for declaratory relief (Civil Rights) (N.D. Cal. 1974).
Kinney Kinmon Lau *et al.*, v. Alan H. Nichols *et al.*, Brief of Appellees F.3d 1 (9th Cir. 1970).
Kinney Kinmon Lau *et al.*, v. Alan H. Nichols *et al.*, Appellant's Opening Brief F.3d 1 (9th Cir. 1971).
Kinney Kinmon Lau *et al.* plaintiffs v. Alan H. Nichols et. al, defendants: Order. Civil No. C-70 627 LHB. F.3d (9th Cir. 1970).
Kinney Kinmon Lau *et al.*, *plaintiffs* v. Dr Edward Hopp *et al.*, defendants: Order (2006).
Kinney Kinmon Lau, *et al.* v. Alan H. Nichols, *et al.*, Appelant's Opening Brief (1971a).
Kinney Kinmon Lau, *et al.* v. Alan H. Nichols, *et al.*, Appelant's Reply Brief (1971b).
Knight, H. (2013) Elizabeth Hall – broke barriers in S.F. schools. *The Daily*.
Krashen, S.D. (1977) Some issues relating to the monitor model. Teachers of English to Speakers of Other Languages, Miami Florida.
Lai, H.M. (1982) *Short History of the Chinese Media in North America*. Chinese Historical Society of America. https://himmarklai.org/keywords/chinese-media/
Lai, H.M. (1994) Unfinished Business: The Chinese Confessions Program. Conference on the 50th anniversary of the Repeal of Exclusion Acts, San Francisco, CA.
Lai, H.M. (2004) *Becoming Chinese American: A History of Communities and Institutions*. Altamira Press.
Lang, P. (1982, February 24) S.F. Groundbreaking for Yick Wo School. *San Francisco Chronicle*, 14.
Lau v. Nichols, 414 U.S. 563 (1974). (1974).
Lau v. Nichols Oral Arguments. Supreme Court of the United States (1973).
Lee, E. (2015) *The Making of Asian America: A History*. Simon & Schuster.
Leeman, J. (2004) Racializing language: The history of linguistic ideologies in the US Census. *Journal of Language and Politics* 3 (3), 507–534.
Leonardo, Z. (2002) The souls of white folk: Critical pedagogy, whiteness studies and globalization discourse. *Race, Ethnicity and Education* 5 (1), 29–49. https://doi.org/10.1080/13613320120117180
Lew, G. (1965) *Gordon Lew's Chinese New Lessons 1*. The Institute of Oriental Culture.
Lew, G. (1966) *Gordon Lew's Chinese New Lessons 2*. The Institute of Oriental Culture.
Lew, G. (1971a) *Dragon Boat Festival*. San Francisco Unified School District Chinese Pilot Program.
Lew, G. (1971b) *Preparing for Chinese New Year*. San Francisco Unified School District Chinese Pilot Program.
Lew, G. (1971c). *The Moon Festival Is Here*. San Francisco Unified School District Chinese Pilot Program.
Lew, G. (1971d) *The Story of Ching-Ming*. San Francisco Unified School District Chinese Pilot Program.
Lew, G. (1971e) *The Story of the Red Envelopes*. San Francisco Unified School District Chinese Pilot Program.
Lew, G. (1971f) *Winter Festival*. San Francisco Unified School District Chinese Pilot Program.
Lew, H.J. (1985) Chinese Representation among SFUSD Administrators. In R. Alioto (ed.) (Low proportion of Chinese administrators ed.). San Francisco, CA: The Association of Chinese Teachers.
Low, V. (1982) *The Unimpressible Race: A Century of Educational Struggle by the Chinese in San Francisco*. East West Publishing.

Low, V. (1999a, October–November, 1999) Advisor's Corner: Elementary School. *Sojourner's Walking Papers*.

Low, V. (1999b, December, 1999) Advisor's Corner: High School. *Sojourner's Walking Papers*.

Lum, J. (2004) *TACT 1969–2004: 35th Anniversary Celebration* (Memories: The Beginning of the TACT Newsletter, Issue.

Lum, J.B. (1969) TACT Does Act: General Membership Meeting Puzzled by Supervisor. *The Association for Chinese Teachers (TACT)* 1 (4), 2–3.

Lum, J.B. (1970) Chinese bilingual department replacement. In M. Reiterman (ed.) (pp. 1). San Francisco, CA: The Association of Chinese Teachers.

Lum, P.A. (1975) *The Chinese Freedom Schools of San Francisco: A Case Study of the Social Limits of Political System Support* (Publication Number 7522484) University of California, Berkeley].

Lum, P.A. (1978) The creation and demise of San Francisco Chinatown Freedom Schools: One response to desegregation. *Amerasia Journal* 5 (1), 57–74. https://doi.org/10.17953/amer.5.1.w3vm70446137v81t

Marsh, D. (1979) The classroom effectiveness of teacher corps graduates: A national assessment. *The Journal of Classroom Interaction* 15 (1), 25–33.

Martinez-Cola, M. (2018) Sympathetic symbols, social movements, and school desegregation. *Journal of Law and Society* 45 (2), 177–204. https://doi.org/10.1111/jols.12071

Matsuda, M.J. (1996) *Where is Your Body? And Other Essays on Race, Gender, and the Law*. Beacon Press.

McHenry, D.E. (1946) Cross filing of political candidates in California. *The Annals of the American Academy of Political and Social Science* 248 (1), 226–331. https://doi.org/10.1177/00027162462480013

Mehlman Petrzela, N. (2010) Before the Federal Bilingual Education Act: Legislation and lived experience in California. *Peabody Journal of Education* 85 (4), 406–424. https://doi.org/10.1080/0161956X.2010.518021

Memorandum and Order Requiring the Parties to File Plans for School Desegregation, 1 (1971) April 28.

Menken, K. (2008) *English Learners Left Behind: Standardized Testing as Language Policy*. Multilingual Matters.

Menken, K. and García, O. (2010) *Negotiating Language Policies in Schools: Educators in Schools*. Routledge.

Mintz, F. (1985) *The Liberty Lobby and the American Right Race, Conspiracy, and Culture*. Praeger.

Mitchell, K.R. (2019) *Bilingual Educational Language Policies in Context: A Multidimensional Examination of California's Bilingual Teaching Authorization* (Publication Number 13896275) University of Minnesota]. Minneapolis, MN.

Moore, S.C.K. (2021) *A History of Bilingual Education in the US: Examining the Politics of Language Policymaking*. Multilingual Matters.

Morita-Mullaney, T. (2014) Leading from the Periphery: Collective Stories as told by English Language Learner Leaders PhD thesis, Indiana University, Bloomington, IN.

Morita-Mullaney, T. (2018) The intersection of language and race among English Learner (EL) Leaders in desegregated urban Midwest schools: A LangCrit Narrative Study. *Journal of Language, Identity & Education* 17 (6), 371–387. https://doi.org/10.1080/15348458.2018.1494598

Morita-Mullaney, T. (2019) The better immigrant seeking genuine inclusivity of all immigrant youth. In E.R. Crawford and L.M. Dorner (eds) *Educational Leadership of Immigrants: Case Studies in Times of Change* (pp. 195–204). Routledge.

Morita-Mullaney, T. (2024) Recentering multiple minoritized languages in dual language bilingual education. In J.A. Freire, C. Alfaro and E.J. de Jong (eds) *The Handbook of dual Language Bilingual Education*. Routledge.

Morita-Mullaney, T. and Chesnut, C. (2022) Equity traps in the deselection of English Learners in dual language education: A collective case study of school principals. *NABE Journal of Research and Practice*. https://doi.org/10.1080/26390043.2022.2079390

Morita-Mullaney, T. and Nguyen, D. (2023) Asian American teachers as interlocutors: Racializing agendas of ascription and skill. *Asian American Policy Review: A Harvard School Kennedy Publication* (33), 55–64. https://www.proquest.com/docview/2808682032?sourcetype=Scholarly%20Journals

Morita-Mullaney, T., Renn, J. and Chiu, M. (2020) Obscuring Equity in dual language bilingual education: A longitudinal study of emergent bilingual achievement, school course placements and grades. *TESOL Quarterly* 54 (3), 685–718. https://doi.org/10.1002/tesq.592

Moscone, G.R. (1970) Senate Bill 1188. In The Association of Chinese Teachers (TACT) (ed.). San Francisco, CA: State Senator George R. Moscone.

Moskowitz, R. (1971, September 13) S.F. Busing to Start Today. *San Francisco Examiner*, 1, 8.

Moulder, A. and San Francisco Common Schools School Board. (1886) Circular H286. In P.o.S.F.C. Schools (ed.), (pp. 2). San Francisco, CA: San Francisco Common Schools' Superintendent.

Moy, G. (1975) Asian Resource Center. In The Association of Chinese Teachers (TACT) (d.). Chicago, IL: Asian Resource Center.

National Education Association (1966) *Invisible Minority: Report of the NEA Tucson Survey on the Teaching of Spanish to the Spanish-Speaking*.

National Teacher Corps Task Force (1965, November 18–19) Agenda from the National Teacher Corps Task Force: Conference on Recruitment and Selection. National Teacher Corps Tasks Force: Conference on Recruitment and Selection, Washington, DC.

New York Times (1971, August 17) Chinese ask court to bar busing plan for San Francisco. *New York Times*.

New York Times (1989, July 25) Berkeley Chancellor to quit and return to teaching law. *New York Times*.

Ng, B. (1971) ESL Staffing at Concentration Sites. In L. Lui (ed.). San Francisco, CA.

Ngai, M. (1998) Legacies of exclusion: Illegal Chinese immigration during the Cold War years. *Journal of American Ethnic History* 18 (1), 3–35.

Ngai, M.M. (2010) *The Lucky Ones: One Family and the Extraordinary Invention of Chinese America*. Houghton Mifflin.

Nichols, A. (1967) *Proposal for a Master Plan for Excellence for San Francisco School System*.

Nichols, A.H. (1991) *Journey: A Bicyle Odyssey through Central Asia*. J.D. Huff and Company.

No Child Left Behind, Pub.L. 107–110, 115 Stat. 1425 (2001).

Nolan, D. (1967, April 25) At the Old Hall. *San Francisco Examiner*, 31.

Office of the Superintendent of San Francisco Unified School District (1978) *Lau Consent Decree Annual Report*.

Office of the Superintendent of San Francisco Unified School District (1980) *Lau Consent Decree Annual Report*.

Office of the Superintendent of San Francisco Unified School District (1982) *Lau Consent Decree Annual Report*.

Office of the Superintendent of San Francisco Unified School District (1983) *Lau Consent Decree Annual Report*.

Office of the Superintendent of San Francisco Unified School District (1991) *Lau Consent Decree Annual Report*.

Okamura, R., Takasugi, R., Kanno, H. and Uno, E. (1974) Campaign to repeal the Emergency Detention Act. *Amerasia Journal* 2 (2), 71–94. https://doi.org/10.17953/amer.2.2.01457t03763w71w0

Okihiro, G.Y. (2016) *Third World Studies: Theorizing Liberation*. Duke University Press Books.

Omi, M. and Winant, H. (1986) *Racial Formation in the United States: From the 1960s to the 1980s*. Routledge.

Order Modifying Consent Decree (2008).
Order: Attorneys for Plaintiff Intervenor (1974).
Page Act of 1875, § 141, 18 (1875).
Palmer, D., Cervantes-Soon, C., Dorner, L. and Heiman, D. (2019) Bilingualism, biliteracy, biculturalism and critical consciousness for all: Proposing a fourth fundamental principle for two-way dual language education. *Theory into Practice* 58 (2), 121–133. https://doi.org/10.1080/00405841.2019.1569376
Palmer, D.K. (2009) Middle-class English Speakers in a two-way immersion bilingual classroom: 'Everybody should be listening to Jonathan right now...'. *TESOL Quarterly* 43 (2), 177–202. https://doi.org/10.1002/j.1545-7249.2009.tb00164.x
Palomares, U.H. and Rubini, T. (1973) Human development in the classroom. *Personnel and Guidance Journal* 51 (9), 653–657.
Pennycook, A. and Coutand-Marin, S. (2003) Teaching English as a missionary language. *Discourse: Studies in the Cultural Politics of Education* 24 (3), 337–353. https://doi.org/10.1080/0159630032000172524
Perea, J. (1997) The Black/White binary paradigm of race: The normal science of American racial thought. *California Law Review* 85 (5), 1213.
Peterson, R. (2020) *Corrupting the College Board: Confucius Institutes and K-12 Education.*
Poon, O.A., Segoshi, M.S., Tang, L., Surla, K.L., Nguyen, C. and Squire, D.D. (2019) Asian Americans, Affirmative Action, and the political economy of racism: A multidimensional model of raceclass frames. *Harvard Educational Review* 89 (2), 201–226. https://doi.org/10.17763/1943-5045-89.2.201
Pratt, B.M., Hixson, L. and Jones, N.A. (2022) *Measuring Race and Ethnicity Across the Decades: 1790–2010 Mapped to 1997 U.S. Office of Management and Budget Classification Standards.* Washington, DC: U.S. Census Bureau Retrieved from https://www.census.gov/data-tools/demo/race/MREAD_1790_2010.html
Public Law 93-380, Aug. 21, 1974, Sec 702 (a.) and Sec. 703 (a)(4)(B).
Public Law 95-561, Nov. 1, 1978. Sec. 703 (a)(4)(A).
Quinn, R. (2020) *Class Action: Desegregation and Diversity in San Francisco Schools.* University of Minnesota Press.
Reisman, C.K. (2008) *Narrative Methods for the Human Sciences.* Sage Publications.
Repeal of Emergency Detention Act of 1950 (1971).
Response of the United States to the Court's Order of August 24, 2006 of Kinney Kinmon Lau *et al.*, Plaintiffs United States of America, *Plaintiffs-Intervenors v. Dr Edward Hopp et al.*, Defendants (2007).
Richardson, L. (1988) The collective story: Postmodernism and the writing of sociology. *Sociological Focus* 21 (3), 199–208.
Robeledo Montecel, M. and Danini Cortez, J. (2001) *Successful Bilingual Education Programs – Criteria for Exemplary Practices in Bilingual Education.* Intercultural Development Research Association. https://www.idra.org/resource-center/criteria-for-exemplary-practices-in-bilingual-education/
Rodríguez-Dorans, D. and Jacobs, P. (2020) Making narrative portraits: A methodological approach to analysing qualitative data. *International Journal of Social Research Methodology* 23 (6), 611–623. https://doi.org/13645579.2020.1719609
Rogers, B. (2006) 'Better' people, better teaching: The vision of the National Teacher Corps, 1965–1968. *History of Education Quarterly* 49 (3), 267–415. https://doi.org/10.1111/j.1748-5959.2009.00212
Rogers, B. (2009) 'Better' people, better teaching: THE vision of the National Teacher Corps, 1965–1968. *History of Education Quarterly* 49 (3), 267–415. https://doi.org/10.1111/j.1748-5959.2009.00212.x
Rogers, H.E. and Nichols, A.H. (1967) *Water for California: Planning, Law & Practice, Finance.* Bancroft-Whitney.

Rosa, J. and Flores, N. (2017) Unsettling race and language: Toward a raciolinguistic perspective. *Language and Society* 46 (5), 621–647. https://doi.org/10.1017/S0047404517000562

Ruíz, R. (1984) Orientations in language planning. *Bilingual Research Journal* 8 (2), 15–34. https://doi.org/10.1080/08855072.1984.10668464

San Francisco Chronicle (1969, February 28) Angry Chinatown debate on schools. *San Francisco Chronicle*, 2.

San Francisco Chronicle (1971a, May 14) Policemen: Build yourself a future with the San Francisco Police Department. *San Francisco Chronicle*, 35.

San Francisco Chronicle (1971b) Resignation request: Kopp attacks busing planners. *San Francisco Chronicle*, 4.

San Francisco Civil Grand Jury (1998) *San Francisco Unified School District Report.*

San Francisco Civil Grand Jury (1999) *SFUSD Implementation of Proposition 227 Report of the 1999–2000 San Francisco Civil Grand Jury.*

San Francisco Examiner (1963, October 9) Supervisor Candidates: Alan Nichols. *San Francisco Examiner*, 35.

San Francisco Examiner (1968a, December 2) Artist to Help Design Bridge. *San Francisco Examiner*, 141.

San Francisco Examiner (1968b, August 18) Protest by Affluent in Chinatown: Urge End to Social Ills. *San Francisco Examiner*, 30.

San Francisco Examiner (1970, January 6) 'Invisible Chinese' Sue Census. *San Francisco Examiner*, 4.

San Francisco Examiner (1971, September 14) Parent's Boycott: Chinatown Plans 'Freedom School'. *San Francisco Examiner*, 1.

San Francisco Examiner (1975, March 12) School board won't send layoff letters. *San Francisco Examiner*, 18.

San Francisco Examiner (1998) Superintendent as jailbird. *San Francisco Examiner*, A-16.

San Francisco Unified School District (1974) *The Chinese Bilingual Pilot Program: ESEA Title VII Program Guide*. chrome-extension://efaidnbmnnnibpcajpcglclefindmkaj/ https://files.eric.ed.gov/fulltext/ED098282.pdf

San Francisco Unified School District (2008) *Master Plan for Multilingual Education.*

San Francisco Unified School District (2023) *Facts about SFUSD at a Glance.*

San Francisco Unified Schools (2008) *Master Plan for Multilingual Education.*

San Francisco Unified Schools (2020, September 16) Facing Our Past, Changing Our Future, Part II: Five Decades of Desegregation in SFUSD (1971-today). https://www.sfusd.edu/facing-our-past-changing-our-future-part-ii-five-decades-desegregation-sfusd-1971-today

San Francisco Unified Schools: Office of the Superintendent (1970) *Biography of Alan Nichols.*

Sanchez, F. (2008) *The Lau Action Plan: Presentation to the SFUSD Board of Education.*

Serrano v. Priest, 584 (1971).

Smith, J.A. (2017, January 25) How San Francisco paved the way for California to embrace bilingual education. *San Francisco Public Press*. https://www.sfpublicpress.org/how-san-francisco-paved-the-way-for-california-to-embrace-bilingual-education/

Smith, R.H. and Carnegie Foundation for the Advancement of Teaching (1919) *Justice and the Poor, A Study of the Present Denial of Justice to the Poor and of the Agencies Making More Equal Their Position Before the Law*. Pub. for the Carnegie foundation for the advancement of teaching by C. Scribner's sons.

Stewner-Manzanares, G. (1988) *The Bilingual Education Act: Twenty Years Later.* Occasional Papers in Bilingual Education, Issue.

Stone, J.C. (1966) The California story continued: Teacher education by legislation. *The Phi Delta Kappan* 47 (6), 287–291.

Stop AAPI Hate (2023) *Stop AAPI Hate: Our Origins*. https://stopaapihate.org/our-origins/

Supplementary Educational Center of San Francisco Unified Schools (1969) *The Chinese Bilingual Pilot Program* [Grant]. San Francisco, CA.

Takaki, R.T. (1995) *Strangers at the Gates Again: Asian American Immigration after 1965*. Chelsea House.
Takaki, R.T. (1998) *Strangers from a Different Shore: A History of Asian Americans* (2nd edn). Little Brown. http://www.loc.gov/catdir/enhancements/fy0914/98218270-d.html
Tape v. Hurley, Pub. L. No. 66, Supreme Court of California (1885).
Targeted News Service. (2019, July 1) Lau Consent Decree Sunsets for San Francisco Unified School District. *Targeted News Service*.
Terrar, T. (2009a) The national teacher corps and resistance to professional education in the 1960s. *New Orleans: Race, Gender & Class* 16 (3/4), 218–247.
Terrar, T. (2009b) The national teacher corps and resistance to professional education in the 1960s. *Race, Gender & Class* 16 (3/4), 218–247.
The Association of Chinese Teachers (TACT) (1971) *ESL/Bilingual Committee Notes*.
The Association of Chinese Teachers (TACT) (1975) *TACT ESAA Project for Cross Cultural Understanding: The Chinese Americans 1975–1976*.
The Association of Chinese Teachers (TACT) (1977a, April) In-Service Workshop. *TACT/ESAA Newsletter* 3 (4), 1.
The Association of Chinese Teachers (TACT) (1977b, April) Progress Report. *TACT/ESAA Newsletter* 3 (4), 1.
The Association of Chinese Teachers (TACT) (1979) Layoff Impact to Chinese Teachers. In Unknown (ed.). San Francisco, CA: The Association of Chinese Teachers (TACT).
The Association of Chinese Teachers (TACT) (1984) *The Association of Chinese Teachers (TACT)*.
The Association of Chinese Teachers (TACT) (1999) *The Association of Chinese Teachers (TACT) 30th Anniversary Publication*.
The Association of Chinese Teachers (TACT) (2004) *TACT 1969–2004: 35th Anniversary Celebration*.
The Lau v. Nichols Supreme Court Decision of 1974: Testimony of Edward H. Steinman Before the Committee on Ways and Means of the California State Assembly. CATESOL (1975) (CATESOL Occasional Papers, no.2), California State Assembly (1974).
Thompson, K. (2013) Is separate always unequal? A philosophical examination of ideas of equality in key cases regarding racial and linguistic minorities in education. *American Educational Research Journal* 50 (6), 1249–1278. https://doi.org/10.3102/0002831213502519
Tierney, D.S., Hendrick, I.G., Ingles, S.A., Mastain, R.K., Brott, R., Fitch, P.A. and Birch, L. (2011) *A History of Policies and Forces Shaping California Teacher Credentialing*. Commission on Teacher Credentialing.
Titus, J.O. (2011) *Brown's Battleground: Students, Segregationists, and the Struggle for Justice in Prince Edward County, Virginia*. The University of North Carolina Press.
Tom, B. (1978) On politics and education in San Francisco: Commentary by the President, Board of Education. *Amerasia Journal* 5 (1), 87–99. https://doi.org/10.17953/amer.5.1.n8305j5h832j5223
Tsukamoto, W. (1990) Bilingual Community Council Annual Report. In SFUSD School Board (ed.). San Francisco, CA.
Turner, W. (1971, September 14) Many shun buses in San Francisco. *New York Times*, 18.
Uchida, Y. (1971) *Journey to Topaz*. Scribner's.
Umansky, I. (2016) Leveled and exclusionary tracking: English learners' access to academic content in middle school. *American Educational Research Journal* 53 (6), 1792–1833. https://doi.org/10.3102/0002831216675404
Umemoto, K. (1989) 'On Strike!' San Francisco State College strike, 1968–69: The role of Asian American students. *Amerasia Journal* 15 (1), 3–41. https://doi.org/10.17953/amer.15.1.7213030j5644rx25
U.S. Census Bureau (1973) *Decennial Census Official Publications: 1970*. U.S. Census Bureau. https://www.census.gov/library/publications/1973/dec/pc-2-1g.html

U.S. Commission of Civil Rights (1974) *Counting the Forgotten: The 1970 Census Count of Persons of Spanish Speaking Background in the United States.*
U.S. District Court of Northern District of California: Modified Consent Decree (2015)
Usdan, M.D. (2006) *Souvenir Journal, Celebrating 50 Years of Service to America's Urban Public Schools.* Council of the Great City Schools: A Look Back, A Current Assessment And a Look Ahead, Issue.
Valdes, G. (1997) Dual-Language Immersion Programs: A Cautionary Note Concerning the Education of Language-Minority Students. *Harvard Educational Review,* 67(3), 391–430. https://doi.org/10.17763/haer.67.3.n5q175qp86120948
Valdez, V., Freire, J.A. and Delavan, G. (2016) The gentrification of dual language education. *Educational Policy* 48, 601–627. https://doi.org/10.1007/s11256-016-0370-0
Van Horne, H. (1970, April 7) Short Changed by the U.S. Census. *San Francisco Examiner,* 26.
Voting Rights Act of 1965, Pub. L. No. 89–110, 78 (1965).
Voting Rights Act of 1965, Pub. L. No. 94-73, 89 400–406 (1975).
Wagner, V. (1998, July 16) S.F. ignores ruling on Prop. 227. *SF Gate.* https://www.sfgate.com/news/article/S-F-ignores-ruling-on-Prop-227-3080497.php
Walton, C., Riddick, L.R., Riesnof, V. and Lum, J. (1971) Chinese Bilingual Director position. In T. Shaheen (ed.). San Francisco, CA: University of California, School of Education.
Wang, L.L.C. (1969, January 14) Chinese Students Association Address on Chinatown in Transition. *Chinese Students Association.*
Wang, L.L.C. (2007) Chinatown in transition. *Amerasia Journal* 33 (1), 31–48. https://doi.org/10.17953/amer.33.1.3246116125188729
Washington, H. (1970, December 18) Longing: Would-be cop tries to measure up. *San Francisco Chronicle,* 1, 18.
Weiner, S. (1972) *Educational Decisions as Organized Anarchy.* [Doctoral dissertation, Stanford University].
Whiting, S. (2021, September 27) Demolishing a 'bridge to nowhere' is first step in $66 million redesign of S.F.'s Chinatown park. *San Francisco Chronicle.*
Wong, J.D., Ng, B., Tom, R., Chan, D.I. and Lui, L. (1970) *Articles of Incorporation of The Association of Chinese Teachers (TACT).* San Francisco, CA: The Association of Chinese Teachers (TACT).
Wong, K. (1977, November 30) Heritage: Recalling S.F.'s own Great Wall. *The San Francisco Examiner.*
Wood, J. (1969, May 9) 5 Teachers refuse to Salute Flag. *The San Francisco Examiner,* 1–2.
Wood, J. (1970, January 23) U.S. funds urged for Chinatown Schools. *The San Francisco Examiner,* 3.
Wood, J. (1971, September 16) S.F. School Board Chief: 'Chaos in Integration Now'. *San Francisco Examiner,* 7.
Wright, G. (1971, July 11) The balancing game. *The San Francisco Examiner,* 3.
Wu, E. (2013) *The Color of Success: Asian Americans and the Origins of the Model Minority.* Princeton.
Wu, F.H. (2018) From the 'perpetual foreigner' to the 'model minority' to the new transnational elite: The residential segregation of Asian Americans. In G.D. Squires (ed.) *The Fight for Fair Housing: Causes, Consequences, and Future Implications of the 1968 Federal Fair Housing Act* (pp. 133–150). Routledge.
Yick Wo et al. v. Hopkins (1886).
YuRat and Jones, W. (1971) *A Frustrating Time was Had by All (The Chinese, that is).* TACT Monthly Newsletter, Issue.
Zhao, X. and Biernat, M. (2017) 'Welcome to the U.S.' but 'change your name'? Adopting Anglo names and discrimination. *Journal of Experimental Social Psychology* 70, 59–68. https://doi.org/10.1016/j.jesp.2016.12.008

Index

Note: References in *italics* are to figures, those in **bold** to tables; "n" refers to chapter notes.

AAPA (Asian American Political Alliance) 134
AAPIs xxii
ABA (American Bar Association) 76
ABC (American born Chinese) 36, 45, 47, 51, 160, 161, 171
Ackerman, Arlene 126
ACLU *see* American Civil Liberties union
ACT (Association of Chinese Teachers) 57, 161, 189, 193–194
affirmative action 193, 197
Alioto, Superintendent 154, 158, 167
Alioto (Mayor) 93, 98
American Bar Association (ABA) 76, 77
American Civil Liberties union (ACLU) 76, 127–128
anti-Black xxii–xxiii
Apodaca, Dr. Rosita 128
Asian American Administrator's Association 177
Asian American Political Alliance (AAPA) 134
Asian American Studies xxi–xxii
Asian American Task Force for the Admissions on University Admissions 145–146
Asian Americans 94, 176
Asian Law Caucus 128
Asian Pacific American Legal Center 128
Asian Pacific Islanders 186
Asians 94
Association of Chinese Teachers (ACT) 57, 161, 189, 193–194

Barbarra, Vincent 73
Barkley, Alice 67
BART (Bay Area Rapid Transit) 52
BBE *see* Bilingual–Bicultural Education
BCC *see* Bilingual Community Council
BCLAD *see* Bilingual Cross-Cultural Language and Academic Development
Bean Sprouts (TV program) xi, 161–163, 164, 172
Berger, Justice Warren E. 88
Berlin, Isaiah 107, 157
Betty, Ms. 138
Bilingual Community Council (BCC) 118, 158, 180–181
Bilingual Cross-Cultural Language and Academic Development (BCLAD)
 license 148, 149, 189
 program 117, 134, 157
Bilingual/Crosscultural Specialist Credential 148
Bilingual Department *later* Multilingual Pathways Department 117–118
 Intake Center 124
 Student Assignment Center 124
bilingual education 19, 20–21, 74–75, 102–103, 125, 147–148
 Chinese-Cantonese 20–21, 22–23, 30, 40–41, 43, 54–55, 174–175, 197
 funds 58
Bilingual Education Act (1968) 44, 53, 131
Bilingual Education Act (1974; 1978) 116, 147, 148, 165
Bilingual Education Reform Act of California (1980) 121–122
Bilingual Individual Learning Plan (BLIP) 123
Bilingual–Bicultural Education (BBE) 114, 115, 120, 179

biliteracy as a strand is segregation 187–188
biliteracy decline 188–189
Boyer, Robert K. 58
Bridges, Ruby 31
Brown, Pat 91
Brown v. Board of Education (1954, 1955) 3, 11, 95, 99, 103, 107, 112, 144, 179
Brynelson, Wade 123–124
Burke, Judge Lloyd H. 83–84, 128, 179, 180
busing xxiii, xxv, 22, 24–25, 59–60, 65, 95–97, 99–107, 175, 193

CAA *see* Chinese for Affirmative Action
CAAs (community action agencies) 76–77
Caen, Herb 70
California
  Assembly Bill 507/80 121
  Assembly Law 1329 (Chacon-Moscone Act (1976)) 120, 121
  Community Colleges 166
  Department of Education 166
  Proposition 13 155
  Proposition 209 178, 179
  Senate Bill 1355 148
  State Board of Education 128
  Supreme Court 10
California: Proposition 227: English for the children: after Lau 125–131
  CAA opposition to 127–128
  enforcement of 128
  funding outside of schools 126–127
  parent roles 125
  school responsibilities 125
California proposition 209 178
California State University 166
Cantonese xxv, 9, 34, 51
  proficiency as mediator of biliteracy decline 188–189
Cantonese-Chinese bilingual program 20–21, 22–23, 30, 40–41, 43, 54–55, 174–175, 197
Carr, Senator (Santa Barbara) 146–147
Carter, President Jimmy 179
census 68, 72–74
Center for Applied Linguistics 113
Center for Educational Telecommunications (CEL) 162
Cesar Chavez Elementary 172
Chacon-Moscone Act (1976) 120, 121

Chan, Rosemary 57
Chew, Laureen 116, 121–122, 132–141, 147–150, 153, 154, 157, 189, **196**
Chew, Wellington 59, 62, 63, 63
Chin, Helen 177
Chin, Lonnie 163, 165, 168–172, 176, **196**
China, trips to 168
China Times 101, 104
Chinatown, San Francisco xxv–xxvi, 28
  Community Children's Center 21
  Neighborhood Legal Assistance League 20
Chinese American Citizen's Alliance 38, 101
Chinese American Democratic Club 178
Chinese BBE program 120
Chinese Benevolent Association (Six Companie) 67
Chinese Benevolent Association (Six Companies) 104
Chinese Bilingual Pilot Program 43–44, 53–54, 64, 86, 118, 139, 160
Chinese Cultural Center 68, 69
Chinese educations asssigned outside of Chinatown: before Lau 45–55
Chinese exclusion: before Lau 3–11
Chinese Exclusion Act (1882–1965) xxv, 3, 10, 14, 15, 58, 163
Chinese for Affirmative Action (CAA) 66–75, 78, 80, 127, 181, 186, 193
  opposition to California Proposition 227 127–128
Chinese names, anglicization of 5
Chinese Primary School 9
Chinese principals: post Lau 165
  an angel in nearby Chinatown 168–172
  far away 165–168
  Irene and the Wah Mei Preschool 172–173
Chinese Six Companies 67
Chinese teachers *see* TACT (The Association of Chinese Teachers)
Chinese Times 38
Chinn, George Y. 98
Choosing equity (2019–2024) xxv–xxvi
Choy, Buddy Tate 67
Choy, Phillip 63
Christian evangelism 5–6
Chu, Linda 25, 26, 27, 28, 34–35, 43, 162
Chuck, Harry 137

Chuck, James 63
Citizen's Advisory Committee on Education (1960) 50
Citizens' Taskforce on Bilingual Education 113
City College of San Francisco 40
Civil Rights Act of 1964 70, 88, 95, 111, 112, 124, 194–195
civil service 69–71
Cleveland Elementary 168
Clinton, Bill 182
collective advocacy: many tentacles: before Lau 56–65
Collier, Irene Dea 158–159, 160, 161–162, 165, 172–173, **196**
Collier, Malcolm 172
color xxii
Commerce High School 53, 165
Commodore Stockton Elementary 22–36, 45, 47–48, 57, 147, 168–169, 194
  Bean Sprouts 162
  busing 99, 100, 104
  Chinese Bilingual School 40, 52–53, 54, 58, 61, 62, 64, 75, 116
  Island of Secret Memories 163
  (later) Gordon J. Lau Elementary 177, 194
  Teacher Corp 137, 138
  teachers 46
community action agencies (CAAs) 76–77
community agencies at the core: before Lau 66–75
Cone, R. 98
'Confessions Program' 15, 58
Confucius Institute of China 191
Consolidated Chinese Benevolent Association 106
Consortium for the National Equal Justice Library (2018) 77
content choices 176
Costa, A. L. 170
Council of Great City Schools' Conference 95
Council on Interracial Books for Children 161
Coutand-Marin, S. 4
COVID-19 pandemic 186
cross-filing 91
'cultural differences' 73–74
culturally inclusive education 52

Dai Go 47
Daily Alta California (1885) 7
Dallas Independent Schools 129
del Portillo, Ray 118
Den, Ms. 129
Department of Health, Education, and Welfare (DHEW) 21, 22, 60
DES (Dominant English Speakers) 114
desegregation 92
Ding, Loni 162, 163, 193
District Project Manager of Title VII 53
DLBE *see* dual language bilingual education
Dominant English Speakers (DES) 114
Douglas, William 111, 144
Douglass Elementary 31, 32
Drumright, Everett 15
dual language bilingual education (DLBE) 114, 187

East West 38–39, 39, 101, 104, 112, 159, 167
Economic Opportunity Act (EOA) 76
educational placement center (EPC) 175, 190
Eisenhower, President Dwight 29, 179
ELD (English language development) placement 123
electoral fusion 91
Elementary and Secondary Education Act (1968)
  Bilngual Education Act (1968) 22
Ellsworth Jones 71 104
Ellsworth Jones, W. 101
EME (Ethnic Minority Educators) 153
Emergency Detention Act of 1950 (McCarren Act) 57–58
Emergency School Aid/Assistance Program (ESAP) 60, 139, 193
Emergency School Assistance Act (1972) (ESSA) 160, 161
Employment Law Center 128
English as a Second Language (ESL) 13, 20, 23, 51, 56, 101, 114, 115, 125, 138–139, 154, *181*
English for the children 125–131
English language development (ELD) placement 123
Enrollment Placement Center (EPC) 130, 182
EOA (Economic Opportunity Act) 76

EPC *see* educational placement center; Enrollment Placement Center
ESL *see* English as a Second Language
ESL/Bilingual/Bicultural: Dreams and Priorities conference 62, 63
ESSA *see* Emergency School Assistance Act (1972)
ethnic enclaves 105
Ethnic Minority Educators (EME) 153
Ethnic Studies program 148, 149
ethnicity 73–74
Evening Bulletin (1885) 105

Feinstein, Diane 93
First Chinese Baptist Church 45, 57
Fisher Act (Licensing and Certificated Personnel Act) 1961 50
Fitzgerald, Mr 49
Floyd, Assemblyman (Gardenia) 146–147
FOBs (Fresh off the Boat families) 47, 48
following the trail xxv–xxvi
Fong, Harold 101–102
Ford Foundation 76
foregrounding xxiv
foreign languages 49–50
Francisco Junior High School 14, 47–48, 56, 59, 62
Fred Korematsu School for Social Justice 31
Freedom Schools of Chinatown 104–107, *106*, 175
  Telesis system 105, 107
freedom to 107
French language 50
Fresh off the Boat families (FOBs) 47, 48
Fritzi of California 78

Garcia, Carlos 181
Gee, Barbara 63
Gee, Stanley 101–102
George Washington High School 47
Georgetown University 77
Gin, Sandra 57
Goldman, Edward D. 83, 84–85
Gordon J. Lau Elementary 177, 194
Gramsci, Antonio 66
Great Society Program 53
Guerin, Geralyn 59
Guey Heung Lee et al. v. Johnson (1971) 102, 105, 107, 111

Hall, Miss Elizabeth 46, 49
Hammond, Alan *see* Nichols, Alan
Hampton v. Mow Sung Wong (1976) **143**, 144
Hattam. V. C. 74
Hayakawa, Samuel Ichiye 135–136
Health Education and Welfare (HEW) 148
  Emergency School Assistance Program (ESAP) 193
Heber-Smith, Reginald: *Justice and the Poor* (1919) 76
Hect, Ken 144
Height, Dorothy 170
HEW *see* Health Education and Welfare
higher education: remedies and remediation 142
  Edward Steinman, Santa Clara University 142–144, **143**
Hill, Irving 87
Hispanic community 74
historicizing 167–168
Holiday Inn 69
Hong, Ruby 57
Hong Kong 173
Hope College, Holland, Michigan 66
Hopkins, Peter 174
Horne, Jennifer 64–65
Horseshoe Plan 59, 60, 99, 100, 103–104, 178
House Committee on Un-American Activities 57
How University 77
huaqiao 67
Human Language Development Curriculum 140
Human Rights Commission 68, 69
Hunt, Dr Jim xxiii–xxiv
Hunter's Point 23, 25, 49, 52, 99, 140, 165
Hurley, Jennie 6

IDEA (Individuals with Disabilities Act) 84
idealistic lawyer and public servant appointed to School Board: before Lau 90–96
immigration 39
Immigration and Nationalization Act (1965) 56, 60, 149, 165
Immigration and Naturalization Services (INS) Confession program 15

Individuals with Disabilities Act (IDEA) 84
Introduction
  Asian American Studies xxi–xxii
  following the trail xxv–xxvi
  language policy xxiii
  narrative policy portraiture xxiii–xxiv, **xxvi**
  racial plotting and continuums xxii–xxiii
Issei xxi

J. Washington Irving school 13–14
Jackson, Jesse 170–171
Jacobs, P. xxiv
Japanese Americans xxi, 17
Jean Parker Elementary 12, 18–19, 22, 40, 51, *52*, 53, 54, 100, 104, 137
Jenkins, Robert 61, 93
Jeu Dip *see* Tape family: Joseph
John Hancock Elementary School 46, 137
Johnson, David 49, 95
Johnson, Lyndon B. 53
  Great Society Program 17
  War on Poverty 76
Johnson, Patricia 49, 95
Johnson v. SFUSD (1971) xxiii, 22, 60, 95, 99, 102, 107, 178, 179
Justice Enterprise company 68

Kam Wai Lau, Mrs 81
Katz, Larry 20
Katz, Lucinda Wong Lee *see* Lee, Lucinda
Katz, Norman 20, 79–80
Kennedy, Edward 17
Kennedy, Robert 93
Kim, Claire Jean xxii
Kinney Kinmon Lau et al. v. Alan H. Nichols (1970) 81, 83
Kinney Kinmon Lau et al. v. Alan H. Nichols (1971) 85
Kitagawa, Megan 29–36
Kittredge, Michael 63
Krashen, S. D. 138
Krueger, George 117–118

Ladies Protection and Relief Society 4
Lai, Andrea 58
Lai, Melissa 24, 25–30, *28*

language as choice 190, 192
language pathways 182
language policy xxiii, 73
language preservation 15–17, **16**
language rights 17, 74, 170, 174, 176, 190
Latino-Spanish speaking families 23, 99–100, 176
Lau, Fred 70–71, *71*
Lau, Kinney Kinmon 18, 20, 22, 191
Lau, Mrs 19–20, 78–79, 191
Lau and its remedies (1974–1985) xxv, 117
Lau architects for language rights 194–197, **195–196**
Lau Consent Decrees (1976 and 2015) 111–124, 170
  Annual Reports 112–114, 180
  comparison of **183**
  identification of eligible students 114, **115**
  language program type 114, 115–117
  Modified Lau Consent Decree to the Sunset 178–185
  trained teachers 117–118
Lau v. Nichols (1974) xxiii, xxiv, 3, 73, 75, **143**, 144, 178, 179, 186, 194, 197
  and Chinese American language rights *xxv*, 20, 79–89, **80, 81**, 97–98, 107, 111–112, 127, 145, 169, 194
Lau v. Nichols Oral Arguments (1973) 88
League of United Latin American Citizens (LULAC) xxiv
Lee, Denise 79–81
Lee, Lucinda 12–13, *13*, 16, 19–21, 22–36, *28, 29*, 43, 51, 74, 78–80, 102, 104, 116, 117, 121–122, 132, 137, 162, **195**
Lee, Sophie 153, 160, 176–177
Lee Guey Heung 102
Lee Quon 73
Leeman, J. 74
legal aid 76
Legge, Charles A. 128
Levin, Gerald 143
Lew, Gordon 26, 33, 37–44, 51, 53, 54, 120, 160, 167, **196**
  books 43, 181
  Chinese New Lessons 41–43, *42*
  East West 68
  Story of the Red Envelopes 43
Lew, Helen Joe 158, 163–164
liberty 107

Life Magazine 170–171
Lim, Darlene 130, 153, 156, 157, 160, 165, 173–176, **196**
Lim, Roland 52
'linguistic isolation' 187
local racial concentration 105
Loomis, Reverend 4
Low, Victor 45–55, 73, 74, 113–114, 118, 133, 138, 165, 166–167, 176, 177, **195**
 The Unimpressible Race: A Century of Educational Struggle by the Chinese in San Francisco 167
Lowe, Leo 64
Lowell High School 17
Lui, Larry 59
LULAC (League of United Latin American Citizens) xxiv
Lum, J. B. 62
Lum, John 57, 63, *63*, 117–118
Lum, L. B. 101–102
Lum, P.A. 106–107
Lum, Phil 57, 63
Lum, Walter 38

McCarren Act (Emergency Detention Act of 1950) 57–58
McCarthy, Emily H. 180–181
McGladery, Mary *see* Tape family: Mary
Mailliard, Congressman 58
MALDEF (Mexican American Legal Defense and Education Fund) xxiv, 128
Mandarin Chinese xxv, 4, 133, 137, 147, 189, 191
Marina Junior High 59
Marshall Elementary School 49, 52
Master Plan for Multilingual Education (2008) 181, 182, 187
Maxwell Jolly, Julie 181
MCD (Modified Consent Decree) 187
META (Multicultural Education, Training and Advocacy) 127
Metcalf, Antoinette 63
Mexican American Legal Defense and Education Fund (MALDEF) xxiv, 128
'missionary language' 6
Modified Consent Decree (MCD) 187
Mohler, Judith 59, 101
Morena, Superintendent 153
Morita, Eugene Takashi xxi

Moscone, George 58
méiyǒu bànfǎ xxii
Moulder, Andrew J. 8, 9–10, 11, 105
Mow Song Wong v. Hampton (1976) 193
Mow Sun Wong v Hampton (1977) 69
Mrs Lau: before Lau 12–21
Multicultural Education, Training and Advocacy (META) 127
Multilingual Pathways Department 181
multilingualism 74, 182, 187
music 26–27

narrative policy portraiture xxiii–xxiv, xxvi
National Association for the Advancement of Colored People (NAACP) 49, 76, 94, 95
National Labor Relations Board v. Western Addition Community Organization (1975) **143**, 143–144
national origin 11, 70
National Teacher Corp 12, 17–18, 51, 52, 53, 137, 138, 157
Native Sons of the Golden *State* 38
Needham, Henry 129
negative liberty xxiii, 107, 197
Neighborhood Legal Assistance Foundation 81
Nelson, Gaylord 17
Nelson, Mrs 20, 21
New York Times 104
Ng, Beverly 58–59
Ngai, M. M. 9
Nichols, Alan 90–98, 172, **195**
Nisei xxi
Nixon, President 139, 168
No Child Left Behind Act (2001) 131
No Child Left Behind Policy (2001) 182
Nob Hill school 105, 106
Noe Valley 99
North Beach Chinatown Council 60–61, 105

O'Connor, Thomas 86, 88
O'Douglass, Justice William 102–103
Office for Economic Opportunity 76
Office of Bilingual Education (OBE) 148
Office of the Auditor General of Caifornia 146
Ollier, Irene Dea 153
Omi, M. xxii

Oriental School, San Francisco 10, 167
Otis, Reverend 4

PACE (Philippine-American Collegiate Endeavor) 135
Pacific Heights School 46
Page Act (1875) 3
paper son status 14–15
Parker, Jean 74
Patrick Henry Elementary 25
Payne, Medora 31–36
Peace Corp 18
Pearl Harbor xxi, 29–30
Pennycook, A. 4
personalized curriculum writers, not publishers: before Lau 37–44
Philippine-American Collegiate Endeavor (PACE) 135
Pledge of Allegiance 52
Portraits of America xxiii
positive liberty xxiii, 107, 197
Pottinger, John Stanley 88–89
Prince Edward County, Virginia 104–105
Princeton Seminary 66
Public Advocates 128
Public Law 94–142 84

Quon v. Stans (1970) 142–143, **143**, 193

race 60, 73, 74, 178–179, 190
racial desegregation 107
racial integration 94–95, 140, 170, 193
racial plotting and continuums xxii–xxiii
Reagan, Ronald 19, 128, 135, 149
'Reggie' found a way: before Lau 76–89
Reggie program 193
Reginald Heber Smith Fellowship 76, 77
Remedial remedies (1968–2018) xxv
remedies and more remedies: after Lau 111–112
    identification of eligible students 114
    language program type 114–117
    late 1970s: building structure within the structure 118–121
    Lau Consent Decree Annual Reports 112–114
    1980s: positions, promotions and pupil proportion 121–122
    1990s: English heavy and bilingual light 122–124
    trained teachers 117–118

remedies and remediation in higher education 142–152
roadmap for narrative policy portraiture xxvi
Rodríguez-Dorans, D. xxiv
Rogers, Harold 90
Rojas, Waldemar 'Bill' 126–127, 128, 129–130
Roosevelt, Franklin xxi
Roosevelt Junior High 59
Ruiz, Richard 186

Saint Mary's Catholic Church 132
San Francisco
    First Presbyterian Church 5
    language rights 75
    legal aid offices 77–78
    Richmond district 94
San Francisco Advisory Committee Education Equality/Quality Plan 92–93
San Francisco Board of Supervisors 90, 91–92
San Francisco Chinese for Education Committee 105
San Francisco Chronicle 61, 70–71, 71, 98, 126
San Francisco Civil Service Commission 71
San Francisco College 17
San Francisco Common Schools 105
San Francisco Examiner 13, 18, 52, 61, 69, 73, 74, 91, 93–94, 98, 105, *106*, 127
San Francisco Neighborhood Legal Assistance Foundation 73
San Francisco Police Department 71, 71, 72
San Francisco State University 26, 46, 48, 49, 50, 134, 147–150
    BCLAD Cantonese program 157
    Cantonese teacher education bilingual program 148
    Intercollegiate Chinese for Social Action (ICSA) 135, 137
    Mulan program 134, 135
    School of Education 148
    #StopAAPIHate 186
San Francisco Unified School District (SFUSD) xxiii, 12, 18, 37, 40, 46, 51, 197
    Asian Pacific Islanders 186

Bilingual Department 117–118
biliteracy as segregation 187
board of supervisors 90
Chinese Bilingual Pilot Program 43–44, 53–54, 64, 86, 118, 139, 160
Chinese-Cantonese bilingual education 20–21
Chinese students 56
Citizen's Advisory Council (CAC) 100
collective strategy 186–187
Constitution and California Educational Code violations 82–89
desegregation 92
Diversity index 179
dual language immersion/bilingual education 14, 187
Enrollment Placement Center (EPC) 130, 182
failure of langage needs 111
Horseshoe Plan for busing 59, 60, 99, 100, 103–104, 178
Human Development Program 139
Hunter's Point Elementary School 23, 25, 49, 52, 99, 140, 165
Language Academy 128–129, 130
Lau Consent Decree Annual Reports 112–114, 180
legal sunsets 178
mandatory busing 99–107
Master Plan for Multilingual Education 181, 182, 187
Master Plans for Bilingual–Bicultural Education 113, 181
Teacher Corp 12, 17–18, 20, 51–52, 53, 137, 138, 157
teachers 56–57, 59, 61–62, 65, 107, 169
Sanchez, Dr. Francisca 181
Santa Clara University 142–144
  language rights and affirmative action **143**
Sarah B. Cooper School 46, 137
school desegregation and bilingual education: before Lau: 22–23
  bicultural over bilingual 36
  the bused and the curriculum 32–33
  content and the curriculum 33–35
  leaving home: bused in 31–32
  staying put: the walkers 23–26
  student constitution 29–31
  student interaction on the playground 35–36
  walkers and curriculum 26–31
school desegregation and mandatory busing: before Lau 99–110
segregated schooling 107, 187–188
Serrano v Priest (1971) 77–78
SFNAACP v. SFUSD (Brown) case 157, 172, 174, 176, 178–179, 190, 193–194, 197
SFUSD *see* San Francisco Unified School District
Shaheen, Dr. Thomas 59, 65
Shelley, John Francis 91
Sherman School, San Francisco 101
shikata ga nai xxi–xxii
Silk Wing Work 73
Sing, Lillian 67, 163, 172
Single Rental Occupancy households (SROs) 72–73
Six Companies 66, 104, 106
Smith, J. A. 127
Spanish BBE progrmas 120
Spanish language 50, 60, 120
Spring Valley School, San Francisco 6, 46, 100, 169–171
SROs (Single Rental Occupancy households) 72–73
Stanford Law Review 90
Steinman, Edward xxiv, 20, 73, 76–89, 90, 95, 111–112, 113, 150, 186, 194, **195**
  Reggie program 193
  Santa Clara University 142–144, **143**
Sterling, Farmer 3–4
Stevens, John Paul 144
Stewart, Don 146, 147
storytelling 140, 141
Sue, Ed 137
Sung, Robert 26, 53, 54, 55n1, 120, 160
sunset and beyond: language as problem, right, resource or choice? 186–187
  biliteracy as strand is segregation 187–188
  Cantonese proficiency as mediator of biliteracy decline 188–189
  dual language immersion/bilingual education 187
  language as choice erodes language as a right 192
  Mandarin is the New English 191
  school choice: selection or placement? 190–191
sunsets 178

sunsetting and choice: co-articulating language rights, affirmative action, and voting rights 193–197
Surh, Hannah 63

TACT (The Association of Chinese Teachers) 56–65, *63*, *64*, 163–164, 168
  Bean Sprouts (TV program) 162–163, 164
  bilingual education 59–60, 74, 117–118, 130, 147, 148, 153, 158–159, 181–182, 192
  community education 158–159, *159*
  curriculum creation and professional development 160–162
  Island of Secret Memories 163, 164
  North Beach Chinatown Council 60–61
  'Project for Cross Cultural Understanding: The Chinese Americans' 160
  teacher layoffs 153–156, *155*
  waivers: not yet highly qualified 156–158
Tai Sui Fong 26
Tait, George 167
TAP (Temporary Assignment Permit) 107
Tape family 3–6, 9, 10, 11, 70, 94
  Frank 9–10, 167
  Joseph (Jeu Dip) 3–5, 7
  Mamie 3–11, 63, 71, 105, 163, 167, 169, 171, **195**
  Mary 4–9, 11, 71
Tape v. Hurley 6, 11
Teacher Corp *see* National Teacher Corp
Teacher Professional Development Library 166–167
teaching as activism (1968–1974) *xxv*
Telesis system 105, 107
Temporary Assignment Permit (TAP) 107
Third World Liberation Front (TWLF) 135, 136–137, 138, 148, 154
Third World Rights Federation activist in the midst 132–141
Thompson, K. 107, 116–117
Ting, Phillip 146
Title VII
  Chinese Bilingual pilot 75, 148, 189
  fellows 165, 166
  grant 20, 22, 26, 27, 28, 52–54, 58, 160

Tom, Ben 63, 100–101, 102
Tom, Dr. Roger 57, 138, 139–140, 141n1, 148, 177
Treasure Island 100
Troike, Rudy 118
Tsui, William 28–29
TWLF *see* Third World Liberation Front

Uchida, Yoshiko xxi
University of California, Berkeley 46, 66, 144–147
University of Chicago 66
University of San Francisco (USF) 166
University of the Pacific, Stockton 148
Unz, Ron 125, 130
US Census, 1970 72–73, 143, 193
US Constitution
  Fourteenth Amendment 11, 82–83, 85, 87–89, 95, 103, 111, 112, 194–195, 197
  violation 82–83
US Ninth Circuits 158

Voting Rights Act of 1965 74
Voting Rights Act of 1975 194, 197

Wah Mei Preschool 165, 172–173
Wales, Virginia 104
WALK: We All Love Kids 104
Walker, Vaughn R. 180
walkers
  and the curriculum 25–31
  staying put 23–26
Wang, Ling-Chi 20, 61, *63*, 66–75, 78, 80, 98, 128, 143, 144–147, 150, 172, **195**
Wang, Ted 128
War Relocation Authority xxi
Washington, H. 70
Washington Irving Elementary 132–133, 137–138
Weekly Calistogan 5–6
Weigel, Stanley Alexander, Judge 93, 95, 100
Whiting, S. 69
Wilkins, Judge Claudia 182
Williamson, Raymond D. 86
Wilson, Pete 128
Winant, H. xxii
Wo Lee 174
Wong, Anna 161, 165
Wong, Christina 130, 181

Wong, Dennis 63
Wong, Germaine 67
Wong, Jones 63, 64
Wong, Larry Jack 137
Wong, Ted 57
Wong v. Hampton 75
Wu, William 63

Yee Foon Sit 102

Yick Wo 174, 176
Yick Wo Early Childhood *see* Sarah B. Cooper School
Yick Wo Elementary 174, 175
Yick Wo v. Hopkins (1886) 103
Yinig Ngoi Toy 102
youth behavior 66–67
Yu Rat 63–64, *64*
Yu Scum 63–64, *64*

For Product Safety Concerns and Information please contact our EU Authorised Representative:

Easy Access System Europe

Mustamäe tee 50

10621 Tallinn

Estonia

gpsr.requests@easproject.com